W9-BWD-439

"Books We're Excited About in 2017" (*CHICAGO TRIBUNE*)

"Books We Can't Wait to Read in 2017" (*CHICAGO READER*)

"Books to Help You Survive the First 6 Months of Trump"

(*CHICAGO REVIEW OF BOOKS*)

"Probing her own experiences with disease and health care, Anne Elizabeth Moore offers scalpel-sharp insight into the ways women's bodies are subject to unspeakable horrors under capitalism."

—*CHICAGO TRIBUNE*

"Sharp, shocking, and darkly funny, the essays in [*Body Horror*] . . . expose the twisted logic at the core of Western capitalism and our stunted understanding of both its violence and the illnesses it breeds. . . . Brainy and historically informed, this collection is less a rallying cry or a bitter diatribe than a series of irreverent and ruthlessly accurate jabs at a culture that is slowly devouring us."

— *PUBLISHERS WEEKLY*, starred review

"Scary as fuck, and liberating."

—*VIVA LA FEMINISTA*

"Anne Elizabeth Moore is the feminist killjoy I want at every party—armed and ready to calmly, often humorously, eviscerate any casual misogyny in the room. Compiling her years of experience as a journalist, this collection showcases Moore's staggering body of knowledge. At the core of several of these essays is Moore's own body and its betrayals in the form of autoimmune disorders and her newly accepted label of disability. Admirably, Moore never lingers too long on her own experience, but instead uses it to reach to different corners of the globe and different eras in American history to diagnose the malignancy of misogyny on bodies beyond her own. Perhaps because of Moore's multiple analyses of various horror films, *Body Horror* seems to remind readers of the iconic line, 'The call is coming from inside the house.' Anne Elizabeth Moore is masterful at illustrating how the ills of capitalism have become so insidious that they are now coming from inside—our houses, our heads, our very cells."

—SARAH HOLLENBECK, Women & Children First Bookstore

"As the subtitle promises, this essay collection by award-winning journalist and Fulbright scholar Anne Elizabeth Moore tackles heavy, complicated issues with biting humor and aplomb, dissecting the ways patriarchal capitalistic trauma plays out on women's bodies and health, both mental and physical. From her keen observations on the 2014/2015 Cambodian garment workers' mass strike and its resulting massacre to her vulnerable, often hilarious insights on the maze of current American healthcare and her own varied ailments, Moore writes with spark and verve."

—LYDIA MELBY, Texas Book Festival

"At turns chummy, cerebral, and incendiary, *Body Horror* holds no punches. This motley crew of essays form an astute and uproarious exploration of the insidious misogyny and ableism bred into contemporary culture. You'll laugh, you'll cry, and you might even rage-vomit. A winner."

—KATHARINE SOLHEIM, Unabridged Bookstore

PRAISE FOR *THREADBARE*

"*Threadbare* takes us down the rabbit hole of the global fashion and textile industry, connecting the dots between the lives of the women who work at Forever 21 and the women who sew the clothes that hang on the racks there. With vivid storytelling and deep investigation, Anne Elizabeth Moore and her team of talented cartoonists prove the strength of comics as tool for translating impossible complexity to our everyday experience."

—JESSICA ABEL, author of *Out on the Wire* and *Drawing Words & Writing Pictures*

"A fascinating look into the lives behind our clothes. From the people who make them, to the people who model them, to the people who sell them, our clothes are part of an intricate network which spans the globe. The art in *Threadbare* helps draw a personal connection to what might otherwise be overwhelming statistics, and gives an intimate look into the way the world is affected by what we buy."

—SARAH GLIDDEN, author of *Rolling Blackouts* and *How to Understand Israel in 60 Days or Less*

"A compelling and comprehensive portrait of the human cost behind what we wear. The sharp, gorgeous, and distressing *Threadbare* will leave you questioning both your wardrobe and the state of the world as a whole."
—TIM HANLEY, author of *Investigating Lois Lane: The Turbulent History of the Daily Planet's Ace Reporter* and *Wonder Woman Unbound: The Curious History of the World's Most Famous Heroine*

"Well-researched, engaging, and full of surprising (and sometimes horrifying) statistics, you may finish reading this book and decide to become an activist—no longer shopping for clothes at your local mall and pressuring your elected officials for legislation that holds clothing manufacturers and retailers responsible."
—LISA WILDE, author of *Yo, Miss: A Graphic Look at High School*

"*Threadbare* is a brilliant amalgam of art, storytelling, consciousness-building, and old-fashioned muckraking. It takes on the enormous project of confronting the international apparel trade, through delving into individual stories and lifting up voices that are usually suppressed or ignored in mass media. The Ladydrawers collective and Anne Elizabeth Moore bring us face to face, literally, with the people most affected by labor exploitation and abuse—and in seeing their faces, we understand the realities beyond the facts. An intrepid journey!"
—MAYA SCHENWAR, editor-in-chief of *Truthout*, author of *Locked Down, Locked Out: Why Prison Doesn't Work and How We Can Do Better*

PRAISE FOR ANNE ELIZABETH MOORE

A "post-Empirical, proto-fourth-wave-feminist memoir-cum-academic abstract [that] makes our country's Mommy Wars look like child's play—and proves . . . why we should be paying attention to Cambodia's record of human rights and gender equity."
—*BUST MAGAZINE* (on *New Girl Law*)

"Attains the modest yet important success of making personal narratives and experience matter to critiques of history and globalization."
—*HYPHEN MAGAZINE* (on *Cambodian Grrrl*)

"A passionate, engaging, heartbreaking, funny, and inspiring book. I want to slip it into every tourist guide to Asia and give a copy to every girl in the world."

—JEAN KILBOURNE, author, filmmaker, and cultural critic

(on *Cambodian Grrrl*)

"Anne Elizabeth Moore lets readers peer over her shoulder as she attempts the implausible. It turns out, the implausible is hard, and funny, and tragic, and illuminating, but once you sign up for the journey she never lets you look away. After reading what this woman accomplished in a few months, you might ask yourself some hard questions about how you spent last summer…"

—GLYNN WASHINGTON, NPR's *Snap Judgment* (on *Cambodian Grrrl*)

"*Cambodian Grrrl* offers a compelling and spirited model of what is possible when media-making becomes a community endeavor. Don't understand why media is a human rights issue? You will by the end of Anne Elizabeth Moore's latest effort."

—JENNIFER POZNER, Executive Director, Women In Media & News

"1000000000000000% punk rock."

—JACKSONVILLE PUBLIC LIBRARY (on *Cambodian Grrrl*)

"Conversational, intellectually curious, and charmingly ragged, *Unmarketable* is an anti-corporate manifesto with a difference: It exudes raw coolness."

—*MOTHER JONES* (on *Unmarketable*)

"[Offers] something distinctly more radical than merely protesting against consumerism: a total rejection of the competitive ethos that drives capitalist culture."

—*LA TIMES* (on *Unmarketable*)

"This is a work of honesty and, yes, integrity."

—*KIRKUS REVIEWS* (on *Unmarketable*)

"Sharp and valuable muckraking."

—*TIME OUT NEW YORK* (on *Unmarketable*)

B.O.D.Y HORROR.

CAPITALISM, FEAR, MISOGYNY, JOKES

ANNE ELIZABETH MOORE

CURBSIDE SPLENDOR

Published by Curbside Splendor Publishing, Inc., Chicago, Illinois in 2017.

First Edition
Copyright © 2017 by Anne Elizabeth Moore
Library of Congress Control Number: 2017936598

ISBN 978-1-940430-88-1
Edited by Irma Nuñez and Naomi Huffman
Cover and interior art by Xander Marro
Author photo by Elizabeth Mason
Book design by Alban Fischer

Manufactured in the United States of America.

www.curbsidesplendor.com

CONTENTS

One of the great paradoxes of writing a book is that the introduction is often the last section set to paper, for as easy as it may have been to write what appears on the pages that follow, it is far more difficult for an author to explain why they felt compelled to write it. Yet as I sit down at my laptop this morning, the Republican-backed Congress has pledged to repeal the Affordable Care Act, or ACA, by a vote of fifty-one to forty-eight, with no replacement plan yet on offer.

This would be the number one priority of women's rights groups in the US, were they not distracted by a very narrow definition of "women's health," as first on the GOP chopping block is coverage for pre-existing conditions. These include the entirety of autoimmune disease as well as most other chronic illnesses—often only uncurable because understudied, and understudied because largely found in the bodies of women. Autoimmune diseases, in which the body's immune system turns on itself, resulting in pain, debility, or worse—I have several—are no different, afflicting a population that is between 80 and 95 percent female, depending on diagnosis. Nearly fifty million US residents are estimated to have such disorders; should the ACA, popularly known as Obamacare, be repealed, the diagnosed are unlikely to be eligible for private health insurance coverage under whatever program replaces current healthcare policy, assuming one does.

The ACA also provided the funding package for expanded Medicaid, and in certain states like Michigan—where I now live—this single economic move has allowed an entire industry to thrive in the desperate economy of Detroit. My entire not-for-profit health network primarily treats folks covered by expanded Medicaid. They have jobs, we have healthcare. The ACA is far from ideal, certainly, but I do not know a soul who has not benefited from it. An immediate repeal, or even a Medicaid restructure, is likely to shutter this massive health facility in a high-needs part of the country, whereupon even my neighbors eligible for and able to afford private insurance will find it that much more challenging to locate a provider. Thousands will be out of work in this state alone. Millions of the autoimmune across the nation—mostly women—will see access to lab tests, health professionals, and life-saving medicines at affordable prices stripped away overnight. Pain will increase for us, first weekly, then daily. Movement will become labored, then difficult, then cease. Many will be unable to get to places of work, or even dress. Livers will be poisoned, breathing will become difficult, blood pressures will elevate, kidneys will fail. A pervading sense of hopelessness will gain traction. Suicide tallies will rise, I guarantee it. And death rates, from a debilitating class of diseases that can be controlled with careful maintenance and testing, and a very minimum of medical oversight, will quickly stupefy.

I wrote this book in case you hadn't figured out yet that what we are facing at this moment is institutionalized misogyny at the service of capitalism. I wrote this book to describe to you how terrifying this truly is. I wrote this book in case it is the last thing I do.

BODY HORROR

Body horror, the goriest of the horror media subgenres, is to my mind the only mode of cultural production capable of capturing this political moment. Also called biological or organic horror, the subgenre is marked by a distinct visuality, which makes it particularly popular for exploration in film. Body horror literature exists, of course: Mary Percy Shelley's *Frankenstein*, Franz Kafka's *The Metamorphosis*, and Charles Burns' *Black Hole* are personal favorites, and hybrid forms like videogames (images from the first-person shooter *Silent Hill* haunt me, years on) and serial television (*The Walking Dead*) fill out the range of ways we can follow along as the known turns into the unknown, the normal becomes disfigured, the comforting emerges as truly terrifying.

Yet the above-named titles are all works of fiction, perhaps inspired by true events or political doings or lived experience, but not in any way beholden to facts. What I am interested in laying out for you in this book is the *experience* of body horror, as a close observer and quasi-survivor—a real-life Final Girl, scruffed and seeping blood from the nose. There are quite a few of us, Final Girls all: survivors of physical and emotional toils so acute they have changed us. In work, entertainment, and medicine—three pillars of global capitalism—women stand witness, too often muted, as their own bodies bleed, mutate, or break down under the simple effort it takes to get through another day.

Contained within this collection are previously published reports and essays on this phenomenon, as well as several all-new works. They are organized (loosely) beginning with the objectively reported and ending in the deep interior monologue I rarely share with anyone. They were written in a dizzying range of circumstances and locales during a time period in which I traveled two hundred days per year, and the period immediately following it, when I could not leave my block, or sometimes even my bed, for several months. (The first essay deserves note in this regard; "Massacre on Veng Sreng Street" shares my experiences covering the largest garment worker uprising in the history of Cambodia, and the government-fueled violence that ended it. It was somewhere between those happy marches and the chilling walks under machine gun sights endured in the nation thereafter that I first noticed something had shifted in my body.) Each essay, however, is rooted in the experience of misogyny, whether mine or others', and the heightening tension that arises from the degeneration, mutilation, or destruction of that (feminine) body.

Of course labeling the horrific makes it less so. I learned this from family friends on the Lakota reservation in South Dakota where I was born, and saw it confirmed later among the survivors of mass killing in Cambodia and those who witnessed the 2008 civil war in the Republic of Georgia. When horror is made banal, a vocabulary for comedy develops. If you don't believe me, just ask the RNs down at your local hematology/oncology clinic for the latest in knee-slappers. Popular psychology will tell us that humor intends to distract and deflect, but jokes also establish a zone of shared experience.

I hope, I mean to convey, that despite my clear and deliberate attempts in these pages to disgust and frighten you, that you still find pleasure and comfort in this book.

WORK I

There was a period not too long ago when I was wracked with pain and could barely type, but this book was late. My slow progress toward completion was due to a recent appointment with a new specialist, a visit long delayed by the cancellation of my health insurance in August under the vindictive eye of a caseworker at the Department of Health and Human Services in the State of Michigan. I spent a month resubmitting the exact same materials I had sent along three months earlier, and finally, my insurance was reinstated in September. But the ailments had racked up in four short weeks, and my new doctor was overwhelmed. Without proper medication, I had lost mobility in both hands. Without access to lab tests, it was unclear if my liver was functioning properly. My blood pressure had skyrocketed, putting me at immediate risk of heart attack, the side effect of a steroid I should have stopped taking, but could not without medical guidance. The specialist's task at that moment was to undo the damage inflicted on my body by the state. My task was to continue operating as if I would survive: eat food, cleanse myself, uphold promises, meet deadlines.

Put otherwise, I was to complete a book cataloging physical debility despite my own increasing physical debility. *I have only ever promised readers I would try not to flinch*, is what I said to calm myself down. *I have made no promises not to flinch.* Yet such projects always raise the question of how much awfulness one should really share, a situation in which writers tend to exercise caution. The novelist Alphonse Daudet wrote poignantly of hiding his suffering from loved ones in order to conserve his relationships during the years he spent in *tabes dorsalis*—a late stage of syphilis in which the nerves of the spine begin rotting away. Published under the title *In the Land of Pain* and edited and translated from French by Julian Barnes, Daudet included his readers among his beloved.

"I don't want my next book to be too harsh," he wrote. "Last time I felt I went too far. Poor humanity—you shouldn't tell it everything. I shouldn't inflict on people what I've endured . . . people should be treated as if they were sick. . . . Let's make them love the doctor, rather than play the tough and brutal butcher."

I adore my readers and wish to guard them from suffering, too, but I couldn't sign off on the collection of essays you're about to read if I agreed that writers have a responsibility to readers to quell harsh descriptions of lived experience. Nor if I found Daudet's writing on pain—often couched in lovely metaphors—to be sufficient on the subject. In recent years, I have adopted a similar approach to humanity, presuming that they, too, are experiencing some form of impairment or suffering, but rather than warranting protection, I suspect that readers desire to see their experiences reflected in the world. (I further quibble with the amount of trust Daudet places in doctors, although I see where it comes from—his, at least, offered morphine, whereas mine have twice now significantly worsened my condition or brought on entirely new diagnoses.) Unlike dear Alphonse, I have found that more folks experiencing physical or emotional pain see it alleviated through literature than through medical advice. (Hat tip to Susan Sontag's foundational thoughts on illness narratives, which I discuss directly in the essay "Fucking cancer.")

More accurate and complete descriptions of pain seem to be required, I am sorry to report, even if it means I play the "tough and brutal butcher." Do not misread this as a desire to dissociate from my own sensations, although that is occasionally helpful, too. To write through and of pain is rooted in a desire to remain present and immediate to one's current requirements for survival. Barnes casts Daudet's collected notes, in his introduction, as descriptions of a decline toward mortality, the writer's final act. In a way, it was: Daudet published nothing else in his lifetime, and the notes he took toward the book on pain did not become one until Barnes came along. Yet there is no explanation as to why, and it seems to me quite possible that Daudet abandoned the project of cataloging his suffering so as not to "inflict on people what [he'd] endured." Indeed, after he stopped writing what became this book, Daudet lived another three or so years. His illness far outlasted any estimates for survival he was offered by his medical team. Daudet did not, in fact, document his own demise. Only the occasionally excruciating experience of being alive.

What I mean to point out is that writing about pain is not the same as writing about mortality—not at all. I love the notion that writing on suffering might always be a conclusive statement: he suffered, but only for a short time, and then it was over. Or: she suffered, and it was for several years, but it was less than two decades. We can place it in the past, and now it is done with. If we could elide pain and death, in other words, I would be all for it. But much of this book was written while I was very much alive, while sharp stings in my right wrist sparked at each keystroke, and I was distracted by a growing numbness in my left arm, and fingers on both hands were nearly unable to bend at the joints to choose between letters. The jolt of a shift key was often too much to take on and entire pages were left to capitalize themselves automatically.

This book is no exploration of mortality. Writing about pain, I would go so far as to suggest, is very much the opposite of writing about death.

However difficult it may be for me to craft—physically or emotionally—or unpleasant for you to ingest, I am at this moment writing about life.

It is considered an act of subversion for women to depict life in any extreme, of course, and this is because women are so rarely offered opportunities to do so. In 2015, the Center for the Study of Women in Film found that women comprise only 19 percent of all directors, writers, editors, producers, executive producers, and cinematographers on the top grossing 250 films. Of all box office genres, women are least likely to work in horror, accounting for only 9 percent of the behind-the-scenes workforce on these films.

I cited similar numbers in a piece for *Salon*,[1] in which I analyzed the content, cast, and crew of seventy-four international horror films, using data submitted by a handful of enthusiasts. Among those films, I found only 5 percent are directed by women, 7 percent are written by women, and 14 percent are produced by women. Onscreen, women are listed as leads in 42 percent of these films, yet appear to lead plot in 48 percent of them—a seemingly minor difference suggesting that the 6 percent of uncredited leading ladies probably got stiffed. (I mean, of course they got stiffed; these are horror movies. But getting underpaid, too? Not cool.)

Of the remaining characters in the seventy-four films I analyzed, 31 percent are female and 69 percent are male. (There is only a single identified nonbinary character in any of the films I examined.) Women die with less frequency than men in horror films—44 percent of onscreen deaths are women's—although not enough to make up for the initial gender imbalance of the ensemble: a total of 32 percent of all female characters die, as opposed to only 23 percent of male characters. It's true, in other words, that a woman onscreen in a horror film is more likely to die than a man. (Here are some numbers to back up that other long-standing joke, about race being a major predictor of onscreen death, as 70 percent of all characters die in horror films, but only 27 percent of them are white.)

The low bar set for signaling the agency of female characters, the Bechdel Test,[2] is still set too high for almost half the films I analyzed: female characters talk to each other about something besides a man in 52 percent of the films, although many pass on technicalities (female characters discussing male demons instead of living men, for example). More than a quarter of the films, 28 percent, contain at least one incident of sexual violence—only a handful of them committed against male characters—while 19 percent of the films contain more than one incidence of sexual violence. On average, however, I found more than one incidence of sexual violence per film, since a few of the films I analyzed use serial rape as a primary plot device. The Bechdel Test does seem a useful predictor for sexual violence in film: movies that pass it tend to have limited rape scenes. However, in a classic perversion of a mainstream trope that still, somehow, fails to benefit women, the Bechdel Test also serves as an indication of whether or not women are granted agency *behind* the camera—fewer women work as writers, directors, editors, or producers on films that pass the Bechdel Test than on films that don't. (Whether this means women are more likely to green-light flat or insulting female characters is unclear, but I look more closely at the degendered nature of misogyny in the essay entitled "Women" in this volume.) Even more disturbing: onscreen female agency is unquestionably punishable by death. Of individual films that contain more female characters' deaths than male, 82 percent pass the Bechdel Test.

It's fitting, in horror, that many platitudes of daily life be reversed—but isn't punishing women who divert their attention from men simply reinstating standard misogynist norms for the sake of entertainment? Films are often said to offer some escape from reality, with giant spiders, evil scientists, and unexplained phenomenon at the ready to distance us from the news of the day. Yet for women viewers of horror, no "escape" is possible. For despite the infrequency of overgrown arachnid attacks in real life, sexual violence occurs onscreen in horror films at the same rate as it happens to women in the world every day.

Horror film is a man's world, even looking beyond the production teams that create it. The most visible fan base, comprised of internet commenters, film critics, and bloggers, is dude-replete almost without exception. Even the cultural imaginary created by the world of horror film, where fears take physical form and may or may not be bested within ninety tension-filled minutes, is constructed by and for men. It's not only the enthusiasts and self-proclaimed experts planting a stake in that fictional world, in other words: there are simply more men granted agency to shape the world of horror, and they populate it with more male characters than female. And while a male horror viewer is granted distraction by that world from whatever banal horrors he may experience in his life—the daily grind of a shitty job or difficult relationship is temporarily obscured by, say, an onscreen shark that's been crossbred with a bear and a torpedo—a female viewer is granted no such respite. Neither is a female character—she may behead the hurtling bearshark with as much aplomb as the next dude, but chances are good she's still going to have to fend off some guy pulling his dick out of his pants afterwards.

This cursory data analysis suggests that an entire genre of film has cohered around men's fears that somehow manages to ignore women's fears entirely. If we take sexual violence as just one example (although period blood, childbirth, or gatherings of naked women around campfires might also suffice) we can reasonably assume that some of the men, if not *most* of the men, who write, direct, and produce horror films believe sexual violence to contribute to the effectiveness of the genre. Now, men aren't experiencing sexual violence as frequently as female characters in these films, nor do men experience rape as frequently as women do in real life. So the fact that men behind the scenes of horror appear to believe that rape heightens tension is not rooted in their own experience of it. Most women probably agree that sexual violence is, well, pulse-quickening, to say the least, and I would never argue for a second that it isn't. But what is clear is that men who make horror films value the impact that scenes of rape and sexual violence can have on their bottom line, which is to say that sexual violence, in horror films, is considered good for business.

Emotional responses to sexual violence may or may not be gendered, I have no idea. We do know that one in every five women in college experiences rape or sexual assault, compared to only one in sixteen men. Many don't report it, and some don't survive it, yet quite a few do, which means more women than men have managed to cope with the impact of sexual violence, in real life. A far greater percentage than female characters who survive it in horror films, certainly.

What I offer for your consideration is this: that perhaps what scares men most—as evidenced by the fears we are given to consume as entertainment in the horror genre—may often be things that women have just learned to work through.

ENTERTAINMENT I

The body adapts easily to pain, but the mind still calculates ways to avoid it. We're told that women don't like horror films—body horror, in particular—because they can't stomach the gross-outs, but it seems more likely to me that women simply crave new experiences. Perhaps an all-male revue of mad scientists, psycho killers, and evil demons offers little new to women, many of whom, after all, regularly experience blood gushing out of their vaginas or, less frequently, tiny beings inside their bodies making absurd demands. Women are too often habituated to unwanted sexual advances in the workplace or on the street, occasionally delivered under threat of violence, or increasingly accustomed to mysterious diseases with bizarre symptoms that no one can explain. Non-binary folk can experience the additional daily horror of living in a society so tied to gender norms that every move is restricted, like the use of public restrooms, or wearing certain clothing items outside of the home. Few horror films of any tradition come close to portraying the banal terrors faced by people who do not identify as men.

Considering the lack of gender diversity in horror films in general, it will not surprise you to find that the body horror subgenre boasts a similar, dude-heavy lineup. A glance at Wikipedia, the site where well-paid, well-educated white men write down what they think the world is like, offers proof: David "*Crash*" Cronenberg, Brian "*Society*" Yuzna, Frank "*Basket Case*" Henenlotter, and Clive "*Hellraiser*" Barker are all listed as foundational contributors to the form. A slightly closer look doesn't offer much to dispute the assessment, either. There's little in *The Fly* (even the 1958 original, before Cronenberg's 1986 remake), *Invasion of the Body Snatchers* (1978), *Deadgirl* (2008), or *The Human Centipede* series (2011–2015)—each also directed by men—that doesn't call to mind those directors or the worlds they've envisioned.

Indeed, Cronenberg and Henenlotter, as well as Marcel Sarmiento and Gadi Harel, co-directors of *Deadgirl*, and Tom Six, the creator of *The Human Centipede* series, have each come under fire for misogyny.

Six, at least, is direct about his negative portrayal of women in *The Human Centipede*, which notoriously features a group of innocents medically attached to see how long they survive when consuming only the waste of the people whose assholes are sealed to their faces. "Politically, it is very incorrect," he explains coolly to *The Guardian*[3] of his infamous film series, in which various unlicensed medical practitioners sew groups of often-female victims together, mouth to anus. When pressed further on his gender politics in the late *Gawker*'s even later film site *Defamer*, however, Six is tellingly dismissive of personal accusations of misogyny. "I absolutely love women," he says.[4] One of the characters in the final film—the third, and easily most offensive of the series—is "an asshole," he concedes. "He's very bad to women. But it's great to write it!"

The warden of the film is a serial rapist, indeed (as well as a murderer and flagrant violator of most civil and human rights), but the charge leveled at Six isn't solely due to this character. In the larger context of this particular film, women have been written out of the script almost entirely, save the warden's sexually abused assistant and a jar full of clitorises the warden snacks on in times of strife. Yet Six asserts that he is just giving people what they want. "Horror audiences, they want to be thrilled, they want to be entertained because they are safe, themselves," he explains, in a tone described as "chipper."

Six's excuse for uninventive storytelling is a common one, but Gadi Harel took a different track with independent film site *ScreenAnarchy* to derail accusations of misogyny arising from his portrayal of a group of boys who find a lifeless woman and hide her away for their entertainment. "She was so easy," he says, praising *Deadgirl*'s lead, Jenny Spain.[5] "But she was also chained down."

Harel's joke is both true and funny, but fails as miserably as Six's comments to defend him from placement in the ranks of vile women-haters. In fact, his statement points to the bizarre situation he has created in which a woman is chained to a table and repeatedly raped and mutilated under his direction, for which he praises her.[6] It's even easier to point out that Six's "love of women" is defensive and apparently quite fair-weathered; elsewhere in the same interview, he compares women to mice, and claims he would never hurt either, which makes one wonder what exactly he believes a misogynist *does*.

No matter. Misogyny, in body horror, is clearly in evidence—as are racism and ableism—yet body horror offers the unique opportunity to explore physicality almost purely. In fact, the loss of body autonomy is central to the form, and bodies of all varieties are explored, often re-cut or re-engineered well beyond the limits of traditional sex, gender, or race—or for that matter nationality, economic class, or even humanity.

It is why body horror, when done well, can elicit a physical reaction in the viewer. A film may be visceral because it is vividly depicted, yes, but it also affects our viscera. In Cronenberg's *The Fly*, for example, Jeff Goldblum's character famously becomes twitchier and more harried and ever more disgusting as his body gradually transforms into that of a giant insect. In the brilliant and hard-to-find *Society*, otherwise a dorky 1980s teen boy coming-of-age film, the underpinnings of the upper class are revealed: orgies and mutations and ritual sex acts between close blood relations are contrasted with standard horrifying bullshit like real estate deals and country clubs. Often, the "victims" in such films are female, whether the subjects of experiments or the corpses left by subjects of experiments. But not always. In fact, we are almost as likely to see a male body mutilated in the subgenre as a female body, as much as the bodies of the latter may be singled out for more extreme abuses, discussed in more dismissive terms, or only present under an inequitable pay scale.

What remains unwavering is that, regardless of a subject's gender—or race, class, or anything else—body horror hinges on the notion of body *normativity*. A subject always starts as "normal" and over time becomes "abnormal."[7] Embedded in the assertion of what is normal, we find a set of presumptions about what roles, behaviors, desires, and appearances are appropriate for everyone. But it is in the assertion of body normativity—and its subsequent, persistent failure—that body horror holds the potential to become a radical visioning tool, a way to explore the possibilities on offer when the abnormal becomes common. Or, to put it more accurately for these modern days, when we acknowledge that the abnormal became common quite a long time ago.

ENTERTAINMENT II

A charmingly gory Canadian film named *American Mary* (2012) can show us how little it takes to upend a master narrative.

Jen and Sylvia Soska's tale is quirky, well-acted, and unpredictable (a feat in a genre in which pretty much the next thing that will always happen is that someone will die). It is a remarkable film on several counts. Given the genre, there is a noticeable lack of gratuitous sexual assault. Mary's rape occurs early in the film, fully contextualized, and is clearly not employed to contribute to viewer trauma. Compare to popular but extremely rapey *V/H/S* (2012), for example, which uses the found-footage conceit to explore six brief tales. Of them, three feature rape or the threat of it as the turning point in stories about men; a planned sexual assault even acts as a plot device in David Bruckner's installment, "Amateur Night." Rape, in horror films, tends to function as merely one aspect of a larger evil ultimately intent on thwarting men's desire. In *American Mary*, however, the rape scene is so understated that you may not even notice when it occurs. However, when Mary responds to her attacker, with deliberation and focus, it is clear that rape need not act as a given within a larger unfolding narrative of terror. *American Mary* presents sexual assault as event, not consequence.

The narrative derives from this moment, as our protagonist leaves school to focus on her own studies once it becomes clear that the price of entry to the aboveground world—in tuition fees and in the emotional distress of regular run-ins with her rapist—is too high. This glitch in her plans is made plot by the fact that she's studying medicine—Mary wants to be a surgeon—and has no intention of giving up her goal upon leaving school.

Not only is sexual assault handled as appropriately traumatic and fully survivable, *American Mary* offers a female character in horror who retains agency—and regains body autonomy—throughout the film. Indeed, whenever she questions her abilities, talent, or value to the world, Mary receives no small amount of positive affirmation for being who she wants to be. She becomes, indeed, a world-class surgeon, highly paid and sought after for her exquisite skill with the scalpel. Even if unlicensed.

Now, don't get me wrong. Mary is also killing people and

mutilating them, or, less frequently, merely threatening them. She's a complicated woman whose innate sense of justice—however much it may not jive with the rest of the world's—never wavers. And while there are flaws in this film, glitches of plot and ill-explained motivations (the film is set in Canada and the protagonist, Mary, is Canadian; while she expresses a hope to travel to the United States, she does not go, and no other explanation for the title unfolds in the narrative), the set-pieces are dead-on (ha ha), the acting solid and unindulgent, and the costuming exquisite. (Leather surgical masks add a particularly nice touch.) Still, the genius of *American Mary* is that feminine bodily autonomy wins out in every struggle.

Yet the film never goes down the rape-revenge route—another subgenre of horror (discussed further in the essays "Vagina dentata" and "Women" in the pages to come). In rape-revenge films, gender plays a central role: a woman or group of women is raped or sexually assaulted, and revenge is enacted on the man or group of men who perpetrated it. These roles are invariable—a male rape victim, for example, could never go on a rampage and kill hundreds of women who had victimized him and have it be considered rape revenge, for his story would simply be about a serial killer. A male protagonist is allowed sexual assault as backstory, if you see the point, which is exactly how sexual assault functions in *American Mary*. Too, the drama is too calculated to be vengeful and the gore too (ahem) surgical for *American Mary* to be classified as rape-revenge. The film is simply body horror, in the serial killer tradition—and just happens to be centered around a smart, strong lady.

Because horror films are formed in the cluttered, fetid bowels of capitalism, and reliant on the underpaid labor, emotional devotion, and silence of feminine players to function unhindered (a final nod to Harel), gender in horror always has meaning. The gender reversal in *American Mary* expresses more about what body horror is capable of than the entire sourced and edited Wikipedia description of the subgenre.

In body horror, humans experience disease or physical

transformation or acts of mutilation, in violation of both nature and the autonomous desire of the so-called normal human subject. If horror film creates a cultural space where fears can be explored in safety, body horror fosters one where the worst fears of the self— the loss of autonomy—can be viscerally enacted but still recovered from. *American Mary* grants a female character autonomy over her own body and the bodies of others. Rare in film, perhaps, but body changes are something women who have been sick or pregnant or had periods have already experienced and managed to survive, not to mention those who find their daily lives changing in fundamental ways after experiencing sexual violence, or under the systemic labor abuses of capitalist production. Body changes are often par for the course, too, in nonbinary lives, whether through breast-binding, hormonal transformation, or surgical operation. Millions upon millions of women and nonbinary people in the world have figured out ways, somehow, to mitigate the fear of appearing abnormal, and navigate the world in droves despite the real dangers posed by a medical system that does not understand them, a labor field that does not value them, and cultural products, like horror films, that revel in their imagined destruction, absence, or elimination for entertainment.

There are quite a few of us for whom body horror is actually kind of banal.

MEDICINE I

A memory from early girlhood: I'm a pig-tailed lass in a cute, frilly dress, and all my friends are playing with Barbies or model horses or making mud pies or drawing princesses. I could be practicing domesticity alongside other girls but I am instead inside, nose in a book, memorizing all the bones of the human body. *Distal phalanx, middle phalanx, proximal phalanx, sesamoid bone, metacarpophalangeal joint, carpometacarpal joint.* I'd memorized the primary bones in the human hand before I left kindergarten, following years of extensive study with a Visible Man toy. ("What about a Visible Woman?" I asked my dad once, a neuroradiologist who was given similar items as gifts all the time, and always passed them on to me. He wanted a son, and that didn't bother me at the time because I liked to go to car shows. "It's the same," he said, although it's clear to me now that it isn't.)

I was seven years old when the *Anatomy Coloring Book* came out in 1977, and I was disappointed. Although I finally had a book that allowed me to pursue a "normal" age-appropriate activity like coloring, it was already beneath my intellectual skills. Not, however, my motor skills; I still have the book. My awkward marker lines bleed well outside the bounds of the occipital lobe, and dull-colored pencil marks lap over the edges of the chambers of the heart. I was barely capable of working the mechanics of a pencil sharpener then, but I could see the book's creators had oversimplified complex systems that I had delighted in. "This book is for babies!" I recall announcing to my mother, who laughed.

My early obsession with anatomy made me a whiz at games like Operation! or puzzles of the human body, and, later, would stun rheumatologists unused to precision on the part of their chronic pain patients. "Are you a physician?" a radiologist once asked me as he wheeled me out of the MRI machine in response to my demand to view scans. "Sort of," I told her, although I didn't elaborate that I am my only patient. For reasons I sometimes still cannot fathom, I didn't go into the sciences, although my obsession with the incongruities of the human body were sated for a good long while with monster movies.

MEDICINE II

Then in Seattle I became athletic. I had until then been exclusively artistic, sensitive of soul. I was partial to black dresses and thoughtful poses, more likely to show off my biceps hoisting a book than a barbell. But I joined a crew team in my thirties, which meant rising at four every morning and carrying a boat out to the cold water by five for two hours of rowing before I went to work at eight. I was dedicated to the sport, so I would also return later that night to practice on the machines before bed at 8:00 p.m. I was an athlete.

Several regattas later, I realized my athleticism was a symptom. I had a disease that causes a rapid increase in energy and I had no other outlet for it. My thyroid had gone haywire and was overproducing hormones; every single one of my body's urges was amplified, first just a tiny bit, and eventually—over the course of several years—by great volumes. It was so gradual that I had not noticed until I was eating several full meals a day and not gaining weight, performing daily Olympic-style training sessions but never relaxing into a reasonable heart rate, always taking in water and always urinating it out again. I was hot all the time. I slept very little. I felt like I was like living three different lives simultaneously, and it still wasn't enough.

I diagnosed myself by way of literature. I read an essay in a literary magazine in which a character describes the slowing of her physical functions and mind, gradually piecing together that all of her disparate symptoms are controlled by a single gland that does many different things in the body: the thyroid. This gland truly is a wonder, controlling our ability to perceive temperature, feel hunger or thirst, urinate or defecate. Heart rate and metabolism are also the domain of the thyroid. In essence, this small gland controls the way that you experience the world, how you react to it, and what you desire from it. I recall the author explaining that her hypothyroidism had caused her to sleep more and eat less; she was convinced that she would cease bothering to function sooner or later, on a biological level, before finally perishing of slowness.

I did not relate in any way to her tale, yet the mirror image it cast of my own physical state was alarming. The night I came across the story, I had eaten a massive dinner, worked out in excess of three hours on two separate occasions earlier in the day, had only slept a few hours the night before, and was finishing off a six pack of beer by myself in a hot sauna. I weighed slightly over a hundred pounds. I had worked a full eight-hour day in a high-stress editing job. I should have been exhausted, and if not exhausted, I should have been prone, either from heat or alcohol consumption. Something was wrong with my thyroid.

When I went to the doctor I told her I was hyperthyroidic; she diagnosed me with Graves' disease, an affliction of the thyroid gland that, less frequently, can cause bulging eyes (Marty Feldman had it) and thick, red skin on the shins. At the time, it wasn't clear what this meant, except that I should have my overproducing thyroid gland removed, immediately. It was thought that this would clear up the problem, although it did not. For the Graves' itself was another symptom, the first indication I had that I might never stop accruing certain kinds of diseases.

AN INTRODUCTION

My own private experiences in the world of body horror also changed the way I watched horror movies. I measure characters now against my own emotional pain or physical deterioration, relishing an environment where normative—even idealized—bodies always go wrong.

Among my recent favorites is *Contracted* (2013) a tale of a woman with a degenerative disease slightly more dramatic than my own. The film opens on LA resident Samantha, played by Najarra Townsend, at a party with stilted conversation and a jilted jealous suitor named Riley. Sam begins to annoy viewers before the party even ends (and this party takes way longer than it should, in screen time—ten boring minutes) and skips out with a mysterious fellow reveler named "BJ" who has slipped her a roofie. The two have vigorous, if nonconsensual, rape-sex in his car: it is the prelude to *Contracted.*

Thereafter, the film is broken into three sections, one per remaining day of Sam's life. During the first, Sam experiences mild, irritating physical symptoms, but the only clue that they will increase is Sam's admission that she thinks she's "coming down with something," fifteen minutes into the ninety-minute film.

On day two, Sam oversleeps, and awakens to discover she's experiencing serious vaginal bleeding, which she writes off as an exceptionally heavy menstrual cycle. Her mother expresses meddling concern; her best friend calls to warn Sam that the mysterious BJ is wanted by police for unknown reasons. Sam goes to work at a restaurant, but falls ill and ducks into a restroom to hide out. We are halfway through the film, and it is difficult to feel invested in Sam's grating character. She is not quite attractive enough to care about in a superficial way. Only the slow pace of the film has held viewer attention until now. Then the spell breaks, and the pace of the film quickens. After the quiet moment Sam takes to herself in the restaurant's bathroom, she urinates quickly. Upon standing, she notices that the toilet has filled with dark, red blood.

She visits a doctor, who asks hilariously vague and unhelpful questions, and helps her not at all. Sam's body continues to erode, and when she meets up with friends later, they express disgust at the changes she's going through, and inform her that BJ is wanted for sexually predatory behavior. By the end of the day she has lost several teeth, and a stray worm has appeared on the floor, dropped from somewhere, perhaps her own body; it's unclear.

On day three ("of three," the title card adds ominously), Sam's mother expresses sincere concern—the first genuinely touching moment in the film. Generally, we are given to view Sam as a white woman of some privilege in LA; her emotional maturity includes responses like dumping as much of a bottle of Visine as she can fit into her eye to address her rapid decomposition and declaring things like, "What the fuck!" as her veins blacken, her hair falls out in large clumps, and blood pours from every orifice. Sam's boss at the restaurant is not sympathetic, nor concerned with the health of his customers. He convinces Sam to come in to work even as her body begins falling, in pieces, into his customers' food.

From this moment on, each new symptom is stomach-churning, no matter how many times we have witnessed similar gore in other movies. Sam's fingernails fall off, her hair clumps out, and blood streams from between her legs in great quantities. All the trappings of femininity in their overblown glory fall away from her, useless. She cannot survive like this in LA.

Sam returns to her doctor, who doesn't help, and her emotional health tanks. She takes some illicit substances. She screams at her well-meaning mom. She flubs an entry into an important flower competition (which viewers, admittedly, had no idea she intended to enter, although it does makes for a tidy conclusion to our metaphor about failed femininity.) Sam loses her shit. As the severity of her illness beings to grow more apparent, she crosses a few remaining social boundaries. A noise-music soundtrack kicks in, and the transformation of a marginally attractive (if totally unsympathetic) young white woman into a terrifying and rabid monster is complete. Sam's revenge against humanity includes a seduction of her admirer Riley, a disgusting scene that ends (spoiler alert) with a clump of maggots falling off his cock.

The very final scene is touching, if bizarre. Sam has evolved into a snarling, frothing rage, still in a pretty dress, threatening all passersby, when her mother appears, screeching her love for her daughter to no recognition or avail—the second touching moment in the film is also its last.

There are several moments of true disgust on offer in *Contracted*, and not just emotional violations, where a loved one is treated poorly and we feel bad. The beloved here are treated with a disgusting, vicious violence—and not just Sam's. All bodies are treated as material, as substance, and we are made to read them as disposable. There's a flat-out gorgeous moment, for example, when

Sam, one eye whiting out and another bleeding, massive open sores from her lip to her chin, hair thinning, fixes her makeup in the mirror. She gazes quietly at her reflection as she decides which shade of makeup will best complement her oozing wound.

In *Variety,*[8] film critic Dennis Harvey called *Contracted* "Eric England's body-horror opus," and claimed it contains "all the ingredients for a nasty black-comedy-horror critique of Los Angeles' most narcissistic, emotionally and intellectually bankrupt sides." The film never becomes that, staying within the bounds of "its very limited goal of simply chronicling one unfortunate young woman's body going to hell over a few alarming days' course," as the critic describes.

What Harvey overlooks, however, is that creating a character with whom we do not sympathize as a human being (whom we may even find repulsive *before* her infection), but identify as a physical body with whom we share only the most basic of functions, is an extremely difficult task. *Contracted*, therefore, nods to the point of connection between humans, the spark of compassion for one another buried far beneath attraction or desire or even sympathy. It is our hint that the visceral humanity of non-normative bodies is at stake in body horror, for normative concepts of bodies and of behavior lie both at the core of this film and at the core of our culture. The stress felt while watching is disgust at witnessing femininity falter, but perhaps it's also concern that femininity isn't that stable to begin with. Neither, perhaps, masculinity. Nor the physical bodies they play out upon.

Sam's disease may be unreal (and Mayera Abeita deserves mention for special effects makeup), but *Contracted* strikes a few notes of truth: Sam's hapless medical doctor, totally unable to respond to the patient before him, may come to act as a totem for the entire medical profession in the pages that follow. Her unsympathetic boss, who can't clearly perceive her ailments, and demands she continue working—he, too, may strike you as common. Sam's growing terror as her body changes for unknown reasons will certainly resonate with other stories you are about to read.

ANNE ELIZABETH MOORE

XXX

You may, in fact, find this book as stressful as any other offering from the body horror genre, and for that I do apologize. I only intend the evisceration to display the experience we all do share of being bodies subject to a harsh, cruel world. And in that shared knowledge, I submit, can be found quite a bit of hope.

—AEM (January 2017)

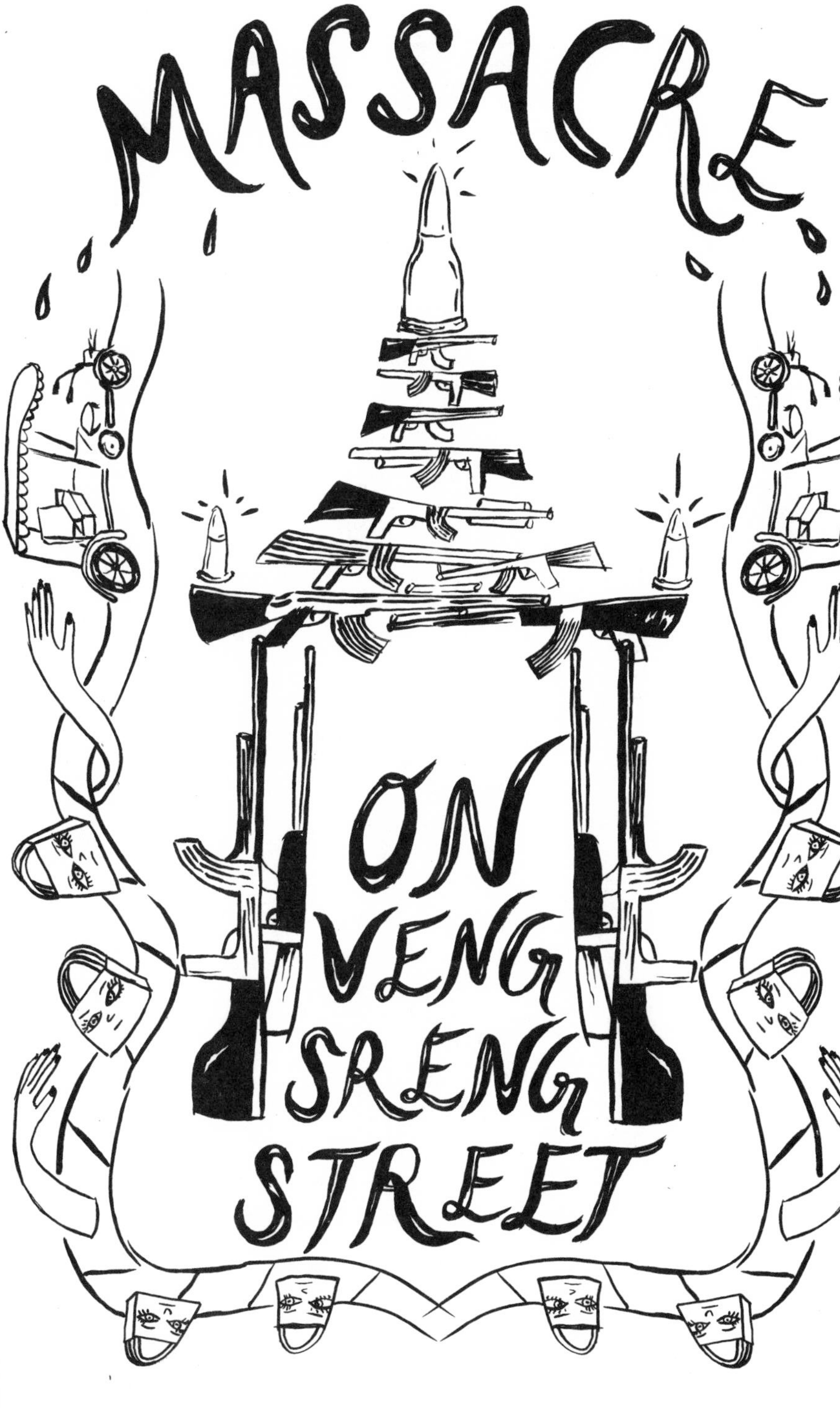
MASSACRE
ON
VENG
SRENG
STREET

By far the most terrifying aspect of the grisly ordeal was that, four days later, everything had returned to normal. The nightmares started then—of adopting a charming baby that harbored evil intentions, ordering a delicious-looking dish in a riverside restaurant that tasted of decaying newspaper, strolling near a pretty pond that sucked me in, all allegories for an event that had unfolded in a less friendly manner than it first appeared it would. I don't nightmare, so the midnight horrors were foreign, the fears of someone who's felt safe for a long time, but knew terror once: indications of a joy gone horribly awry.

The second most terrifying aspect was that, five days before routines reemerged, Cambodians seemed cheerier, more open, and to be having more fun than I had ever witnessed. My experience in the country was limited to the previous seven years, but I'm judging by the thousands of them I saw out in the streets then, beaming, brightly clothed, cheering themselves on for being together in public. The people of Cambodia are renowned for buoyancy and wide smiles, however arduously and famously long has run the nation's strife. The Southeast Asian country's recent history includes periods of severe poverty, intense civil war, rule by the UN, a Vietnamese occupation, the Khmer Rouge regime, an unjustified American bombing campaign, French colonization, and more poverty—generations of desperate hunger and oppression only disrupted by a brief period of national independence from the mid-1950s to the 1960s when people still didn't have enough to eat, but felt proud and hopeful. Arguably, Cambodians were happier during the political demonstrations that started at the end of 2013 than they had been in almost half a century.

That was before the prime minister, baited by the opposition party, cracked down on the protests—the largest the country had ever seen—with machine guns. At least five were killed, more than forty injured, and twenty-three arrested on Veng Sreng Street in Phnom Penh on January 3, 2014. The next day, thugs hired by the ruling party moved into Freedom Park, the designated protest zone, and beat those who didn't immediately run for their lives. Helicopters freshly donated by the Chinese were buzzing overhead. The day after that, vigils were held while military police in riot gear and trucks ready to dispense razor wire dotted most street corners in the city center. The day after that, although a general strike had been rumored, garment factory workers instead headed back to jobs or fled the city entirely, moving home to the provinces and accepting the poverty of rice farming when the possibility of getting gunned down by police under charge of a democratically elected government was the other option. And the day after *that* was Victory Over Genocide Day, the day thirty-five years prior that Cambodia was invaded by the Vietnamese, who ousted the Khmer Rouge but then stayed to rule the country, which many remain angry about.

That was the day things went back to normal. The normal from before. When fear caused silence. When protests were disallowed, and gatherings of more than ten people in public space simply didn't happen. When people refused to talk politics. When no one accused anyone of murder, although everyone knew murders had occurred.

♦ ♦ ♦

Freedom Park was like how people talk about Occupy Wall Street. Of course, "occupy" means something different in countries that have seen—or admit to having seen—military occupations, so few in Cambodia had heard of the Occupy movement. My experience of Occupy Chicago was abrasive and sexist, but others found their politics there. *Everyone was so friendly! We were all in it together!* This was Freedom Park for me. Far more important, this was Freedom Park for the thousands of Cambodians who spent time there, most without a history of political engagement to compare the experience to.

Each time I visited in December 2013 and the first days of January 2014 there were more people in Freedom Park, marchers from rallies and strikes corralled by Cambodian National Rescue Party (CNRP) leaders Sam Rainsy, Kem Sokha, and Mu Sochua. Newcomers came from the provinces, lured by pictures on Facebook, the social networking site of choice in the newly wired culture. People who didn't know each other made sure others had enough food, re-villaging the urban setting. Freedom Park was a "park" not in the Jens Jensen sense, but in the "momentary respite from the roadway" sense; it was a bricked slab with a few straggly trees here and there, to which occupiers tied tarps to create shade for themselves and whoever wandered by. It seemed in all ways the opposite of the Khmer Rouge days, when city dwellers were forced into the provinces, food was hoarded when available at all, and neighbors couldn't be trusted not to report you. Freedom Park was beautiful and happy. Whatever may have felt unsettling for a moment dissipated quickly.

On my third visit, I was befriended by a newly arrived group of garment workers. I had been reporting on the Cambodian apparel industry for five years; garment workers liked me because I openly coveted their fashion sense, and tried to speak Khmer to them and failed. I acted like the girl who can't ever quite break into the cool group, which is exactly how I felt. A crew of six waved me over and gave me some peanuts; I ate them, although I am allergic.

I asked how long they'd been there. They told me three hours. I asked how long they would be on strike, and they explained, nearly in unison, "It depends on the GMAC." The government had announced, just that day, a wage raise to $100 per month. It was a concession to the protests that had greeted the Garment Manufacturing Association of Cambodia's (GMAC) wage-raise announcement a few days previous, to a mere $95. I asked if they were satisfied with the one hundred dollar figure. They were not.

"If the government does not give the salary of $160, all the employees want to change the prime minister. They don't want him to lead again," one told me in response. Another repeated it, verbatim. It sounded canned. Several days later, after the $160 wage raise no longer seemed achievable, many garment workers would tell me that they didn't care about the government. They just wanted to be able to afford meat that wasn't rotten.

The $160 wage was a figure of some dispute. It's significantly higher than most living wage estimates in the country, but the CNRP had promised to raise the minimum wage for garment workers to $150 during their campaign. When they lost the election in July 2013, the government was forced to announce a wage-raise inquiry, eventually floating $160 as a goal for 2018. The CNRP and unions began demanding it immediately, and rally participation soared. Sam Rainsy, the bespectacled president of the CNRP, repeatedly told workers to fight for it, whatever the cost. He told them he would support them, and protect them, throughout their struggle. The government had a history of violently cracking down on protestors, shooting demonstrators and striking garment workers with impunity. Kem Sokha, the CNRP's second in command, announced onstage at Freedom Park one day that the workers were not afraid to die. (This turned out not to be true, but we wouldn't find that out for a few more days.)

In a photograph I took on January 1, 2014, the garment workers are flashing me a sign, raising seven fingers in the air. It is a reference to January 7, Victory Over Genocide Day. The scuttlebutt I'd heard had a general strike planned for the sixth, leaving the seventh open to celebrate a day of renewal, the day the prime minister steps down, opening up the way for a true democracy in Cambodia. It's possible something darker was planned if the strikes didn't succeed; my Khmer had dwindled in recent years, and even if my tutor had taught me words for destructive activities, I'm certain the giggling garment-working ladies would never have said them to me.

We'll call my translator and tuk-tuk driver Nike. It's a pseudonym I've chosen to protect him in case the Cambodian government reads this, but it's a faithful one: like his real nickname, it was chosen to signal the automatic respect and honor the nation craved, primarily available to the poverty stricken masses by way of the brand names that passed through their hands in the garment factories, quickly and easily.

Nike was attractive and lean, and raising two kids: a son he was educating and a daughter he'd sent off to live somewhere else; he didn't tell me where. On a tuk-tuk driver's salary (about $250 per month a couple of times per year, but $100 per month is more common, with occasional stretches when almost no money comes in at all), Nike could barely afford the bribes necessary to keep his son educated. Although the government is supposed to pay teachers, they often do not. When they do, it's very low (only $50 to $70 per month for elementary school educators), so teachers request "thank you money" from the kids' parents so they can eat. Going rates at Nike's son's school were only 1,000 Riel per day, or about a quarter in USD, but $7.50 per month was more than Nike could afford. Education is not the only supposedly public service that actually requires substantial personal investment—they all do. It's what a nation awash in corruption looks like, and no amount of clever sloganeering by NGOs has curbed it. It is just how Cambodia works.

That's one of the reasons folks took to the streets at the end of 2013 and early 2014, before the massacre on Veng Sreng Street in Canadia Industrial Park, one of the country's Special Economic Zones. Corruption has kept steady pace with increasing cash flow into the country, and it's eating away people's chances for financial growth, or even stability. Corruption was not, however, the only reason—not, for example, why Nike was keeping a close eye on the protests since they started, nor why every morning began with his query about whether I had seen the latest developments "on Facebook."

Corruption hits some harder than others. It's a particular burden on women trying to survive on garment-industry wages, and most working women in the country are. Besides garment work, there's not much an uneducated woman can do in a country with entrenched gender roles besides sex work, which (with Khmer customers) pays a little less than teachers' salaries before the bribes, or food vending, which pays about the same. A job at a grocery store or on the cleaning crew of a university pays about $60 per month. If women can afford higher education, there's teaching—high school teachers can make twice as much as elementary school teachers—but Nike's already demonstrated how, with limited funds, educational opportunities for girls often suffer.

It is still worth noting that, even at $80 per month—the wage in place when the protests started in November—garment workers made more than many in Cambodia. At the $100 wage, they would make more than most. And at $160, they would be among the highest paid laborers in the country, mostly women, and remain one of the only workforces with a legally protected minimum wage. Perhaps most significantly, the wage increase would have been won by a popular uprising against the ruling party—a stunning display of political power.

That was never a likely scenario. The Khmer Rouge regime remains a recent memory for many, including the prime minister. Hun Sen was only a senior-level cadre in the regime before he worked in the Vietnamese government and then headed up the Cambodian People's Party (CPP) to win the first official general election in 1993. He's stayed in power ever since—partially due to his embrace of garment industry money—so it was difficult to envision an outcome that included his agreement to double the current wage for garment workers.

Yet the arguments for a wage increase beyond any recent estimates of a living wage were compelling, if largely unvoiced. The population of Cambodia is around fifteen million, and the garment industry labor force around four hundred thousand. As a body, these laborers are surprisingly influential: as the third largest industry in the country, wages from garment work support the nation's second largest industry, rice farming. If you distill this economic model down to a single countryside family, imagine how it might change mealtime dynamics when the girl no one could afford to educate five years ago becomes the family breadwinner. Her workplace needs grow vital to family sustenance. This effect, multiplied by four hundred thousand, is why garment workers were said to have been the driving force behind the sway toward the CNRP, the opposition party, in the July 2013 election.

Some suggest that this sway was larger than official election tallies showed: the results of that contest remain under dispute, which is another primary reason folks from all over the country gathered at Freedom Park toward the end of that year. Charges of ballot-fixing and coercion at the polls plagued the CPP's declaration of victory, as they have plagued Hun Sen since his first election over two decades beforehand. In that time, he's led the country to the first economic prosperity it's ever seen. His nickname is "strong man," and a whole lot of murders, politically motivated and otherwise, can be linked to him. He's also one of the longest-serving leaders of any nation, a factoid that doesn't sit comfortably with those familiar with how democracies work. Yet Cambodians feel gratitude for whatever relief from abject poverty his policies have brought, and that is tough to overlook. Still, even official results—offered by the ruling party, natch—show that the CPP lost a record twenty-two parliamentary seats over the summer. The CNRP won twenty-six. The tide was clearly changing.

Yet the CNRP's Sam Rainsy is an ambiguous figure, too. While many like him simply because he's not Hun Sen, he spent years in self-imposed exile in France, unengaged in significant political developments, including the fight for higher wages in the garment industry. He had helped to establish one of the most important apparel worker unions in the country, although his dedication to workers lags in crucial moments. Many workers told me in near whispers that they wanted a change in government leadership, of course, but would be just as uncomfortable with Rainsy as prime minister as they were with Hun Sen.

◆ ◆ ◆

The day Varn Pov was arrested, Nike hardened.

Pov was the leader of IDEA, the Independent Democracy of informal Economy Association, an ad hoc union for informal workers like tuk-tuk drivers, food vendors, and sex workers—someone I had met a few years previous, and respected—and, I discovered, a friend of Nike's.

"How you know?" Nike demanded when I informed him of the arrest, his eyes getting big.

"Twitter," I told him. He used "Facebook" and "the Internet" interchangeably, but hadn't yet embraced mobile microblogging. Nike folded his hands and leaned angrily on his tuk-tuk. "He a good man." He looked at me again and spit out a word in Khmer that I did not understand. Then, uncharacteristically, punched the back of the seat he'd been leaning on a moment before. He paced for a minute, and then said, "OK. Now I take you to Freedom Park."

It was not a question posed deferentially, service provider to client—it was a command, a role reversal. I now offered him something more significant than cash for driving me places and translating Khmer: I offered him international eyeballs on what he could sense was about to happen in Cambodia.

He drove angrily, no longer chatty, for several minutes. Then he whipped out his phone—a dangerous if common distraction while driving a motorcycle, but he had things on his mind. When he got off the phone he shouted back at me, over his shoulder: "Anne. You know, I concerned about the human rights."

"You should be," I agreed.

The arrest of Pov and nine others on January 2 was the first retaliation the prime minister had taken against demonstrators calling for his resignation in 2014, but this was an old tactic of Hun Sen's that often preceded violence. In 1991, the CPP had over one hundred opposition party members killed while the UN ruled the country, Human Rights Watch has charged. Six years later, the prime minister's bodyguards led a grenade attack on a Rainsy-led rally. Sixteen died and over 150 were injured, shortly in advance of the general election. Only months later, in 1998, hundreds of potential political enemies of Hun Sen's died or disappeared. After the results of that vote were announced, thousands of protestors swarmed the streets of the capital to demand a recount or new elections. Riot cops then cracked down and cleared the protest site.

When Nike and I arrived at Freedom Park that day, we were greeted with chants of "Hun Sen Must Go," the rally cry of the moment.

Who cuts the tree?
Hun Sen
Who stayed in the pagoda and ate all the food?
Hun Sen
Who hurt the monks?
Hun Sen
Who killed the pop star?
Hun Sen
No More Corruption / Hun Sen Must Go

The chant had emerged after a December 10 rally in Siem Reap. The allegations it lists against Hun Sen are so commonly understood as to be undisputed, and indeed, the prime minister himself acknowledged the lot once, laughing off the idea that he would resign over such trivialities. Illegal logging has flourished throughout the country; an activist threatening to expose it was killed by military police. The prime minister studied in the pagoda before ordering the dispersal of monk protests, over both landgrabbing and, more recently, a Buddhist relic rumored to be stolen in revenge for an unpaid government salary. He also had an affair with a pop star who, later, turned up dead.

In a speech delivered that same day, Rainsy elaborated on the chant's allegations, with descriptions of how the Vietnamese were stealing jobs from hardworking Cambodians and comparing Hun Sen to a woman for refusing to take responsibility and step down. The xenophobia and misogyny caught him a few rebukes from human rights organizations, and another from within his own ranks, by women's rights leader (and former parliament member) Mu Sochua. But xenophobia and misogyny can pull in support, too, especially when economic fears run rampant.

An elderly, toothless farmer in Freedom Park offered an example in conversation with Nike. He was from the Kandal province, southeast of the capital, and had been camping in Freedom Park for three days. "I want to change the government," he told Nike in Khmer. He wore a white shirt and a krama, the traditional Cambodian scarf, tied around his waist in a skirt, a style many city folk have abandoned.

"The government cut down the trees, stole the land from the people . . . and now they lost their relic of the Buddha," Nike interpreted for my tape recorder. The farmer could have been anywhere between sixty and eighty, and elaborated at some length on the forced evictions that have often preceded the development of land by CPP party members or their cronies. But what he was really upset about, Nike translated, was that the Vietnamese held the contracts on the logging in the Kampong Speu province and many tourism sites in the country. Which was true.

To the farmer's left, a younger but somehow more haggard-looking man broke in to explain something to Nike. He went on for several minutes, uninterrupted, spitting as he spoke. The only words I understood were "Viet" and "Nam," and when he ran out of vindictives, Nike translated the tirade succinctly: "He does not like Vietnam."

As we left the park that day, a song blasted through the area, bouncing off the street's metal roofs and lone, nearby skyscraper, heralding Sam Rainsy a national hero.

♦ ♦ ♦

I'm foreshadowing—I can't help it. There was a sinister tinge to the air, although I was perfectly capable of overlooking it at the time. The truth is, thousands of happy young Cambodian women—smiles bigger than entire heads—were swarming the streets and the park, openly waving at me for the camera, chatting, hugging me, cheerfully declaring themselves political actors, agents of social change. During my first trip inside the garment factories in 2010, I had to give a pseudonym to the name of the factory and could take no pictures of the women that agreed to talk to me; still I could only convince every fifth or sixth worker to tell me what she thought about her job. No one told me their name. Tuk-tuk drivers would hush you in those days when you mentioned the prime minister, fearing that the wrong word in response would get them jailed or worse. Even the comparatively comfortable middle class resolutely shook heads, reminding me that change does not come overnight, and that patience would be rewarded, before falling silent. An odd way to respond to the name of the prime minister.

In contrast, the visual that sticks with me from the earliest days of 2014 is a swarm of giggling young women, dressed electrically. Cambodians joke that the way to tell a Khmer women from a Vietnamese woman is that the Vietnamese woman only likes to wear one pattern at a time, paired with a solid color. Cambodian women like to wear many patterns, a mish-mash of symbols and cute animals, clever if misspelled slogans, nearly incandescent colors. All together! As many as possible! She might wear a hot pink top and bright green hoodie with an American flag printed on the back with jeans, flowered socks, colorful shoes. They have plenty of time to concoct good outfits: they spend eight-hour days working in the factories where clothes are made, plus two hours of often mandatory overtime, and if they aren't able to afford or find a fell-off-the-truck version of something they like, a whole other batch of clothes eventually returns to them, cast-offs from the US and EU, cheaply sold by the bulk in one of the city's many markets. More garments are discarded every year as production rates increase, last year by 20 percent—an ever-expanding volume of apparel that garment workers both create and look great in.

Perhaps because my pictures from that time are so filled with vibrant color, I can only describe being on the streets of Cambodia at the start of 2014 as the experience of pure joy.

♦ ♦ ♦

Around 9:00 a.m. on January 3, workers gathered along Veng Sreng Street. Many were striking to demand the $160 wage, but some had other concerns: back pay at some of the nearby factories was still owed to workers. The mood was light, however. One striking worker told me that, more or less, the protest was a big dance party.

Quietly, in the background, a military unit gathered. Later identified as Brigade 911, an Indonesian-trained force with an unruly history including participation in the 1998 election-related violence, they dressed in sparkling new riot gear. They arrived by truck. They took out their guns, AK-47s and Norinco Type 97A Assault Rifles. Then, as a livid young man named Kha Sei told me in front of a clinic on Veng Sreng, "they fight the dancers."

Warning shots were fired over the heads of protestors. The crowd threw rocks and sticks in response. Police answered with live rounds, killing at least five, injuring and arresting many more. Several of the injured or arrested later claimed they weren't even protesting. One was a food vendor, working nearby, seeking to feed her family by selling food to protestors.

"When the police shoot the people, one guy died over there," Kha Sei pointed to a spot a few feet away. "He's still alive? The police shoot more."

"Were all five factory workers?" I asked. There had been no confirmation of this at the time, but Kha Sei, in his blood-red t-shirt, seemed to know all the players.

Sophy, a garment worker in her early twenties who was also there that day, crossed her arms and looked disgusted. A third friend, who didn't give his name, said yes. "But many more than five," this friend added. He pointed to a wall fifteen yards to our right, marking the property of the Sunwell Shoes Company. "They throw one body there. Many others, they take away in the car." (Missing persons reports emerged later, although the official death toll was not raised.)

A striker standing near Kha Sei was shot. He mimed how he and two friends carried the gunshot victim to the medical clinic where we now stood, not thirty feet from where MPs were shooting, a point across the street Kha Sei pointed out to me. The clinic director turned them away. "He was scared about the government," Kha Sei said. The striker died. He stood over the spot, glaring angrily at the ground. I looked away out of respect.

Kha Sei spread his arm behind him, gesturing to the ruined clinic at our backs. "So we do this," he said. The building had been destroyed, gutted—everything smashable smashed, everything wrenchable hurled to the ground and stomped on. The sign bearing the name of the clinic was riddled with holes, clearly caused by one young man on another's shoulders, one holding on while the other punched. The group chased out a woman who had just given birth, then tore through everything in sight.

Two days later, the clinic was still a pile of rubble, testifying to an anger not released but delayed. The angry trio I interviewed stood at its entrance, glaring at everyone. The nameless friend's parting words to me were a comment that the garment workers were no longer demanding $160 per month.

"Now we just need machine guns," he said.

◆ ◆ ◆

Victory Over Genocide Day was not the day of change the garment workers had signaled for my camera after all; it was instead the day Hun Sen held a special ceremony for a visiting Vietnamese delegation, to publicly thank them for their country's assistance in bringing an end to Cambodian bloodshed thirty-five years beforehand, even though a civil war continued to rage thereafter, and the bloodshed had continued. The bloodshed of two days prior, too, went conspicuously unmentioned. It remains true to this day that the Vietnamese profit from tourism to genocide sites and Angkor Wat, the largest religious monument in the world, and Cambodia's beloved symbol of unity, strength, and pre-Khmer Rouge history. It is also still true that illegal logging hauls frequently end up in the possession of Vietnamese companies, and few investigations result. People remain angry about the post-Khmer Rouge occupation, and the extranational profiteering it allowed. Today, hostilities toward Vietnamese immigrants often result in violence, or death.

Many garment workers had already left the city to return to the countryside, but those still in Phnom Penh on January 7 went back to work that day or the next. People fell into silence. Even Nike and I spoke less frequently. The country mourned, privately, each individual silently allowing hopes to dissipate, one by one. From the outside it may have appeared as if none of it had ever happened: Not the exhilaration. Not the horror. I might have ignored the whole grisly ordeal myself, if the nightmares hadn't started then.

But there was no ignoring it. In the earliest days of 2014, most Cambodians had taken to the streets in joy and hope for change. The government had turned on them, and many had died. The experience will never be forgotten, but it may never be publicly acknowledged, either.

A version of this essay was originally published in the Los Angeles Review of Books Quarterly.

By the mid-1920s, the nascent feminine hygiene industry in the US was in peril. Women, all a-flutter about their recently acquired voting rights and whatnot, were persisting in the questionable activity of crafting their own sanitary products by hand. Following a tradition passed down by generations of matriarchs, panty liners were still being sewn from castaway fabrics—hence the phrase "on the rag." This presented a massive barrier to the handful of companies eager to get into the menstrual pad business. Who can blame these diligent entrepreneurs? They were missing out on valuable consumer dollars! So forward-thinking lady-product manufacturer Johnson & Johnson hired a team of efficiency experts to research the matter: Frank and Lillian Gilbreth, a husband-and-wife duo who combined their interests in industrial engineering with a study of psychology (and in their spare time, raised twelve children).

That the Gilbreths were offered the market research contract as a duo is significant, because the Nineteenth Amendment was still new, and because they had a dozen kids, and because Frank died before the undertaking began. So Lillian was in a unique position to both innovate the field of market research—the Gilbreth firm was among the first of its kind—and to do so as a single woman. (The kids kept up the housework; their travails are immortalized in several *Cheaper By the Dozen* films.)

Hiring a woman for the job, even if "the job" was to look into the habits of other women, was unheard of, although some saw Gilbreth's 1926 solo venture as a further expression of growing equality between the sexes. Johnson & Johnson, for its part, perhaps sensed that her status as a career woman and single mother might boost their own marketing efforts among that exact demographic. That Gilbreth was also in the process of inventing the field of industrial psychology—making her, at the time, the standalone expert in the world on how consumers might feel about products, not to mention her ability to speak better even than her husband about the unique values of feminine products—surely played a role in the company's progressive decision to allow her to honor the contract on her own.[1]

The company's problem was simple: "catamenial bandages," as menstrual devices were called at the time, were not selling. Gilbreth's theory was that they did not adequately address women's needs. After all, Johnson & Johnson's main market competition was not other companies, it was the intended customer base, who had been fulfilling their own needs just fine, *thankyouverymuch*, for generations. Commercially-available sanitary napkins were uniformly bulky, heavy, and uncomfortable, which Gilbreth set about proving in interviews with around a thousand women of diverse ages regarding their monthly needs. The resulting market research outlined a matrix of availability, adequate clothing protection, comfort, disposability, and inconspicuousness, all of which, when combined, would create a sort of menstrual product magic that ladies would be unable to resist. That, at least, is what Gilbreth's final report suggested, and Johnson & Johnson concurred. Perceiving immediate salability in her ideas, the company generated patent after patent after patent based on her findings, quickly outpacing the production capabilities of other feminine hygiene product makers, who strove to improve their own designs when Johnson & Johnson's new lines emerged, just to stay in business.

Ninety years on, nearly 6,500 patents for sanitary napkins have been granted. The devices have become uniformly practical in that time, ensuring comfort, leakage control, and disposability—and can even biodegrade, absorb foul odors, or remain entirely unnoticeable when worn and disposed of as advised. It is no hyperbole to claim that the bulk of these advancements are the result of one single woman's labor, nor would it tax imagination to further credit the thousand or so other women she tapped for input. Yet these women's efforts go entirely unacknowledged in the realm of intellectual property: the rights to profit from the feminine hygiene field—as assured by the US Patent and Trademark Office (USPTO)—remain about 95 percent male-owned.

◆ ◆ ◆

Equality between the sexes indeed.

One frequently sees cited today that, nearly a century after achieving the right to vote in the US, women continue to make up 51 percent of the population but only 18 percent of the US Congress, and continue to earn, on average, a mere 77 percent of what men do. (Factoring for race allows us to see that only white women can expect this comparatively high percentage of a male colleague's dollar.) Implicit gender bias crystalizes in the realm of patents, which are held by a pool of inventors only 7.5 percent female.[2] Commercial patents have been granted to an even smaller percentage of women, just 5.5 percent.

This has shifted slightly over time. A massive push prior to Y2K had women earning science, technology, engineering, and math (STEM) degrees twenty or thirty times more frequently than in years past, and a change in patent holdings was one clear result: In the 1990s, 1.4 percent of all patents issued in the United States named at least one female inventor. By 2002, this percentage had grown to 10.4.

The wage gap has shifted a bit as well. It narrowed by approximately half a penny every year—at least until a decade ago, when it stagnated completely.[3] Women's participation across all patent-earning fields dropped during that same time period. Progress toward gender equality, in other words, came to a halt in the US just a few years into the new century.

Such stagnation is usually attributed to a mythological "ambition gap" between men and women. Women, it is often said, simply don't ask for what they want. However, this has been debunked by two different studies of the US labor force.[4] It turns out, women do ask for as many salary increases as men, but their requests are usually denied.

Patenting remains one of the most persistent sites of gender disparity. In 2010, the National Women's Business Council discovered that the USPTO had record-high numbers of successful female applicants. Yet bias remains: "The ratio of successful women patent applicants to successful men patent applicants varies from a low 73.36 percent in 1986 to a high of 93.57 percent in 2002," the report states. Which means that, even in the best of years, only 6.43 percent more women than men are denied patents.

◆ ◆ ◆

Gilbreth's dedication to ensuring women access to menstrual products they might actually use allowed the feminine hygiene industry to survive and soon thrive. The field quickly grew to offer a stunning variety of contraptions and palliatives, all intended to further mask the menstrual cycle as women entered, and then gained standing in, a male-dominated workforce. Noting that no concurrent moves have been made to socially normalize the regular occurrence of menstruation (the notion that Hilary Clinton might use a restroom for any purpose whatsoever was enough to set off presidential contender Donald Trump after one 2016 debate, for example) may spark the realization that the entire sanitary product industry exists to allow women to pass through an arena dominated by men without raising alarm. (Continue on this thought trajectory for too long, however, and you'll discover that far more effort has gone into the innovation of menstrual pads than into the establishment of women's rights. I do not advise this for those who already suffer from depression.)

Devices new to the market in the last near-century therefore vary in both considerateness and usefulness: tampons, for example, absorbent insertables intended to soak up menstrual blood, take some adjusting to, as does the menstrual cup. Each carry potential hazards that range from embarrassing to life-threatening, but both allow for unimpeded movement with little blood overflow. (Unless you're on a heavy day, and you sneeze.) Douches, on the other hand, intended to eliminate lady smells, come with fairly serious health hazards. They temporarily wipe out odor-creating bacteria, but also eliminate odor-eating bacteria, subsequently killing off your body's ability to regulate its own smell or, more dangerously, fight off infection. Other sprays, ointments, and geegaws abound, each purporting to serve the basic purpose of masking half the world's natural bodily processes from the other half. Not to get too twelve-year-old-boy about it, but it's difficult not to burst out laughing at the ridiculous products women are urged to make use of just to experience the pleasure of going outside.

One stand-out product in the feminine hygiene field is the lowly sanitary napkin disposal bag. It is possible that you have never seen any, so let me describe them for you. First and foremost, they are bags, a fact central to their oft-mocked status. Usually paper, although occasionally plastic, they are intended to house soiled feminine products, shielding their contents from view of other restroom users. They have no other purpose. Because you are extremely unlikely to require them in the privacy of your own home, such bags are found most frequently inside the stalls of women's restrooms, although never on the shelves of your local drug store.

Basically fancified scraps of paper to wrap waste in, the devices come heavily decorated. Sanitary napkin disposal bags may be festooned with happy, ladylike figures engaging in playful activities, such as tennis or dancing, or covered with gay flowers. Some may feature a stick figure in a dress delightfully throwing an object into the garbage. Others recall a traditional—frequently, Victorian—notion of femininity, and thus convey decorum. (The ad copy for a stainless steel garbage receptacle, into which such a bag is meant to be placed, similarly claims it "adds a touch of class to any restroom.") Class-striving discretion is important—these bags do hold a specific kind of very dirty garbage from which other garbage, presumably, must be protected—but on the whole, sanitary napkin disposal bags strive to express ease of use, tranquility of mind, or maybe even "fun."

The bags' lighthearted design schemes contrast starkly with manufacturers' overt marketing strategies. These can be found on product descriptions in office-supply catalogs, promotional copy intended for the purchaser, rather than the user. Sanitary napkin disposal bag producer Scensibles, in the section of its 2012 annual report labeled, "The Problem," states: "It's bigger than you think. Now let's talk about it . . . "—the subtext of which is that women's hygiene is a massive but unacknowledged disaster that only you, from your noble perch as office supply manager, can address. The website Teens'n'Parents goes a step further: "Disposal of Sanitary napkin is the major problem polluting the environment [sic]." (Not mentioned, of course, is the pollutive output from sanitary napkin manufacturing plants.) The nicknames used when the products appear in books and films and on television are no less alarming: sani-bag, individual feminine hygiene receptacle, lady bag, and even, "vagina bag."

The ambivalence between the design and marketing approaches is fascinating. While ads intend to browbeat the purchaser into addressing "The Problem" of seeping lady juice with a hefty order of sanitary napkin disposal bags, the product itself goes out of its way to assure users that they are behaving correctly, without effort, and possibly even enjoying themselves. One suspects that the bifurcated messaging is no accident, merely gendered for perceived audiences. Case in point: a recent trade mag op-ed by Scensibles founder Ann Germanow[5] pits the issue as plumbers (95 percent men, nationally) and company bill-payers (CEOs of Fortune 500 companies, as an example, are 98 percent male) versus tampon users, coded here as women. (That biology and gender do not faithfully align has apparently not yet occurred to the sanitary napkin disposal bag community.) "A recent janitorial services blog confirms that if no acceptable alternative for disposal is offered, women ignore the signage and flush anyway," Germanow states authoritatively.

Certainly, the message embedded in the product's very existence is as gendered as the restrooms in which the bags can be found, a wordless reminder to all who identify as women that the monthly waste of menstruators must be pre-bagged, a clear indication that it is more disgusting than all other forms of waste, combined. "The number-one bacteria hot spot in a woman's restroom is the 'sanitary' napkin disposal unit," Germanow contends in her op-ed. Perhaps that lady-waste container can more properly be viewed as a breeding-ground for neoliberal subjectivity, a stealthy mixture of individually targeted fortitude and self-doubt that can only be assuaged by the relentless purchase of beauty products. If the impact of these bags on the psyche seems brutal, however, let's pause to reflect on their impact on the planet. The paper waste, plastics, and manufacturing byproducts created will surely fail to decompose in our lifetimes.

At first glance, the individualized feminine hygiene waste receptacle appears ridiculous. On closer inspection it may just horrify.

◆ ◆ ◆

All told, little good can be said about sanitary napkin disposal bags. That is, unless you care about gender equality. For these tiny, decorative, gore-encasement devices do more than any other product in the field of feminine hygiene to eliminate the earnings gap between men and women.

Nearly 4,000 patents include the phrase "feminine product disposal," but very few of these have been awarded for bags created to house soiled feminine hygiene items. In sum, slightly fewer than fifty patents have been granted for sanitary napkin disposal bags—each, legally speaking, a unique approach to personal containers intended to whisk lady waste away from public view. Considering that they really are only *bags*, let's keep in mind, it should perhaps astound that almost fifty different patents have been awarded for innovating methods of placing unseemly waste inside a container before it goes into a larger receptacle for regular garbage disposal.

In truth, receptacles intended for the exclusive disposal of used sanitary napkins are made largely unnecessary by Gilbreth's extensive efforts. Menstrual products today continue to be self-contained, unnoticeable, and spill-proof, as per her 1926 recommendations and the subsequent slew of patents that arose from them. Most stalls in women's restrooms do come equipped with small trash containers for such waste, which could, in a worst-case scenario, be wrapped in paper, conveniently located in the immediate vicinity of toilets throughout most of the Western world. If a small trash container, or any toilet paper, is for some reason absent in each individual stall, most likely there will still be a trash container in the restroom proper. In a worst-case scenario, it is true, in a public restroom, other women may see you and be forced to acknowledge that you menstruate, which they are also likely to do on a regular basis (and if they do not, they will certainly not be surprised that you do). Defenders of the sanitary napkin disposal bag—manufacturers, plumbers, and building owners, for the most part, with whom I have engaged in spirited online conversation—tell us that the primary purpose of such bags is to remind women that sanitary products are not to be flushed down the toilet. How shockingly inefficient! A sign in a stall would do just as well, or eliminating the potential for more paper waste entirely: include plumbing lessons for young women in home economics courses at the middle school level.

Sustained consideration will lead you to wonder whether sanitary napkin disposal bags might not be capitalism's ideal form: an environmentally and emotionally destructive, eminently saleable, necessarily disposable, and cheaply manufactured good with little to no unique functional value around which a dedicated audience can be manufactured and endless profits derived therefrom. All part and parcel of a larger project, to mask the natural bodily processes of half the population. They are truly exemplary, these feminine hygiene products; all the moreso for being such a humble—even, dare I say it, useless—invention.

However fully the bags themselves perform and entrench misogyny, however, their design and manufacture promise a gender equitable future: of forty-six patents for feminine hygiene personal-sized waste containers, fourteen are held by teams including at least one man and at least one woman.[6] Twelve are held by men, and twenty by women. Therefore a percentage of profits from the sani-waste bag industry ultimately go to 30 percent mixed-gender teams, 26 percent men, and 44 percent women. To get more specific, patents on bags that protect trash from truly offensive girl garbage are owned by a staggering 59 percent female inventors.

This is where capitalism gets interesting. Because the profits into which sanitary napkin disposal bags are eating are not those of the 2 percent of women CEOs of Fortune 500 companies, nor are sani-bags being purchased with the seventy-seven cents that women are taking home for each male coworkers' dollar. A predominantly masculine economy, driven by a fear of girl blood, is funding a pool of nearly 60 percent female inventors.

Lillian Gilbreth would certainly have been proud. Gender equity is finally within reach! The question we must ask ourselves, ninety years since her efforts—not to overlook the uncredited labor of thousands of other women—saved the flailing feminine hygiene industry, is whether we want it under these conditions.

An earlier version of this essay was published at The Baffler.

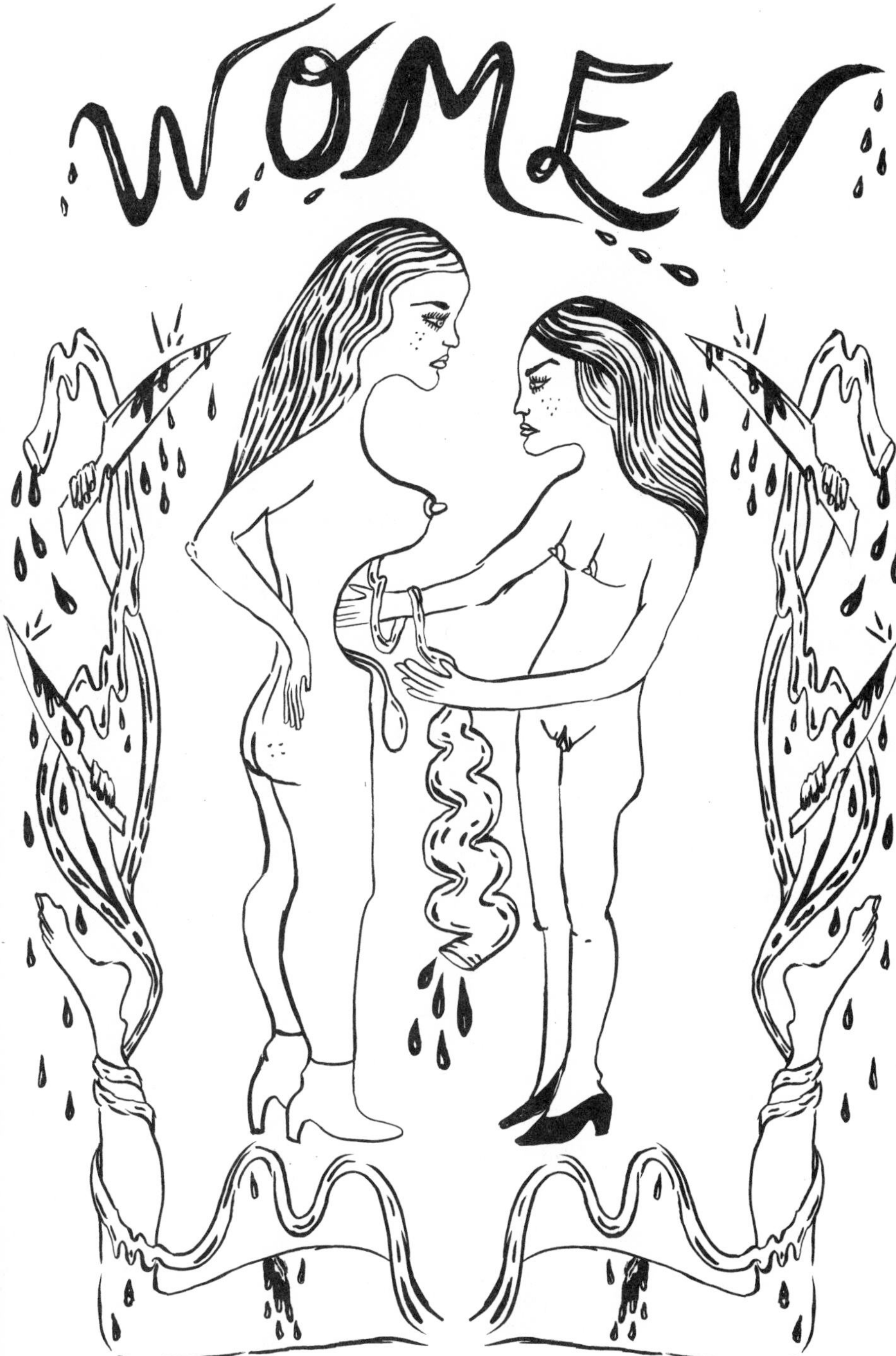
WOMEN

Arguably, Lucky McKee's *The Woman*—heralded in promotional materials as "The Most Controversial Film of 2011"—is merely a close study of justifiable misogyny. Not that low-level, "no girls allowed" stuff we see in locker rooms these days, either. Misogyny as ideology, as spirituality. An abiding rejection of femininity, manifested in a violence so wretched and grotesque it becomes all-consuming, self-explanatory, and deeply righteous. It leaks from onscreen characters and encompasses the theater, the living room—viewers of McKee's film are placed, for a time, in the uncanny position of acquiescence. It is uncomfortable. For although I live in a world that demands my destruction in a myriad of ways every day and I have thus learned to follow the logic of misogyny, I have no desire to *feel* it.

McKee's film lays groundwork carefully. A five-minute opening sequence follows a feral woman through the woods. She is nurturing and careful, but also bloodsucking and unkempt, so definitely wild. A jump cut to Peggy, the teenaged daughter of a happy-enough-seeming family at a backyard barbecue—isolated and inconsolate—establishes this film as one about *gender issues*. Heavy-handed, but not unclever, McKee then ticks off a list of familial dysfunctions as the rest of the clan parades across the screen. Peggy's brother, Brian, watches with glazed eyes as his youngest sister, Darlin', gets roughed up by neighborhood boys. Their mother Belle (played by an unusually unhinged Angela Bettis) acts deflective and abused around her husband, even in public, even at a party. Upon repeated viewings, it's clear we are witnessing emotionally and sexually abused family members re-enact their domestic roles for neighborhood innocents, but you don't so much notice this on first viewing.

And that husband, Chris Cleek (Sean Bridgers). There is nothing remarkable about him. He is brash and aggravating, and believes his jokes to be very funny. You have met him at family barbecues several times yourself. He is a lawyer, and he likes to hunt. When he goes off into the woods, he finds The Woman there, in the wild, through the site of his rifle. A deep bass line kicks in, the scene goes slo-mo, and we are suddenly in a rock video. She emerges from the water and arches her back, sexually, for him, as she redresses herself. He wants her, and not just to fuck. He wants to own her; a possession, a catch, a prize.

So he takes her. Chains her up in the cellar, and eventually, introduces her to the family. Not as a person, but as his thing, to wash and feed and use at will. Of course for sex—she's not a person in his mind, but a masturbation aid. She isn't human, she's a wild woman, but also just a woman. The metaphors fall away quickly, thin veils that, until this moment, have kept Chris Cleek and by extension every other self-important lawyer/hunter/father you've ever met at a backyard family barbecue from going on a rape-and-murder rampage. The veils are labeled: society, respect, family, love, and when the last one falls away, we have only the patriarch, finally unhinged but honest, ranting against womanhood as he pummels every female in spitting distance to the ground.

In the last twenty minutes of the film, there are no more metaphors, only raw and pure misogyny explored to its fullest, without restraint. It is messy and sticky, like an underserved man's well-earned orgasm. Belle, too late, speaks up. This is not tolerated. A meddling lesbian teacher, interfering, accidently unearths a family secret. She is punished. Peggy balks. She is beaten. Brian, revealed to be the psychopath and rapist he has been trained to be for his entire life, is rewarded. Finally, the men—having imposed total dominion over the women—set to tearing each other apart. And then, the tables are turned, sort of, although maybe put back where they belong?

We'll return to those, the discomfiting final moments of the film, and pause to answer the question surely forming in your mind:

How is this not the most offensive and depraved hate speech ever dressed up as entertainment and put on public display in the history of man? The studio's marketing team would like you to believe that it is, but it is not. Because this film is not exclusively a performance *of* misogyny; it posits that misogyny might emanate, also, from women. It therefore imagines an abiding detestastion of femininity as something over which women may have control, even agency. *The Woman* degenders the misogynist, allowing misogyny a pervasiveness and logic that very closely mirrors reality. Believe it or not, that misogyny might exist in all of us is, actually, quite a hopeful notion.

♦ ♦ ♦

Let's consider this about misogyny: if we want to lay all the blame for all the problems of the world at the feet of men—AKA "the patriarchy"—we certainly may. Plenty of people do and they make their arguments quite well, whether they are dusty academics or eleven-year-old girls. There exists plenty of evidence, after all, to back up such claims. The adoration of the masculine as protector must also decry the feminine in all non-submissive forms, and who better to advance such a ridiculous notion than men?

Unfortunately, "because men" doesn't provide a terribly satisfactory answer to the question of how a deep, anti-feminine undercurrent came to run through all of culture and society, providing an ethos for our very socio-economic structure. To hold as true that misogyny is wholly inescapable but emanates exclusively from men, we must also believe one of two things: 1) that women, who truly do exist in every corner of society, even if we cannot see them or do not acknowledge them, in point of fact do have no power, or 2) that women are party to the same flawed thinking as anyone else, as men, as the patriarchy, and therefore tend to use what power they do have toward disastrous ends, at least where gender equality may be concerned. The first construct strips women of agency—itself a misogynist act—while the second degenders misogyny and makes women complicit in it, blaming them, in part, for their own oppression. Yet it also offers a modicum of control over an otherwise external, and often overwhelming, force.

Now these strokes are overly broad and the gender binary easily disprovable, but the question I'm getting at is this: Would we rather our cultural products *perform* misogyny, or hold folks accountable to it? We could push this question further, for even an abiding belief in the gender binary is an act of violence against those who do not fall neatly into it: Would we rather *perform* transmisogyny or hold folks accountable to it?[1]

Most of us familiar with the term, in hoping to ultimately eliminate the need for it, would likely prefer a notion of misogyny that held folks accountable to gender-based violence in all forms. For filmmakers, however, the question is not always so simple. Consider, for example, Lars von Trier's *Antichrist*. "Accusations of misogyny are routine in discussions of Mr. von Trier's films," the *New York Times* summarized in a 2014 review of *Nymphomaniac*, following a tally of the harsh brutalities his leads are forced to endure throughout his oeuvre. (Rape by gang of sailors, rape by entire town, genital mutilation, and murder are such standard von Trier fodder that many were disappointed that 2011's *Melancholia* merely ended with the world melting.)

The *Times*, however, decreed von Trier *not* a misogynist, based on the ample evidence the director himself has supplied, proving he believes women to be capable of performing under the most extreme circumstances in his films, upholding their narratives in the entirety in almost every single case. Indeed, the evidence for von Trier's non-misogyny grows, for he found his original draft of *Antichrist* to be *not misogynist enough*, so he hired "Misogyny Expert" Heidi Laura, *a woman*, to deepen the abiding woman-hatred in the film.

For the film performers von Trier works with, the answer to the question I pose above is easy: they would rather perform misogyny— that is, perform the experience of it. They do so commendably. It is not in their job description to hold anyone accountable to anything, and performing actual misogyny has got to be a far cry more interesting than mildly reflecting it as the girlfriend or mother of a protagonist, who may not even have a name, much less a battle scar. The hope of such women actors, expressed in countless interviews and public statements, is to perform something well enough that indictment will follow—although by others, and later.

For von Trier, however, the question is more complicated: he wants to perform misogyny, but he wants to do it deliberately. So well, in fact, that he will find the folks who know the most about its effects and pay them to provide pointers on the stuff, even if they are women, because there are many many things that they are better at than men. (Suffering, apparently, is another skill he evidently believes women hold unique talent in.) His is a thoughtful performance of misogyny, and I submit that we are intended to believe that its aim is to hold others accountable for unchecked, undeliberate, unthought-ful misogyny elsewhere.

Yet the women in von Trier's films all accept devastation, and that's worth considering too—even Justine, Kirsten Dunst's lead in *Melancholia*, submits to the world-ending scenario despite her otherwise fully narcissistic behavior, making no effort to shift the course of nature toward something more befitting her own interests, which otherwise dominate the plotline of the film. Von Trier may be performing misogyny with a considered delivery and purposeful intent, but his leading ladies hardly bother kicking against the pricks, as it were. The world they envision either allows for a great deal of unchecked feminine disapproval, or it will destroy itself and they will submit to it. Von Trier's misogyny may be intentionally con-structed, in other words, but without agency, his female characters are still left to its whims. They are not hopeful films.

Lucky McKee, arguably a lesser artist with a much tinier vision—certainly a genre filmmaker—takes a far more expansive view. His horrific universe is filled with horrible people committing horrible acts, too, although in his films can be detected another possibility:

a future in which misogyny may be eradicated. What might it take to build that world? At the end of *The Woman*, we begin to have a sense.

♦ ♦ ♦

"We belong to the gender of fear, of humiliation," French theorist and filmmaker Virginie Despentes writes in *King Kong Theory*. "The other gender. Masculinity, that legendary masculine solidarity is formed in these moments and is built on this exclusion of our bodies. Pact based on our inferiority."

What Despentes is posing is observation, but also prescription. By acknowledging the precise site of misogyny—as based in women's own fear, humiliation, and inferiority—she perceives her own complicity in it.

Despentes also offers a corrective. She suggests eliminating that wellspring of gendered fear and humiliation with a display of power. "Going to gigs was the most important thing in my life," she writes, in a passage describing her own violent rape after hitchhiking to a show. "Worth putting myself in danger for. Nothing could be worse than staying in my room, far from life, when so much was happening." She will not apologize for her brazenness, or dwell in her naïveté. Despentes has simply weighed the options available to her, as a member of the "gender of fear," and opts to acknowledge the danger by walking toward it. Experiencing it. During her own rape, she had a knife that she did not use. She writes:

> *A powerful and ancient political strategy has taught women not to defend themselves. . . . But women still feel the need to say that violence is not the answer. And yet, if men were to fear having their dicks slashed to pieces with a carpet knife should they try to force a woman, they would soon become much better at controlling their "masculine" urges, and understanding that "no" does mean "no."*[2]

Her knowledge of the political strategy used to keep women acquiescent, even when bodily integrity is at stake, is personal and deep: "I wish I'd been able to escape the values instilled in my gender that night," she writes, "and slit each of their throats, one by one. Instead of having to live with being someone who didn't dare defend herself, because she's a woman and violence is not her domain, and the physical integrity of the male body is more important than that of the female."

Despentes detects, in other words, her own misogyny. She was complacent to it, and allowed it to take place on her own body, allowed herself to become evidence of it, proof that it lived within her. Not a condition she was all that amenable to, in the end: she writes that she would prefer to carve it from the necks of her attackers—cutting it symbolically out of herself—than live with it inside her.

My own rape was less violent, and not the site of awakening to my own misogyny. That took more time. The realization that, as an editor, I tended to discredit submissions of women writers contributed. My disregard for feminized labor—care work like nursing and early childhood education—started to become clear. Additionally, my sense as a very young person that other young women were "competition" instead of "allies" helped me see that "the patriarchy" wasn't keeping "women" down—I was. Learning to hate other women had taken time, too: My complacency to misogyny was honed over years of watching good, kind, well-meaning friends comply to the gender-based oppression on display in others, then embodying it themselves. My own rape should probably have been years earlier, in fact, as I was trained by a violent, racist, overbearing, alcoholic father to comply to his every whim from birth. Yet by the time it happened (at a party, there was drinking, everyone was acting crazy, verbal consent impossible in a foreign country where language skills are shaky), it felt so thoroughly natural that it took a decade to notice a violation had occurred. By the time I named it rape, it was already far in the past. By accepting it, unnamed, for so many years, I know that I have the capacity to overlook it if it happens again right in front of me. It is possible that I will let it happen to someone else. Perhaps I already have.

What I know, therefore, is that the shyness, reticence, fear, and humiliation Despentes points to—it needs to be stamped out. In myself and in others. Unlike Despentes, if I went back and slit the throats of everyone complicit in my rape, the bodies left open and bleeding would not only be those of men. That, in fact, is part of why it took so long for me to identify my experience as rape: because I did not understand that women are capable of misogyny. I thought my female friends by definition could not stand by and watch my bodily integrity be violated. Now I remember the time that they did.

If I could borrow Despente's carpet knife and cut the misogyny from my favorite female friends, I certainly would. The submissive reaction of women to the dominant, violent culture, the way that they—we—have conformed to and upheld a dynamic that stripped women of agency and which they—we—accepted without adjustment—if I could find it in their bodies I would carve it out. If I could locate it in myself I would remove it and watch it die.

◆ ◆ ◆

Film depictions of rape are diverse and telling. Take the classic rape-revenge fantasy *I Spit on Your Grave*. Originally released under the superior title *Day of The Woman*, Meir Zarchi's 1977 film is brilliant, horror or no, rape-revenge fantasy or no. Although replete with unexamined class problems—spoiler alert: the idle rich win out over the struggling poor, in the end—there are few more accurate depictions of American culture than this little gem.

What distressed American viewing audiences (and why you may never have heard of it) is that the film takes Despentes' pronouncement—that rape may be controllable if women learn to defend themselves with violence—seriously. And because it does, both the critical reception and the viewership of the film have been curtailed. The lesson on offer is how deeply abiding misogyny is, and how intrinsic to capitalism.

The film follows an urban transplant—a writer named Jennifer Hills—during her summer sojourn in the country by the lake. Her tranquility is broken, repeatedly, by four young men from town, and she grows agitated. Eventually, they nab her, bring her to a remote area of the forest, and rape her brutally and repeatedly. When they finally leave, we witness her struggle to stand and then slowly return home; there they are awaiting her and, again, attack. Three of the young men convince a fourth, who has some form of intellectual impairment, to kill her. He cannot, but claims that he did. Her recovery takes weeks, and when she reemerges, the group of rapists turn on each other in fury that she survived. United they may have been a threat, but once divided, she seduces each handily. *Coitus Interruptus*: she then kills each attacker in as brutal a manner as she can muster. It is remorseless and ever so slightly thrilling.

Jennifer does this impassively, played by a sensibly stoic Camille Keaton, Buster's granddaughter. That she was married to Zarchi at the time undercuts the force of the film a bit—onscreen she is a serenely composed, self-aware, independent woman, both before and then a while after the rape. Her stage presence is commanding: it alone is worth audiencefuls of appreciation. Yet can a woman be depicted as remorseless without a supportive, offscreen husband?

Critics didn't care, and panned it out of hand. (Inspiring a cult following, of course.) Roger Ebert gave it zero stars and called it a "vile bag of garbage ... sick, reprehensible and contemptible," getting the thrust of the film dead wrong overall but sprinkling in a muted, off-key cheer for "feminist solidarity."[3] (Barf.) Tasteless, irresponsible, and disturbing are common insults hurled by critics, and certain characters receive unfair portions of blame: namely the "retarded" rapist Ebert points to and the "sick"/"sadistic"/"degraded" female protagonist. Britain used the film to push for tighter control over film standards—censorship. Without the cult following the critical depreciation inspired, the film would have been effectively buried.

Carol J. Clover attempted to set the record straight in her 1992 book *Men, Women, and Chainsaws*. Providing an overview of the film's negative critical reception, she qualifies its inclusion in her tome on gender and horror by restating the purpose of the book: "To offer an account not just of the most but of the least presentable of horror," nearly apologizing for the nod to the existence of the offensive garbage. She says that she does not "fully share" the negative views of the film—noting one interviewee's suggestion that it be made compulsory viewing on high school campuses—and correctly identifies the film as not as shocking and less valueless than critics charged. She suggests that *I Spit on Your Grave* fails because it never adopted a masculist viewpoint, in which gang rape would be let off the hook as acceptable, and makes excellent points about individual culpability for violent actions—each rapist blames the others, at some point, or blames the victim, which begins to raise larger questions about how rape occurs. Yet whatever social value she may find in the film, Clover ultimately condemns it as artless.

It's not true—long ponderous scenes of tranquility and solitude effectively underscore the plotline of the film, which lend it quite an arty sense indeed—but more interesting is Clover's point about the gendered POV of the film. If it is true that Zarchi's film failed to adopt a masculist viewpoint, and that this caused bigger meltdowns in the reviews section and at the box-office, we can surmise quite a bit about how allegiant we expect culture to be to the logic of rape and misogyny.

Strongly allegiant, it may be safe to say. Let's take the subgenre of horror the film sits in as a first example. From a certain perspective, contextualizing a film as "rape-revenge fantasy" is a problem in itself. We do not have burglary-revenge fantasy films, although plenty of movies begin with a thieved item and continue under a plot dictated by its reacquisition. Movies in which kidnappers or terrorists are hunted down are not characterized as kidnapping- or terrorism-revenge fantasies. Kidnapping and terrorism are too correctly situated already as legitimate crimes to need to justify them as revenge-worthy. Too, films in which rapes occur in the first place are not termed woman-revenge fantasy flicks. In fact, sometimes they are just "fantasy," if they are distinguished in any way at all. Rape, in fact, is the standard. In horror, in film, and in culture. Only retaliation against it is marked and unusual.

This is not to say that rape is inevitable, or common, or necessary—only that we do not condemn it thoroughly when it occurs. I didn't, when it happened to me. Untold numbers of women don't, either, some under confusion of what does and does not constitute rape. Confusion is more common in some circles than others—as Missouri House Rep. Todd Akin's more recent claims of the impossibility of pregnancy in the case of "legitimate" rape indicate. Cultural confusion allows for a legal one. As Despentes writes, "With rape, it's always up to you to prove you didn't really give your consent." In *I Spit on Your Grave*, Jennifer doesn't bother proving anything to anyone. She simply extracts revenge.

I Spit on Your Grave allows for a cultural imaginary in which the domain of women is violence, both serene and justified, as Despentes suggests it should be. But culture has a way of enforcing adherence to norms, even if tiny pockets of resistance can be found; few know this as well as Despentes, who has also made films that were considered rape-revenge fantasies, and were censored. Her theory therefore holds, that "rape is a well defined political strategy: the bare bones of capitalism."

In the end, capitalism marked *I Spit on Your Grave*. The film was problematized by critics like Ebert, who labeled it a deviation from the standard and acceptable depiction of gender politics and culture. Then the film was censored, for those same reasons. The domino effect continued. The film developed a small, cult audience—perhaps the best capitalism can do for women, in the end.

For fans of narrative diversity, as well as those who would prefer the eradication of misogyny, this presents a real problem. A truly great film, the fatal flaw of *I Spit on Your Grave* is that it fails to privilege a masculist worldview. This has kept it from wider distribution, critical acclaim, and audiences of all but the most dedicated enthusiasts. Could *I Spit on Your Grave* function as a social imaginary, allowing a possible future in which more men refrain from forced sexual assault out of fear of getting their dicks cut off in bathtubs? We simply don't know, under capitalism—people would have to see it, first.

◆ ◆ ◆

So we do not have *Day of the Woman* to look to, but we do have *The Woman*. The 2011 film somehow escapes the problematic rape-revenge framing—because Chris Cleek is given top billing?—but otherwise is set against this same sordid media history, and my theory is that what popular success McKee's film has seen is due to its primary contention that women deserve the oppression they get. Most of the run time of the film, in fact, is obsessively devoted to its masculist viewpoint—the exact one lacking in *I Spit on Your Grave*.

In McKee's tale, every female character eventually cannibalizes, consuming herself or others due to starvation, mistreatment, or a fear that is misunderstood to be love. You can read this as a metaphor if you like, but some of these women straight-up eat people. It is a cultural mandate, yes: in this world dominated by a hateful lawyer and his shitty rapist asshole serial killer son, the only means of feminine survival is to sacrifice your body or that of the nearest replacement female. You may starve if you do not consume the flesh of another. Women onscreen hold equal responsibility to men onscreen for the oppression of women, no question. (One of the smart turns of the film is that certain bizarre leaps in plot are blamed on a female character's unrelated medical condition, Anopthalmia, the absence of one or both eyes: literally, a lack of ability to see. Women in *The Woman* are horrible because they *are incapable of adopting a feminine viewpoint*.)

Then McKee's film takes a sharp turn. Until then a sheerly brilliant metaphor for present-day sexual politics, the narrative falters in its resolution. In the final moments of the film, the feminine returns to nature and nurture, and the masculine is left to rule society and culture: a false dichotomy based on a misguided assertion that gender is biological and cultural politics rooted therein. We will not know what Despentes may have taken from a world in which women make violence their permanent domain within an existing culture; McKee has women stepping back from society entirely, allowing it to remain the dominion of men.

A truly radical narrative might have destroyed this false dichotomy, already breached, or supplanted each with each: What would a society look like if women simply protected themselves in the world into which they are born? Then again a truly radical film would have featured a soundtrack and production by people who are not men, thus creating an economic infrastructure to support non-male cast and crew (as, somewhat awkwardly, von Trier occasionally does). A visionary filmmaker might even have followed through on Despentes' suggestion that men can learn to refrain from rape and women can learn to embrace the violence of self-protection, and given us a glimpse of what that might look like.

The Woman isn't, therefore, a radical feminist film. But by siting misogyny in women, it offers a glimpse of a future over which it can be controlled and eradicated.

A portion of this essay was originally published on The Blog is Coming from Inside the House.

A FEW THINGS I HAVE LEARNED ABOUT ILLNESS IN AMERICA

1. Sit with a friend through cancer treatments because you love her, not because you believe she would do the same for you. She won't. Cancer changes people, and it makes people vulnerable. If your friend survives, she will want to reinvent herself. She will *need* to reinvent herself. What I mean is: your friendship is probably over, once your friend beats cancer. You will help them do that—survive—but your only reward is likely to be that knowledge. You may, later, go through cancer treatments yourself. It is possible that you will do this alone. Even if you sit with three different friends through cancer treatments. What is important to realize is that you helped them survive because you are good at survival.

2. Your best doctor is your body. Hopefully you will also find other doctors who have more training in and experience with illness than your body does, but I would not count on it. Weigh professional opinions and theories against how a medication feels in your palm, or what comes to mind while it digests in your stomach. Avoid processes that allow the administration of treatment to get too far away from your own hand. Not because you should not trust other people—you should—but because it matters if you shake before you give yourself an injection, or if your heart aches every time you go in for new lab tests.

   Another way to say what I mean: notice what makes you feel bad, and avoid it in the future. I have found that most people do not know when they feel bad. I personally did not learn how to tell when I feel bad until I turned forty-four.

3. Many people will offer advice. No—everyone, in some way or another, will offer advice. Some will tell you to change the way you eat, or how to feel. They may suggest you find a better doctor, as if you do not live daily with the failures of modern medicine. Others will tell you how you can make it easier for them to understand what you are going through, or demand that you be patient with them. You must try not to laugh. If people grow annoyed at your behavior, they may repeatedly ask what is wrong with you, even after you have told them one million times that you are sick. Still others will believe resolutely that you have done something wrong. They will say, "a-ha," at the wrong time when you relay an anecdote, or forward articles to you about smoking, yoga, or drinking tap water. They do this out of kindness, but what is being said is: you are failing to live up to my expectations of you.

   If you bother to listen to other people at all—although I can understand why you would not—you may wish to translate everything anyone tells you into the phrase, "I care about you more than I myself realize, more than I am currently capable of expressing." Do this without speaking, inside your own head. It is only for you.

4. This is important: do not hate your disease. If you can, try not to hate anything at all, but that may be too hard. You have a right to be angry. Still, hate is for people who feel they have nothing to lose, for people who are comfortable sitting in judgment of others. Most important: hate takes time and energy. Time you could be devoting to far more important pursuits, like laughing at jokes, or research. Hate only inspires more hate; what you need right now is love.

5. When someone discovers you are sick, do not be surprised by their cruelty. For example, someone may say, "Oh, my

grandmother committed suicide when she was diagnosed with that!" Or an acquaintance might give you false information about your disease. This will happen, surprisingly frequently, with doctors. Friends in media and entertainment will write you into stories as a character, taking your hard-won experience of survival from you without permission and using it to advance their careers. You may see yourself become a morality tale for hard living, dangerous choices, sexual promiscuity, eating meat, lack of religion. You may find your high school best friend does this, or your auntie. It is what people do: use what they come across for their own purposes. You cannot blame them, but you do not have to be around them.

Another acquaintance, after a frank conversation about your illness, may comment, "Wow. It's terrifying that such a thing could so easily happen to me!" Laugh at that person. Laugh at their narcissism, at a worldview that believes that illness picks and chooses victims for a moral or ethical reason, or any reason at all. Laugh at the fact that they feel safe when you know that they are not. Hope that they remain safe, because an unjust comeuppance for narcissism is illness. But do not trust that person. Do not trust anyone who takes from you in your moment of greatest need.

6. Others will avoid you. *Most* will avoid you. They do not want to deal with mortality, yours or their own, or what strikes them as worse than death: frailty, weakness, disability. This will make you deeply sad for the world, and for yourself, that you may never speak to your best friend again, to any of your best friends again. If you ran a company or organized events in your neighborhood, those people—whose lives you worked hard to support—may not gather around you. Let me tell you this because no one else will: people are awful. I am sorry that you will feel alone much of the time. I am sorry for every doctor's appointment and

bad-news phone call that you have to endure by yourself. I am sorry about the time that pharmacist was flirting with you until he looked at the drug you came in to pick up, and paled. I am sorry that an insurance agent once called you to demand $986 to pay for the test result that indicated a $1,200 per-injection drug prescribed by your doctor had given you a new disease. I am sorry for the bitch on the bus who couldn't see you were in pain so complained loudly for three miles that you wouldn't give up your handicap seat for her shopping bag. I am sorry that the energy you once spent making others laugh or dressing up for parties or planning elaborate adventures is now used to fill weekly pill containers, do tai chi, visit specialists, or trying to stay awake.

I am sorry it seems so easy for others to forget you are important.

7.   Another way people might react to your illness is by saying quite effortlessly: "What can we do, your community?" It may take a year to hear this question, or longer. You may think you will never hear it. In truth, you might never hear it. You will expect to hear it when you post on Facebook about a negative test result or mention to a small group of friends over coffee that your doctor is concerned. The crucial question will not come then. It may not come when you fail to show up for birthday parties, although it is clear that your absence has been noted. It may not even come after a week when you cannot answer the phone, or when you do not have the energy to respond to emails. When you effectively disappear from the face of the earth.

You will be made aware then that people are gossiping, but you will also be aware how few of those asking others about you have ever actually asked you how you are. Everyone will feel that they have expressed concern and wished you well, but the actual number of people who will do so is quite low. You may see, in other words, the evidence of community forming, but it will still take time for its benefits to be offered to you.

Try not to sob when this happens. The friend who finally mouths these words will believe she is the hundredth person to say, "What can we do? How can the people who care about you show it?" Do not mention that you don't know if you believe in community anymore, or which exact community members have hurt you beyond repair. Do not test her faith in the power of people to gather in support as yours has been tested. Just answer her question.

8. Your European friends will make what seems to them to be very logical suggestions: request a paid leave from work, go to a health spa for a month, begin receiving disability compensation. Supplement your Western medical treatments with Chinese medicine. These treatments may not be affordable or in some cases available to you in any way. Your European friends will be baffled by the cruelty of the State. It will not make sense to them how a rich nation can so severely take advantage of its population. This is important: do not attempt to answer their follow-up questions, because a whole lifetime can be wasted describing the injustice you are currently experiencing. It does not need to be yours.

9. Even if you have been assured the most basic of care by federal policy—however minimal indeed for those whose diseases are little understood in the first place, and for whom there are therefore no effective treatments—you may suddenly find yourself in your doctor's exam room, crying over the threat of its repeal. You doctor may face personal threats from the same administration: perhaps she was born in a country from which others have been denied entry to the US by surprise executive order, or fears annulment of the law that allowed him to enter

a same-sex marriage with his partner of several decades. Certainly your doctor faces a potential job loss. Your doctor may also cry. However it is possible that your doctor could say, "I have a plan." Then your doctor may detail the black market prescription dispensaries, back-alley lab testing facilities, and unsanctioned exam rooms around the city that will allow you to survive. You may wonder if this is a movie, or a trap. The sliver of hope, however, will buoy you. Let it.

10. You will learn to get by on very small kindnesses. These are often gifts so tiny they mean nothing to those who dole them out. A fruit basket sent by the secretary of a man you worked with once, whom you have never met in person. He is an acquaintance of a good friend that you never heard from, post-diagnosis. A heartfelt but single-line email from a colleague on the other side of the country; an extra warm hug from someone you respect but do not know very well; an angry email from someone in your same line of work, someone who rightly tells you to buck the fuck up when you have professed a desire to give up; someone who does not mind that you are sick, but cares enough to see past that, and spot that you are about to make an irreversible mistake. Over the course of a month, you may only experience one such event, or you may not experience any at all after several years. But if you do, and you thank these people later, they will not remember what they did. They will have no idea that they saved your sanity or your life, that collectively and without even trying, they have created a world you are desperate to stay in for just a little while longer, no matter how difficult.

11. I'm going to be honest with you. I have no reason not to be. I do not know you, and we may never meet, but I can say without a doubt that your doctors may not be telling you the truth and your friends certainly aren't. Drugstore clerks honestly do only want your money. RNs have plenty of other patients set to take

your place. Your company can do without you just fine. Your pets will even move on. (I am not saying that people do not love you. They do.) Yet this moment of horrible honesty is required, so here it is: there is a chance that you will not make it through this, whatever "this" is for you. You may die soon; you will certainly die eventually.

Peer at that statement. Ignore that it is sorrowful and unkind, even as you also admit that it is true. Take it as a reminder to care for what you love, and a plea to be courageous in defiance of unspeakable cruelty. If you do not make it through this— whether it is, this disease or this economy or this political regime or these very, very difficult days—let us remember you as someone who loved very deeply.

Do not let us forget how much you cared.

"My mom was a model and I was expected to follow in her footsteps," Sarah Meier tells me over Skype from her home in Manila. At fourteen she did, living the NYC top-model lifestyle for twelve years before moving back home and accepting gigs on a radio show and as an MTV VJ. She was even set to host *Philippines' Top Model* before the show was cancelled, when she took a gig editing the country's premier fashion magazine, *Metro*. I feel compelled to mention that she's got big green eyes, long straight hair, and glowing, flawless skin. She's beautiful. It is, after all, an important part of her job.

What I'm impressed by, however, is Meier's thoughtfulness. She spent over a decade attending up to ten castings per day, each filled with panels of critics offering professional and often conflicting opinions about what was physically wrong with her. It started to wear, she explains. After a few years, she noticed a creeping sense of self-doubt. It afflicted others, too.

"Really, really, really nice girls turned into horrible creatures," she says. She's referring to her endless string of model roommates. The agencies that administer model contracts also arrange for housing, but the expenses come out of employee paychecks, a standard fashion industry variation on the sharecroppers' company store. The day a new roomie moved in was always great, Meier recalls. But, she adds, "Three months down the road, they're putting Nair in each other's shampoo bottles."

Reality may be crueler, even, than reality television, but the real-life travails of models don't necessarily arise out of professional rivalry. "You could be looking at a blonde-haired, blue-eyed girl, and you're not in competition with her at all"— Meier has light brown skin and dark brown hair—"we're not going to be up for the same jobs, ever. We're not even sent to the same castings. But the way in which we view each other is competition. Like, 'Do you have a better body?' 'How can you get away with eating that when I'm here suffering?' The animosity begins to build. Not just animosity for other models. It becomes animosity for anybody that's happy. Anybody that's living a normal life."

Close students of class politics will recognize Meier's cutting flourish as a textbook description of proletarian alienation. Except, of course, few of us are inclined to think of models as workers. To judge by their portfolios, models spend an inordinate amount of time at swanky cocktail soirees, cavorting on Caribbean beaches, or drunkenly weaving down urban thoroughfares, laughing at passersby with their heels in their hands. Yet even models like Meier, at the top of the modeling food chain in New York, can find the stylized mimicry of the good life they perform for the camera an intolerable, degrading grind. And with vicious campaigns of interpersonal one-upsmanship as virtual conditions of employment, a spectator might consider looking beyond the images of la dolce vita studiously crafted by the industry to ponder just what kind of self is being assembled as an object of choice for ornamentation and adornment.

In other words, the toxicity inherent to the modeling caste is a feature, not a bug—it's doled out to all comers, no minor flaw in an otherwise efficient system but a condition of the job. It is, in short, a labor issue.

◆ ◆ ◆

The charge that models have a rough go of it, however, has not yet caught the popular imagination. After all, the posh surface of the industry gleams with overclass self-indulgence. Even the breed of feminist politically awakened by Beyoncé's 2014 VMA performance can tick off the profession's glaring ideological sins: its misogynist conflation of Woman, always, with salable object; its role in lionizing impossible-to-maintain beauty standards; and its casual enactment of reflexive female consent in the realm of sexual power—the complex of predatory prerogatives we've come to name rape culture. As a result, labor activists and feminists alike suffer an understandable exasperation when confronting otherwise prosaic labor concerns. Fighting for fair wages or adequate child labor protections in an industry so steeped in—foundational to—the iconography of male privilege can seem like petitioning the Koch brothers to join Code Pink.

Then comes a sneaking suspicion that most models haven't spent enough time in the real world to fully comprehend that unjust treatment may not be heaped upon them because of their job, but because of their gender. A cognitive dissonance arises when a seemingly pampered sector of the leisure class stumbles upon a millennia-old pattern of gender oppression as though its members were the first group to encounter it. Why should I care about pay equity in the modeling industry, in other words, when I suffer it daily as a journalist and college professor?

Modeling is, by any reasonable measure of working-class drudgery, a decidedly elite career. Even insiders, pointing out unfair labor practices, describe an "exclusive ... hyper-wealthy country club-like industry" and complain that agencies take too high a percentage of presumably lavish salaries.[1]

Indeed, Meier prefers to characterize her taste of the lush life in positive terms: "I know what a really expensive car feels like to sit in. I know what it smells like," she tells me. "I've tasted some really incredible food and seen some really beautiful places in the world." But country clubs and expensive cars come staffed, a nuance some may overlook. Former cover girl Jennifer Sky, in a call for actors' union SAG-AFTRA to grant models entry, casually mentioned that in her model apartment, "We didn't pick up after ourselves or clean the floor."[2] It's hard to work up much in the way of labor solidarity for people who seemingly don't bother to, you know, *labor.*

As the rallying cry for models to organize has gained volume in recent years, the cause of solidarity with other labor sectors has lagged. What models do is sell, not construct or argue or plan, and any effort to stir them into militancy inevitably ends up navigating the narrow catwalk between cause marketing and genuine labor organizing. Visiting the website for the advocacy group Model Alliance in 2015, for example, opened a pop-up ad for a sexy lady calendar that temporarily blocked you from reading a draft of the Models' Bill of Rights. The calendar "features twelve models who the Alliance feels represent female empowerment and diversity in the American modeling industry," according to the site.[3] Sure enough, the sexualized pouts of twelve women smizing through a variety of skin tones adorn each month of the year. The draft bill of rights, on the other hand, proposes concrete measures to end wage theft, ensure fiscal oversight of agencies, and minimize child labor—decidedly unsexy fare, especially when set against the calendar's high-gloss array of seductive poses. The master's tools may not dismantle the master's house, but check out how great they look in action!

Yet when you peer beyond the pouts and cognitive dissonance, you gradually come to realize that the struggles facing the women paid to act out patriarchal notions of beauty, glamour, and worldliness are not so different from those that assail the figures with whom we've long associated the intersection of fashion and politics: underpaid and overworked garment factory employees. Neither, for that matter, are models' demands much different from those we hear from any other woman involved in the global garment trade, at any phase of production or distribution.

◆ ◆ ◆

My first peek inside a garment factory, in Cambodia in 2009, was a quick one. People who don't work there are not usually allowed in, and certainly journalists are denied entry out of hand, so I lied to the guard in Khmer and faked a heedlessness common to Americans traveling in Southeast Asia. I breezed through the entryway, gaily commenting on the rumbling in my stomach as I headed toward a crowd of young women at a picnic table. The guard caught me after two steps. "It is not a restaurant," he told me in gruff Cambodian syllables. "You must leave."

He glanced at his weapon—an AK-47, the ubiquity of the guns a holdover from the Khmer Rouge era—so I exited the factory gates and joined a crew of mostly young women in the back of another Pol Pot holdover, a decommissioned Chinese military vehicle. My translator joined me to help ask them about their jobs. At first they didn't respond, only shared with me their meager lunch. There is no freedom of press in Cambodia, and workers are explicitly warned not to speak to reporters. My translator told them not to worry; that I was just a tourist who likes clothes. This characterization of me as a guileless fashion fan cheered them, and they agreed, finally, to answer questions.

They were, in all senses, model employees: adorable, pleasant, and happy in their jobs. This last strained my credulity, as it was a blisteringly hot day—they all are, inside the factories—and the five girls and single boy in the back of the truck didn't have enough food, but couldn't afford more. In 2009, the monthly minimum wage was only $55. (It has since more than doubled, but the cost of living has risen, too, and the current monthly minimum earnings of garment factory workers in Cambodia, $128, still fall significantly below all monthly living wage estimates.) Statistically, we'd need another four girls to jam themselves in the back of the tiny truck to represent the current gender ratio of the Cambodian factory workforce, but there simply wasn't room. (The number of employees in the sector has doubled since 2009, too.)

Some in this group packed jeans to ship to China and North America, although it's rare for workers to know where wares end up. Under global Fordism, most only grasp what passes through their field of vision, and the fashion industry is notoriously decentralized. Nearly all that's required to establish a garment's provenance under international trade regulations is the momentary labor of sewing in a "Made In" label—the primary means by which globalization can be tracked by consumers, about to be done away with under new World Trade Organization regulations.

Still, the destination of most Southeast Asian-made garments is predictable: 70 percent of all apparel produced in Cambodia is imported to the United States. While Asian countries, particularly China, lead denim exports, the US still drives consumption of those too, accounting for nearly 40 percent of jeans purchases worldwide. Unlike most apparel, these jeans are made in a single factory—the sole male in the lunch bunch was a cutter from the very front of the line.

Yet his placement at the earliest stage of production didn't offer a substantial difference in vantage point on the group's complaints of labor abuses, many of which were reminiscent of the early days of the Industrial Revolution. The International Labour Organization (ILO)-backed monitoring agent Better Factories Cambodia (BFC) regularly documents the extent to which Asian garment work remains impervious to basic labor and safety regulations. During the 2008 inspections, monitors discovered that some factories weren't meeting minimum wage pay standards, particularly for casual workers, whose ranks only increased after the global economic recession later that same year. Legally required maternity leave pay was granted to only three-quarters of the workers who requested it; only two-thirds of workers requesting sick pay received it. And even these discouraging numbers don't track the vast group of workers who have not been informed of their rights to demand them. Half the companies in the ILO survey failed to meet basic health and safety requirements, and 92 percent were found to illegally mandate overtime work. Wage theft was frequent, commonly carried out through management flacks, who omitted or mischaracterized pay stub translations to employees who were unable to read. Health facilities, mandatory under Cambodian law, remained understaffed, when they were available at all.

When I asked the Cambodian workers about their future prospects in the industry, it became immediately clear how differently women and men view garment work as a career. The first difference between the male workers' responses and their female counterparts' emerged when I asked about their futures. I wanted to know if the female workers hoped to advance in the factory. They only smiled. My translator prodded them with greater eloquence, but this had no effect. Finally, I asked outright, "Would you like to be managers?"

The women broke into raucous laughter. "Oh, they would like," my translator explained through their giggled uproar. "But, no time." Time to study accounting, earn a high school degree, attend college, he continued, which would also take money. Most of their funds—only $55 per month in 2009, keep in mind—were sent back home to support family farms. That's why young people in Cambodia get sent to the city to work in the first place. Approximately 20 percent of the country's fifteen million residents survive on the incomes of nearly half a million workers working in today's garment trade. The family tradition of shipping daughters off to work leaves Cambodia's already weak bureaucratic state scrambling to document the ever widening epidemic of underage labor. Official documents are easy to fake and not always required, and a young person's genuine interest in helping the family may mean she's willing to lie about her age, even if she knows her real birth date, which several generations of Cambodians do not. So while underage workers throng the garment factories, reliable statistics on the problem of child labor are almost impossible to collect. Girls face other barriers to advancement, too: only 6 percent of the garment factory managers in the country are women, most of whom are owners' relatives. For these women to advance in the factories, in other words, they would have to have been born into the business.

The young man stayed silent as his female coworkers described their fates. He knew that he would probably make manager if he wanted to, or get another job if he didn't. His colleagues also lacked the simple sovereignty over their own persons that he could take for granted. A 2006 BFC study found that around 30 percent of the garment factory workforce experienced sexual harassment on the job. A more recent 2012 report from the ILO found that number had dropped to 20 percent—a decline almost certainly stemming from the increase in male factory employees during the industry's expansion.

My hosts' twenty-minute lunch break ended quickly and they waved goodbye. In a few hours, three of the youngest would walk home together after work, to the cramped factory housing unit they shared with three other girls to save money, and make a meager dinner. After that, they'd fall asleep right away, because it would be late, and because they would have to get up early the next day and do it all over again.

◆ ◆ ◆

We recognize labor and human rights violations when they occur on the production end of global fashion, but any close look at the display sector will reveal a distressing litany of similarities—beginning with the tendencies of garment factories and modeling agencies alike to prey on young women. (A feature they share with the marketing divisions that stoke demand for the products of both industries.)

"It's a brutal world," Meier says, recalling her entry into the display-side workforce. "They do want you to come in at the age of thirteen, fourteen, hoping that you'll hit your prime at seventeen." A 2012 Model Alliance report found that over half the models surveyed had started between thirteen and sixteen; another 1 percent had started earlier. More than half of those underage were never or were rarely accompanied by a legal guardian to castings or jobs. (The Model Alliance sample size was small—85 completed surveys, from the 241 who received the form—but so is the modeling world. The US Bureau of Labor Statistics, or BLS, tallied only 4,800 working models in the country that same year. It's a growing field, however, as 2015 numbers indicate 5,800 total models working in the US—an increase of 21 percent over just three years.)

Then there are the long, irregular hours. Models report working fourteen- to twenty-hour days without advance notice, a practice so consistent it shows up in the BLS job description: "Many models work part time and have unpredictable work schedules. Models must be ready on short notice . . . and the number of hours worked will vary depending on the job."[4] The lack of scheduling predictability was also a complaint of warehouse workers I spoke to at a facility in Joliet, Illinois, who ship out clothing by the ton to Wal-Mart and fast-fashion chains. The practice is slightly more troubling in warehouse work, given managers' habits of locking employees into facilities during shifts, supposedly to minimize theft. Working long, irregular hours is of particular concern to parents, both in warehouses and in factories. In Cambodia, childcare options are few and expensive, so factory workers must delay having children, ship kids back home to grandparents, or invest in a good deadbolt and hope for the best during the workday.

For all fashion workers, the pressure to remain malnourished is high, although it is only one of many health and safety concerns in the industry. The 2013 Rana Plaza collapse in Bangladesh, in which more than 1,100 workers died, pointed to one common health crisis that plagues garment employees—dangerous working conditions. In Cambodia, mass faintings that started in 2011 but continue today point to another. Studies found that in the regular course of any given month, between tens and thousands of workers fall to the ground in a faint from a combination of undernourishment, long hours, heat, and bad air.[5] Workers in a Chicago H&M in summer of 2011 told me they left their job en masse when the AC conked out and they began to feel light headed and faint in their store. Some H&M employees have access to company health insurance plans, although other fast-fashion outlets, like Mango, Zara, and Forever 21, do not. (In developing nations, health insurance does not often exist. Regulated garment factories are often required to maintain medical staff, but just as often will let that requirement, among many others, slide.)

Of course, the health concerns facing models are often less evident than indicated by mass fainting incidents: according to the

Model Alliance survey, 68 percent of the workforce suffers from anxiety and/or depression. A quarter profess drug or alcohol dependency, and around a third lack health insurance. Undereating is pervasive—31 percent of models admit to eating disorders, although individual culpability is in question when undereating becomes a job requirement. Supermodel Amy Lemons was advised to eat only a rice cake a day.[6] Others are offered more subtle hints—often backed up by contract stipulations—to lose inches from hips, thighs, or rear.

Jennifer Sky, former *Maxim* and *Sassy* cover model turned *Xena: Warrior Princess* regular, says the industry gave her PTSD. In an emotional YouTube video, she describes unsupervised foreign travel as a child and a lengthy shoot in a swimming pool, when her legs turned an unattractive shade of blue.[7] She was scolded for it, and years of such criticism began to wear on her, just as they did on Meier. Sky's emotional health tanked.

"The caste system on a set is specific and hard to navigate. And, while the model is the focal point, he/she is most often (unless she is a supermodel), at the bottom of the social caste," she elaborated via email. "The model must conform to what the makeup artist envisions for his makeup, even though he is placing his vision on her face. Same goes for the hairstylist and the clothing stylist. At each station, the model must fit into her role, even before she steps in front of a camera. No wonder most models I have ever met are so unsure of where they stand with anyone and always questioning, massively insecure. Because they are never offered any voice or source of security. Their body is a commodity for other people."

Emotional neglect, little sustenance, and unpredictable hours would create rough conditions for any worker under the age of eighteen, but the industry that sets the standards for beauty and desire in our culture is also a big-money honeytrap for male predators. The poster boy for this ugly tradition is "Uncle" Terry Richardson, one of the highest paid photographers in the world, who got his start at *Vice* before moving into couture and celebrities. He has been regularly named in sexual assault and harassment complaints since 2005, for on-shoot behavior including non-consensual jizzing, offers to make tea from used tampons, and demands that models squeeze his balls. (It's hardly a surprise that Bill Cosby, too, has evinced a strong preference for models in his long string of alleged sexual assaults.)

"This is an industry that obviously lends itself to sexual harassment at the workplace," Jennifer Sky tells me. But it's not just models and factory workers: retail thrift store employees and warehouse workers are also targets of verbal or physical aggression and unwanted sexual advances. One worker in the Joliet warehouse told me she was raped by her manager, fired when she filed a complaint, and only reinstated after several co-workers joined protests in solidarity. Other fast-fashion warehouse workers say that sexual harassment at facilities is high because of the relatively few female employees and extensive surveillance equipment common in the Foreign Trade Zones where warehouses are situated.[8] (One might expect surveillance equipment to protect against worker abuse, until one realizes how easily the surveillors can find opportunities to commit such abuses themselves.) Even in supposedly sustainable second-hand fashion, the industry perpetuates the hypersexualization of female laborers: complaints have been filed against Apogee Retail Inc., owners of the for-profit Unique Thrift Store chain, for sexual harassment and abuse.

Model Alliance found that 30 percent of models experience inappropriate, on-the-job touching, 28 percent feel pressured to have sex with someone at work, and 61 percent express concern over their lack of privacy while changing clothes. Only 29 percent feel they can report sexual harassment to their agency, although two thirds of those who have taken this step discovered that their agencies didn't bother to respond. Eighty-seven percent have been asked to pose nude without advance notification, which is a requirement for many agencies.

It's troubling enough to realize that models under the age of eighteen are routinely asked to strip for cameras without advance notice or supervision. But what makes the practice even more disturbing is that, in many cases, it's all perfectly legal. Agencies are able to recruit heavily from the preteen set thanks to a loophole carved out in the Fair Labor Standards Act of 1938 known as the Shirley Temple Act, which requires individual states to pass their own laws protecting child performers or farm workers. New York is one of many states that passed such protections—although eighteen others have not—and in late 2013, Model Alliance successfully petitioned New York to reclassify print and runway models under the age of eighteen as child performers. This category would assure that underage models can only work with state-approved permits, and are entitled to limitations on the hours they work, while also guaranteeing them regular breaks, educational accommodations, and chaperones for those under sixteen. Compliance has been slow, but some in the industry say they've seen a slight upward trend in models' ages since.

There's a far more insidious ripple effect in play, however, when a culture sanctions very young girls as symbols of sexual availability. "Dressing little girls up to sell women's clothing affects the way women feel about themselves," Sky says. "It affects the way men treat women. Why do we have such an out-of-control rape culture? Well if you look at the images of 'women' that advertisers are selling to us . . . [they] are of underage girls, cast as victims, their bodies taking on broken-doll positions, their eyes vacant, helpless, and submissive."

These images may demean individual models, but their cumulative effect also demeans the consumer, Sky charges. "How do you learn to memorize something? You repeat it over and over until is in your subconscious," she explains. "It doesn't take advanced behavioral science to pick up the messages being sold to us."

Still, if you're the one selling the message, you might be able to make your individual peace with its pernicious content—provided the price is right. But here's another counterintuitive truth about the modeling profession: models earn significantly less than you think. BLS suggests models in the US earned only around $19,300 in 2013, the year following the Model Alliance survey, which breaks down to a mean hourly wage of $9.28 per hour.[9] (This is about half the mean income in fashion photography, a male-dominated field, where workers earn a mean of $37,190, and about one-fourth of the annual earnings for fashion designers, who also skew dude, and take home a comfortable yearly income of $78,410.) Retail sales workers across all industries earn mean annual incomes of $21,890, with big clothing retail chains claiming a workforce that's 85-95 percent female. Warehousing and storage workers, who tend to be male, earned an annual mean in 2013 of $29,630.

Look more closely at those earnings. The $9.28 per hour models earned in 2013 represented just 83 percent of the $11.50 per hour living wage in New York that year;[10] while median earnings reportedly rose for models in 2015, the living wage did, too, and the gap between the two persists. The most recent BLS tallies have models earning 91 percent of a living wage, which is certainly a higher percentage of a living wage than factory workers take home in Mexico (67 percent), Guatemala (50 percent), Vietnam (29 percent), or Bangladesh (14 percent). It's also true that part of a model's wages may be offset by the country-club lifestyle and, ahem, low food budget. Yet a percentage of a living wage, however high, is still not a living wage—what stands out, across the spectrum of fashion-related labor, is that the pay for jobs dominated by women isn't intended to ensure survival.

Worse than low pay, however, is no pay. A recent report on Haitian garment factories found that every single one of the country's twenty-four garment exporters was failing to meet the national minimum wage, paying on average only two-thirds of what the law required.[11] Garment workers just outside of Delhi, India, who suffer gender pay discrimination as a matter of course, have had unexplained deductions and delays in payment diminish their paychecks as well.[12] Indeed, workers at retail-outlet warehouses regularly face the range of practices known as wage theft. Laborers at a Walmart supplier in California, for example, won a lawsuit in 2014 for $21 million in back pay,[13] and workers at a Forever 21 warehouse filed a similar claim in 2013, claiming that their bosses didn't compensate them for overtime, or provide them with meal or rest breaks on the job.[14]

Models have likewise reported that agencies dock pay over such offenses as having gained too much weight;[15] it's also common, models claim, for agencies to delay paychecks for months on end. Agencies charge for tests, visas, portfolios, delivery fees, etc.—all deducted from earnings before payout, and not always tallied for workers' financial records. Additionally, some designers "pay" in "trade"—apparel that is often too small to sell to anyone else and too flimsy to withstand the rigors of everyday wear.

"As we know, stuff does not put food on the table or a roof over one's head," Jennifer Sky elaborates. She's now left modeling for writing, but still sits on the Model Alliance advisory board and advocates for change in her childhood profession. "It is the extreme arrogance of the fashion industry that someone like Marc Jacobs, who runs a massive global corporation, would not pay twenty young women $500 each to walk in his show instead of 'gifting' them a garment or two."

But, as is the case with exploited warehouse workers, models face enormous structural barriers to getting their grievances heard, let alone resolved. Agencies guard against costly legal action by claiming that models are independent contractors, not employees. The temp agencies where warehouses contract for labor do the same. This designation leaves workers uncovered by many of the sexual harassment protections that apply to other classes of employees. It also just makes organizing difficult—and dovetails neatly with fashion's individuality-forward ethos.

"To offer no protections is absurd," Sky contends. That's why she wants to see her fellow models form a union. "We empower the worker who is selling us the goods; we too will become empowered. We make the fashion industry use adults to sell adult clothing; it will have a huge global impact."

Modeling rests on the shaky foundation we may wave off as "beauty standards," but its relentless reification of the displayed model-consuming self has far more distressing implications in a democracy than mere aesthetic preference would indicate. Models are not merely selected to reflect—read: entrench—cultural norms, but with every turn before the camera or on the catwalk, they're also empowered to invent them anew. The modeling industry strives to offer that unique combination of recognizably desirable and wholly inoffensive; models are charged to be serenely unattainable objects of beauty at the same time that they must remain studiously and generally unchallenging, for the big spenders in white, mainstream, heteronormative America.

Racial discrimination is paramount. Meier, remember, initially excused the animosity she felt from other models because she wasn't competing with them for jobs. As a woman of color, she simply couldn't have put in for the same marquee gigs that her white counterparts would be offered; the industry is founded on the practice of physical discrimination. Meier's career path, she felt, was distinct from other (white) models'—even though the Supreme Court decreed in 1954 that separate but equal is not equal at all.

Designers seem never to have heard of *Brown v. Board of Education*—or if they have, it hasn't occurred to them that they, too, preside over an enormously influential institution devoted to educating American taste preferences. So it took more than fifty years before racial discrimination among models gained wider public attention. A 2008 *Vogue* article headlined, "Is Fashion Racist?" prompted a burst of adverse publicity that had industry leaders swearing to beef up diversity practices in 2009, only to lose interest in the project again once the new spring colors hit the runway. Since the entire industry is virtually unregulated, no one seems to have proposed target numbers or quotas, and old patterns, in fashion, always reemerge. The number of black models at New York's Spring

Fashion Week hit a low in 2013, and the number of white models—83 percent—a high, with some thirteen companies hiring no models of color at all.[16] By Fall Fashion Week 2016, the number of white models had dropped slightly to 75 percent—still not anything close to what a reasonable outside observer would call "diverse."[17]

When I ask Meier, who is Asian-European, about racism in modeling, her eyes widen. "It's part of the job," she says after a moment. "You develop a thick skin knowing you're going to be discriminated against because of your physical attributes and race or whatever anyway. You take it as part of the job."

Throughout our conversation, Meier had often paused to reconsider her experiences. Unlike Sky, she's not involved in the movement for model's rights, which helped to keep her replies from parroting any broader advocacy agenda. ("I come from the Philippines, where I don't think there are labor laws," she joked at one point.) She took a long pause here before continuing. "This conversation has opened me up to the idea that maybe some of these things aren't actually OK," she tells me. "But . . . they seemed completely OK. I accepted them. I didn't know that I couldn't."

Not knowing has consequences, of course, which is why the models' rights movement is important—although only as important as the movement for all fashion workers' rights. That, however, is substantial: by some estimates, between one-sixth and one-seventh of all working women in the world labor in some sector of the fashion industry, making it the field of commerce perhaps more responsible than any other for women's economic repression around the globe.

Organizing fashion workers has its challenges. We tend to see each workforce in this vast system as distinct to job description—models, retailers, warehouse workers, and factory employees each special little snowflakes, doing their part to keep consumers rebellious but stylish. However, each sector has more in common than it appears: the fashion industry submits its entire workforce to the same system of global Fordism that governs the race to the bottom in apparel manufacture. The more the cutter and the packer are kept at separate ends of the line on a single factory floor, the less likely they are to communicate concerns about the factory they work in. Likewise, when factory workers are segregated from retailers, warehouse workers, and models, these related workforces are unlikely to collectively challenge the global garment industry's systematic disenfranchisement of women as workers and as consumers. For dressed in factory uniforms, sensible slacks, or glittery couture, women remain first-order targets of oppression as workers for the fashion industry—which targets them again as they line up to pay heavy markups in stores.

Still, organizing—even across Fordian divisions—within a single industry may not erase the core problems of fashion—or of modeling. "I don't know many models that have come out whole," Meier tells me honestly. "Not many come out of it feeling empowered, or confident, or having life skills to progress with anything other than their physical attributes. Models are some of the most insecure people I know. Period. And that's not healed by becoming a more successful model. That's healed by getting your ass out of it, completely."

A portion of an earlier version of this essay was published as "The Catwalk Sweatshop" in Talking Points Memo.

VAGINA DENTATA

The re-emergence of feminism as a successful marketing strategy in late 2012 (think: Naomi Wolf, Sheryl Sandberg, Beyoncé) led to a lot of talk about vaginas, setting the stage for the most gynecologically obsessed presidential election campaign cycle in US history four short years later. Grabbing women "by the pussy" became a talking point on morning shows, as did whether or not candidates should use the ladies room at debates. Let's not forget what the Vagenda of Manocide brought to the table!

Following years of work by community media strategists and clever social justice campaigners, it was also becoming clear in the 2010s that speaking *for* unheard voices was no longer acceptable; there was always a burgeoning writer or cultural producer within a marginalized community perfectly capable of outlining their own needs. "Nothing about us without us," goes the international rallying cry, now popular among sex workers, but first brought stateside by disability rights activists in the 1990s. While neoliberal feminism certainly raised the market share of those willing to speak *about* vaginas, I mean to point out, not so much of this talk emanated from *actual vaginas*.

Very few dare to let the vagina speak for itself, and such visionaries are never whom you'd expect. Take Wolfgang Büld, whose low-budget horror film *Angst* of a decade earlier lays the imaginary groundwork for a genuine feminist uprising, far beyond anything hinted at in Sheryl Sandberg's *Lean In*.

Let's be clear: Büld is no feminist, of any variety. He's a punk documentarian and exploitation filmmaker. However, if we define feminism as advocating for equal political, economic, and social rights for women, it's going to be hard to define self-proclaimed vagina biographer Naomi Wolf as such, either. She seems primarily interested in building a following for herself—a quasi-religious one, even—than in establishing conditions where "following" isn't the only way women can achieve power.

In truth, I can't pretend I'm any more interested in Wolf's vagina—nor, for that matter, her *Vagina*—than I would be if, say, anyone else I thought was a big dork wrote a book about something I had been operating exclusively without oversight or input for my entire life. Like cats. This is provable: I don't read books about cats, either. (Although I might be compelled to read a book about a particularly interesting cat.)

Wolf's 2012 cultural history *Vagina* does not interest me, but the critical debate around it has me fascinated. Take Zöe Heller's brilliant take in the *New York Review of Books*, which is worth reading even if you think Naomi Wolf is a big dork. Or hate vaginas. Or have never heard of "books" and have no intention of trying to figure out what to do with them.

Heller opens her essay tallying appearances of the near-ubiquitous orifice:

> "*Vagina pride*" *is now part of the common culture. Television celebrities like Oprah Winfrey speak publicly and with cheerful affection of their "vajayjays." (The conservative watchdog group Parents Television Council calculates that the use of the word "vagina" on television has increased eightfold in the last decade.) The Vagina Monologues,* Eve Ensler's theatrical celebration of the female sex organ, has become an international franchise, endorsed and performed by glossy Hollywood stars and even Michigan state representatives. More than one website now exists for the sole purpose of allowing women to share and compare pictures of their vulvas in "a supportive context."*[1]

However, Heller adds a moment later, this apparent flowering of love for the special flower between many women's legs is not enough for some:

Naomi Wolf would counsel against such complacency. In her
new "biography" of the vagina, she warns that her subject is in
danger of being trivialized by its cultural ubiquity. The vagina,
properly understood, is, "part of the female soul" and the
medium for the "meaning of life itself." In order to free female
sexuality from patriarchal calumny, pornographic distortion,
and some of the damaging myths of second-wave feminism,
it is essential, she argues, that women reclaim the "magic" of
the vagina and restore it to its rightful place at "the center of
the universe."

The critical response to Wolf's book made one thing clear: that
the self-proclaimed feminist figurehead had begun speaking out of—
how shall I put this—the wrong orifice. Not the one she had titled
the book after. I say this with some hesitation: I quite liked Wolf's
first memoir and feel some sympathy for a woman who is simply
forging a publishing career like any other outspoken and excessively
branded man. My patience evaporated, however, when Wolf fired
back at critics via op-eds and social media posts with an argument
cribbed from notes scrawled in Women's Sexual Liberation 101.

"I come from the feminist school that believes knowledge is
power," she writes in the September 11, 2012 *Guardian*, in a screed
clearly intended to paint her detractors as those who delight in ignorance. Citing Tee Corinne, Shere Hite, and other anointed feminists
of yore—and operating under an unexamined transphobia—Wolf
charges detractors with misunderstanding her pro-sex argument
and follows this up by hinting that they might be prudes and/
or illiterate.

It was a dramatic détournement from her intention to speak
for the vagina: now she was chastising those who did not heed her
exaltations of it. At which point her spiritual defense of the particular kind of orgasm she personally enjoys, and suggests others work
toward, too, took on a tone we can only call vagsplaining.

The whiff of sanctimoniousness can be detected from a

distance, although the book appears to have emerged from a less anointed platform: a crisis with the workings of Wolf's own nether regions. After some years of truly delightful orgasms, she explains in *Vagina* (I gather; I'm quoting from Heller's review), Wolf suddenly suffers inadequate ones.

"It was like a horror movie," she describes, according to Heller. It is not clear to me that Naomi Wolf has ever seen a horror movie, of which perhaps one in a thousand is concerned in any way with women's sexual satisfaction. Still, a real horror movie about a malfunctioning bikini area holds more opportunity for ending the oppression of women than Wolf's *Vagina*.

Enter Wolfgang Büld. (Get it? Penetration joke.) His 2003 film *Angst* depicts horrors unimaginable, I imagine, to Naomi Wolf. For one, lead character Helen (played by Fiona Horsey) is frigid, and doesn't enjoy either spiritual or regular orgasms. "That's huge," Helen scowls when her date pulls out his dong, after he abuses her emotionally for a bit. Then he rapes her. I'd soften the description with the term date rape, but we're intended to view him as purely malevolent: he crosses the line from coercion to plain-old physical violence when he traps Helen in a car window and penetrates her from behind despite her screaming protests. Then he disappears. For rape isn't the only horror this film explores: Helen's vagina talks. And eats people.

It does not eat their clothes, which is awesome, if a little confusing. And the vagina's diet is not restricted to people. Sometimes it's perfectly content to chow down on some phallic-looking meat products from a jar in the fridge. This, however, doesn't concern Helen much. She's only freaked out when her vagina demands men. "Feed me!" it cries from her pants.

It's all told in that classic 1970s sexploitation-horror manner, wherein victim tallies mount in titillating shot after titillating shot, each more elaborately pseudosexual than the last. Often a scene will be played for laughs, a moment of respite intended to deepen the coming horror, although sometimes the comedy is unintentional.

Always a gory detail, an overly descriptive color-saturated glimpse of what the imagined terror might look like, if stumbled across in lived human experience. Then a piece of sound equipment in a corner of the screen will remind viewers that, in real life, vaginas don't eat men. *Angst* seems filmed in a place that is either Germany or America or England, and no one seems to know or care which. It's impossible to get lost in, because the cast is all self-consciously self-conscious: *we are acting in a film in which* . . . seems to lead off every stage direction.

What viewers are supposed to *feel fear for* gets a little lost: Is it a vagina that eats? A vagina that eats men? A vagina that has unconventional tastes? Such an ambiguous monster does not inspire much terror, yet from my perspective, the real horror is that Helen seems disenfranchised from her own sexual needs. Every time her pussy consumes some abusive dickwad or another, leaving a fresh pile of laundry between her legs, she grows more horrified at her own body's behavior. I'd probably need to read or call Naomi Wolf to find out what she'd think of this (neither of which am I interested in doing), but I believe she'd find Helen's response perfectly agreeable. Of course one should find unspiritual, anti-procreative sex appalling! Someone died! I admit there is a logic there.

Still, I'm inclined to wish that lanky Helen had gotten the gist of her own body's desires a bit more. After all, every man she meets *is* a rapist. Or a date-rapist, or just a jerk. Including the doctor she goes to for help. Including her stepfather. Her primary love interest, whom she shuns to protect, kills someone with an electric knife. Sort of by accident, but the act does out him as a murderer. He repents and she forgives him, the lesson being: harming someone isn't inherently problematic. The problem is finding joy in it. Helen refuses joy, even as she learns to listen, quite literally, to the sexual demands of her body.

Helen has been gifted with a seemingly impossible situation: to satiate her physical needs, someone will always die. Imagine the masculine figures in cultural history for whom this is true, in the horror genre or otherwise: werewolves, vampires, the titular character of the television program *Dexter*. Every army commander in every war film ever created. Every military commander in every war unfilmed. We may not gender the act of murder as exclusively masculine, but certainly the imagined pleasures to be had from it remain the domain of men.

All of which make *Angst* a bit of a mess, both in terms of gender politics and in terms of character motivation. Occasional scenes—an oral sex attempt gone awry is one truly creative and stunning example—shine. Others do not: apparently I'd stopped watching the film fifteen minutes before the end and didn't notice. (Now that I have seen the ending, I'm not sure it added anything.) Granted, a horror movie about a remorseless murdering cunt would not necessarily be improved with solid acting or logical plot development. It's always going to be messy. I could have used a messier *Angst*, in truth.

Now don't get confused—there's another 2003 film that came out, also called *Angst*, about something totally different. Something related to angst, probably. Büld's movie has little to do with angst, which is possibly why it was also released under the name *Penetration Angst*, but should have been released under the name *Talking Vagina Movie*. For Helen does not feel mere angst. She feels confusion and remorse and self-hatred and survivor's guilt. Vagina dentata's not much fun for anyone, in Büld's view.

Yet *Angst* strives not at all toward metaphor, presenting an endless string of rapists as men being men, and Helen as one woman among many, possessed merely of a particularly unique flower between her legs. She's ashamed, purely, of her body's needs, but this is never drawn out to echo the shame women are generally made to feel when pursuing any of their own desires. Yes, for Helen to feel satiated, someone will always die, but even according to the logic of the film, her lady garden's Vagenda of Manocide is a true public service. The world in which a genuinely murderous cunt is both satisfied and appreciated remains, sadly, elusive.

So Büld is no feminist hero, to be sure. Nor did he intend to become one. His film came about when someone told him he could make exploitation movies in the UK for super cheap, and if they were shot in English, they were guaranteed an audience through DVD sales. By the next day, he'd combined three bad ideas he'd previously rejected into a single story, and production began. (In an interview with horror blogger MJ Simpson, he describes the failed scripts as: "The man-eating vagina, the Siamese twins . . . and some bank robbers getting stuck in a nudist camp. Each of these ideas were not long enough for a feature film, but they had something in common: they were all dealing with the fears of sex."[2])

Angst, therefore, contains no explicit feminist agenda. In fact, Büld labels his oeuvre "intelligent exploitation." "I like so-called B-movies," he tells Simpson, "but most of them are made badly: weak screenplays, bad actors, boring visuals. My intention was to produce high quality in this genre." Indeed, the filmmaker wades directly into misogynist waters when he suggests in the same interview that the film is about "a vagina that works the wrong way: instead of giving life, it absorbs life. I leave the interpretation—if it kills for real or only in Helen's mind—to the audience." In Büld's view, it seems, he may simply have created another film about a crazy chick and her bloodthirsty beaver.

Limitations of both narrative and filmmaker aside, however, what *Angst* offers is much more than a film about a vagina that works the wrong way (meaning: one that does not do what it is supposed to do *for men*). *Angst* establishes an imaginary in which women might value their own desires and heed their unusual bodies, a point slightly further along a continuum of the ways we imagine vaginas work than we have ever seen fit to explore before. Self-proclaimed vagina biographer and vagsplainer Naomi Wolf, on the other hand, has done something far more limited and frustratingly prescriptive: she has merely established her view of the way vaginas *must* work. Weirder, she has established herself as their savior.

One of these directives emulates patriarchal oppression, and it's not the one you'd expect. For what Büld suspects, that Wolf can't fathom, is this: disrupting systems of gender oppression—or the much milder version of same, exploring new narrative forms—can only come from allowing the oppressed to speak for themselves. And that is going to get messy.

The lesson lost on both, however, remains the central concern for any feminist leader in the running. Truly disruptive anti-oppression work that tackles gender disparity must allow the oppressed the opportunity to explore their own joy, wherever it comes from. Even if it causes discomfort.

An earlier version of this essay was published on The Blog is Coming from Inside the House.

CONSUMPCYON

Marian is a bright young woman living in Toronto in the mid-late twentieth century, an employee at a small market research firm who spends her off-hours juggling an attractive but hard-to-please boyfriend, an irresponsible roommate, a tittering gaggle of office-mates, and unenvied friends stuck in the baby-making grind. She is well-educated and able-bodied, and filled with all the hopes and dreams a woman could imagine for herself before the Feminist Revolution took hold: Marriage, she supposes, to a man, and kids, maybe, eventually? Friends to entertain, certainly, in a nice home, although come to think of it, Marian isn't entirely sure what she wants. In fact, Margaret Atwood's 1969 novel *The Edible Woman* (Atwood herself called it "protofeminist") is primarily concerned with what Marian *doesn't* want, and how her disinterest is culmi-nating in physical symptoms. Marian, a product of—and an import-ant cog in—consumer society, eventually finds herself unable to consume. "This is ridiculous," she says to herself when she first encounters her problems with food.[1] What, our protagonist won-ders frequently, could possibly be wrong with her?

Atwood is short on details of Marian's life before her digestive issues arise, toppling with them her status as able-bodied: the book opens with the entirely forgettable sentence, "I know I was all right Friday when I got up." The author is similarly stingy with elements of Marian's person, as well as with precise descriptions of her emerging ailments. Still, there are plenty of words between the opening sen-tence and the appearance of Marian's consumptive failures some 170 pages later, and many of them, upon close inspection, reveal them-selves to be cleverly feminized alarm bells. As Marian grows increas-ingly concerned about her inability to eat, she becomes alienated from her own body—reflected in a shift from first- to third-person narration between the two halves of the book—and increasingly unable to articulate her concerns: she stops being "all right" sometime after Friday, but because Marian never verbalizes her concerns, the reader doesn't have any clues when she gets sick or what form her illness really takes.

What we gather about Marian in the first half of *The Edible Woman* is that she is white, Canadian, upper-middle class, and professional—"normal," we're given to believe, if a bit reticent to contradict the insufferables she seems surrounded by. Her character is filled out in the negative: she is "not blonde," she disapproves of her roommate's drinking habits, she backs away from conversations about child-rearing. Marian desires not to bring offense, clearly, but Atwood designs her inoffensively: she is Everywoman, that literary device into which Atwood's largely white feminine readership might slot themselves. In the common parlance, Marian is "relatable."

Yet Marian's apparent normality is a large part of the trouble, for there is no visible manifestation of her problem with food. She does not develop a tumor, for example, or appear alarmingly frail to any of the other characters in the book, nor does she gain weight. As the adage goes, seeing is believing; not seeing, therefore, leaves one at risk of not being believed, although Marian offers no explanation whatsoever for why she can't eat, so is in no danger of being discredited. The reader only ever knows that, to Marian, the problem is quite real. Yet without any detail regarding symptoms, the reader also has no clue if the problem is biological or psychological.

A "refusal of her mouth to eat," it's called at one point; the blame for her disability placed on "whatever it was that had been making these decisions, not her mind certainly." Her jaw fails to open, she cannot lift her fork, she is hungry but finds she cannot take a bite—Marian has been diagnosed by successive decades of readers as vegan, anorexic, nervous, allergic, hysterical, and a victim of our hyperconsumerist environment.

It might be more to the point to diagnose her, simply, as a proto-Everywoman—and Atwood a visionary. Recently, ailments remarkably similar to Marian's have become quite common among relatively young North American women—including well-educated upper-middle class whites. A 2014 study[2] found around 11 percent of the population worldwide—three-quarters of them women, with twenty-five to forty-five million living in the US—diagnosed with irritable bowel syndrome (IBS), for example, a diagnosis often bestowed upon patients with symptoms and concerns as vague as Marian's. Alongside dozens of other autoimmune diseases—many with food aversions of unknown biological or psychological provenance—IBS has, in the nearly fifty years since Atwood first envisioned something like it, become a modern epidemic.

◆ ◆ ◆

Marian's troubles arise one night at dinner with her fiancé Peter when she can't finish a steak. Her standard diet of TV dinners, packaged puddings, and boil-in-the-bag entrees often leaves her craving something freshly made, so she rarely leaves leftovers when she goes out. Yet she can neither clean her plate, nor offer any reasonable explanation to Peter for her sudden disinterest in the meal. Although she keeps up appearances in the coming days, her difficulties only worsen.

"The day after the filet, she had been unable to eat a pork chop," Atwood writes. All meat is out. Soon Marian finds she can no longer stomach a growing list of foods: next is dairy, and shortly after that, vegetables. Her primary concerns are social, for she continues attending parties and dinners, but resorts to hiding food whenever she finds she cannot finish it. The third-person narrative voice further confounds readers seeking details of the protagonist's digestive troubles, and it becomes difficult to trust Marian's description of events as accurate.

The novel ends tidily, in a too-neat domestic scene in which Marian symbolically offers herself up for consumption but, rejected, ends up consuming herself. Deeply rooted social norms—like that convenience food is harmless, for example, or that single women crave marriage to eligible bachelors—now overcome *like that*, Marian is cured. She can eat again and, newly single, can offer her symbolic self up for other men to eat, too. Marian is back on the market, as it were: Atwood's joke about Marian's re-entry into consumer society.

It reads false and, as we will soon see, it is false, at least for the millions of women in North America who suffer ailments resembling Marian's. Yet on all other fronts, the book is unusually prescient, even for an Atwood novel. For *The Edible Woman* is not only a story about consumerism, about the body's need to eat as biological phenomenon and as cultural metaphor. It is a story about broken political economies and their impact on the physical self.

Take the difficulty in diagnosing Marian, for example, which comes from her seemingly normal existence. She works in advertising—*ahem*, "market research"—and intends to marry a good-looking young lawyer. Obviously she is surrounded by brands, and thinks about how they might fit into her life for a good part of every day. She considers ads, and whether she likes them, even outside of the office: she has internalized her role as a consumer so thoroughly that she is apt to have a product for dinner that she worked on during the week. Her friends are having children—both in and outside of wedlock (although those who start outside of it quickly want in). Her future, in other words, seems clearly planned.

Unfortunately Peter, her good-looking, young, lawyer-fiancé, has no positive interpersonal attributes. He is dismissive of Marian, and the sex they have is perfunctory and passionless. He enjoys hunting and then describing the animals he has killed over dinner. He is a bore, and a bit of a letch, but it is unclear how much of this Marian can perceive, because her behavior is either predictable for a character of that time period—she deflects to him more and more over the course of the book—or inconsistently written, which is unlikely, since Atwood tends to create characters with rich interior selves. The reader experiences the friction between the two potential explanations for Marian's submissiveness through a simmering rage, an experience common to gender-minded readers of works written before the second wave of feminism. At the time, of course, marriage represented one of the only paths to financial security for women, aside from being born rich. (Women in the US couldn't have credit cards in their own names until 1974, for example.) So readers won't be surprised that Marian pursues marriage, even with a partner she acknowledges—although only occasionally, and via interior mono-logue—is imperfect. After all, financial security is necessary to lead the well-branded life she clearly desires. Marriage, therefore, is not something Marian finds negotiable.

Yet something is wrong. That Marian's entire life trajectory is thrown into question when her consumptive issues arise is one clue that the book is about far more than mere consumption, but the *New York Times* missed it in its 1970 review:

> *As her wedding day approaches, Marian quite literally begins to lose her ability to consume things. First she rejects steak, finally she cannot even stomach salad. A case of bridal jitters, says a married friend. Or, as I think the author means us to half-seriously see it, a piece of truth-telling dementia that is a symbolic answer to lying sanity. Not to eat or be eaten up like a confection of calculated flavors might be her heroine's unconscious aim and Miss Atwood's symbolic sense.*[3]

The thesis that "consumerism" is the entirety of the problem that Atwood means to point out likely held a certain logic—maybe even an unwashed allure—when the review was published. (A tried-and-true revolutionary of the 1960s recently told me that, by the 1970s, he had believed capitalism was over. It seemed clear to him and his colleagues, he said, that culture had reached peak consum-erism. Then he laughed.) The onset of Marian's ailment, however, isn't a reaction to food itself, nor the infiltration of ads, brands, sales pitches, and jingles into her world. Her revulsion is triggered instead by an awareness of how it all works together, a glimpse at the man behind the curtain and what he's preparing for her back there.

Marian is not, in other words, symbolically over-satiated by the "confection of calculated flavors" on offer. Here, her body prepares to reject beef for the first time:

Watching [Peter] operating on the steak like that, carving a straight slice and then dividing it into neat cubes, made her think of the diagram of the planned cow at the front of one of her cookbooks: the cow with lines on it and labels to show you from which part of the cow all the different cuts were taken. What they were eating now was from some part of the back, she thought: cut on the dotted line. She could see rows of butchers somewhere in a large room, a butcher school, sitting at tables, clothed in spotless white, each with a pair of kindergarten scissors, cutting out steaks and ribs and roasts from the stacks of brown-paper cow-shapes before them. The cow in the book, she recalled, was drawn with eyes and horns, and an udder. It stood there quite naturally, not at all disturbed by the peculiar markings painted on its hide.

She cannot finish her steak, and it's not because she's already full, symbolically or otherwise. The "Planned Cow," she later calls that steak, and soon adds the Planned Pig and Planned Sheep to her growing list of food restrictions. What rankles her is not solely that meat is flesh: it is that an entire system is devoted to keeping her from realizing that meat is flesh, a well-regimented design incorporating safety scissors, clean uniforms, and dotted lines, all in place to ease and conceal the elaborate machinery that turns living bodies into food. Consumption is not distressing her, nor the culture that facilitates it. Instead, she is repulsed by the economic and political system that create them—marked more by the factory, the uniforms, and the workers than the presentation of cows as meals.

Nonfiction food writer Michael Pollan describes a similar scene in *The Omnivore's Dilemma*. At the meat counter in your local super-market, he suggests, "you encounter a species only slightly harder to identify" than in the produce aisle, where foods tend to retain something of their original form. "[T]he creaturely character of the species on display does seem to be fading," he notes, as more and more the animals on offer for consumption "come subdivided into boneless and bloodless geometrical cuts."[4]

The Planned Cow. The Planned Pig. The Planned Sheep. Who is behind them? What Marian's body begins to reject is the contraption that offers them up. The friendly face of industrialism hides not only the assembly line from the consumer (Marian), but also from the consumed (the cow, who seems perfectly content with its role in the proceedings, however short-lived it may be). Of course, these two roles are fungible: "Every time she walked into the supermarket and heard the lilting sounds coming from the concealed loudspeakers she remembered an article she had read about cows who gave more milk when sweet music was played to them," Atwood writes. "But just because [Marian] knew what they were up to didn't mean she was immune. These days, if she wasn't careful, she found herself pushing the cart like a somnambulist, eyes fixed, swaying slightly, her hands twitching with the impulse to reach out and grab anything with a bright label."

Therefore it's not totally wrong when Marian's married friend attributes her stomach troubles to wedding jitters—the "piece of truth-telling dementia" noted in the *Times*. For marriage is simply another stage of the assembly line's conveyor belt to which Marian feels strapped. *The Edible Woman* also predicted correctly that fem-inist sci-fi of the era to come would liken hell to a reasonably happy marriage to a businessman or tenured professor, replete with kids and a dog. Joanna Russ' *The Female Man* (1975) draws such a compar-ison; *I, Vampire* by Jody Scott (1984) contains a harrowing nightmare sequence in which a morally ambiguous character's death results in an afterlife of baking, child-rearing, and hubby-coddling. (It is how we know the bloodthirsty lesbian has met her demise.) As she plans her wedded life, Marian may well be seeing the pathway open up on a dystopic Stepford Wife future. (Ira Levin's *The Stepford Wives* was published only three years after *The Edible Woman*.)

Yet Marian isn't balking exclusively at marriage itself, or even just marriage to charmless Peter. At one point following their engagement, she finds him acting inscrutably, and she imagines he must have purchased a marriage guidebook, to match the camera and legal manuals on his coffee table. "It would be according to his brand of logic to go out and buy a book on marriage, now that he was going to get married; one with easy-to-follow diagrams," she thinks. She uses loving words, but soon her body is rejecting her placement on this assembly line, too.

What triggers Marian's illness is her glimpse of the elaborate system she feeds into and from, a multi-use machine with a myriad of moving parts, all of which push different aspects of her life toward a single end-goal. Her every move, consumables inclusive, has been predetermined, and her clothing, relationships, and even reproductive goals (she is annoyed to discover) selected for her in advance. It makes Marian sick. Atwood doesn't name the system her protagonist glimpses, but we now know it's called capitalism.

◆ ◆ ◆

Rachel is a mid-twenties pharmaceutical graduate student in Kansas with three dogs, three cats, and a fantastically attractive boyfriend named Alexey. Rachel is quite pretty herself, with long dark hair, clear skin, deep dark eyes, and a strong, sincere smile. Like Marian, Rachel's planning to marry soon, but she's been having some digestive issues, and managing them is taking up a lot of her time.

Luckily her boyfriend is patient and supportive, even when their dinners together make her outrageously ill. "Alexey and I have found some really good frozen pizzas," Rachel writes in a 2009 post on her blog. "[W]e split a pizza one to two times a week and by split I mean he has two thirds of the pizza and I eat the rest. ... In the past, I have gotten some heartburn from it and definitely a ton of gas build up, but it's never made me sick. Last night was the first time it did."[5]

Her story, instructive in its detail, continues. "Immediately after I finished the last piece," Rachel writes:

> *my stomach felt extremely bloated. I had to stand up it hurt so bad. When I tried to sit down, I literally felt like my stomach was going to explode. . . . Then out of nowhere came the urgency, so I ran up to the bathroom. . . . The feeling of needing to get to a restroom with no time to spare is horrible, and experiencing it out of nowhere in a crowded place or somewhere you can't leave quickly is terrifying.*

Rachel goes into some detail regarding diarrhea and nausea—she's got a fear of vomiting that makes the latter particularly unpleasant—and expresses gratitude that she was not only able to get through that pizza night without throwing up, "but also that I only had to take GasX." Other brands whose products she cites would be immediately recognizable to her readers, many of whom suffer similar symptoms ("Pepto" and Immodium are her go-tos), as would the cycle of illness she describes:

> *I hate it so much when foods I've eaten for months with no problems suddenly cause me to have an episode. I had just said to my mom earlier that day that I thought I was finally regaining control of my life and not living it in fear of what food was going to hurt me and make me sick again. All I ate today was cereal because I didn't want to get sick again. I am so sick of cereal. Just when I think I'm in the control, my body steps in to remind me how much of a joke that really is.*

Rachel's tale of pizza-related torment was published four decades after *The Edible Woman* was released. Although her story has much in common with Marian's, the only thing she mentions reading on her blog is her own blog, which she uses to catalogue her IBS. It isn't a platform for self-pity, however; her blog offers the public service of community building. Commenters regularly leave notes on this post, about pizza and IBS, as well as on her other posts, which may be about diet, drug regimen, the social anxiety of living with this particular disease, planning a wedding with a chronic illness, or plain old poop. Rachel's been blogging approximately once a month for seven years, and her readers often leave notes to thank her for writing, or briefly describe their own similar stories. ("Reading your blog post, it honestly sounded as if I was reading one of my own journal entries," one writes.) Commenters frequently note how desperately they have been searching for stories that reflect their own experiences. (One example: "My sister has been dealing with this for the past 2 years and people really have no idea just how much of an issue it really is. It totally changes your life!")

However, irritable bowel syndrome is hardly rare. A relatively common diagnosis given folks that experience discomfort in the large intestine, including cramping, abdominal pain, bloating, gas, diarrhea, and constipation, it's something of a catch-all diagnosis, bestowed upon sufferers with symptoms but no recognizable disease (although IBS does often evolve into something more clearly defined, like ulcerative colitis). You may not even know if your friends have it: as may be surmised, propriety keeps the diagnosis from coming up in most polite conversations. Internet discussions, therefore, which offer both a degree of anonymity to sufferers and, presumably, the comfort of writing from a controlled environment, do not infrequently result from Rachel's posts, although her blog is not the only one to tackle IBS, nor the only one to do so from a personal narrative standpoint. Others offer insight into recipes, drug regimens, new treatment options, fitness routines, legal advice, or other aspects of living with IBS. (There is, for example, a YouTube channel devoted to toilet jokes from someone going by Positive vIBS.) There are, in fact, countless blogs by people who suffer a range of gastrointestinal disorders and autoimmune disease—*Ali on the*

Run looks at marathon training with Crohn's, for example, while *ChronicBabe* covers a wide range of chronic illnesses.

Reading such blogs offers a glimpse into the suffering of what the American Autoimmune Related Diseases Association (AARDA) estimates to be one in five Americans afflicted with autoimmune conditions. The primary struggle of the afflicted (like Marian's) is to understand why their bodies have betrayed them, and to do so, input from other sufferers is required. Even the least talented writers have dedicated readers and commenters, so community seems to be forged not around talent, but out of sheer desperation. Most blogs are kept by women, who make up approximately 75 percent of the diagnoses of autoimmune disease worldwide. From a labor perspective, we should note that the keepers of such sites probably aren't getting paid for blogging, or are at best offsetting site update fees (in the tens to low hundreds of dollars per year) with ads, so most of the work of blogging could be described as the unpaid emotional labor of creating resources for a community that cannot find sufficient help anywhere else. Whether or not bloggers have day jobs may also be relevant—it is notoriously difficult to have the most common autoimmune diseases officially recognized as disabilities and receive social service benefits, despite the inability of sufferers to consistently meet the demands of day jobs. Let's situate this, too, in the context of a capitalist—as opposed to consumerist—society. The work Rachel and other health bloggers do fills a medical need for patient-focused lifestyle and wellness conversations currently untended to by privately funded, profit-driven healthcare systems, who consistently defund support groups, online chat spaces, and counseling services that could provide similar.

That symptoms just as mysterious as Marian's would become quite common in the decades that followed *The Edible Woman*'s publication was certainly unforeseen. But because mysterious feminine digestive troubles and invisible ailments have started to gain medical recognition in recent years, they have lost some of their comedic bite. In fact, "half-serious," "dementia," and "lying," are only a few of the pejorative descriptors the *Times* lends a scenario in which a woman simply can't eat whatever is put in front of her. It is only through the steadfastness of Atwood's pen, it seems, that we refrain from considering Marian a wholly unreliable narrator. "[P]eople suck, in general, when it comes to accepting and respecting IBS as a real issue," Rachel writes in a blog post entitled "Wedding Series: In Laws." I'm apt to let her speak for the millions of other sufferers of understudied diseases. Today, people with similar symptoms are often passed from doctor to doctor for several years—the average is seven—before receiving a diagnosis. Many have watched as their symptoms are written off as psychological—the medical-industrial complex version of the *Times*' "lying."

The problem, however, might not lie in millions of women's heads. A 2001 study at the University of Maryland found that, although women in general have lower thresholds for pain than men, and tend to experience it for longer, their symptoms are often treated less aggressively.[6] In emergency rooms, for example, women wait for pain medication an average of sixteen minutes longer than men, and are 13 to 25 percent less likely to receive an opioid medication. A separate study in the esteemed *New England Journal of Medicine* showed that, among cancer patients, women were significantly less likely than men to receive adequate treatment for their pain.

Researchers remain baffled by these findings, although Hoffman and Taznian told lifestyle news outlet *Mother Nature Network* in 2015 that they'd come across a handful of recurrent explanations in interviews with medical staff. These include presumptions about men being able to manage pain better, and not complaining about it until it was "real;" some women's ability to birth children, which is thought to imply an ability to manage any amount of pain; and women's presumptive tendency to exaggerate and complain instead of describe sensation accurately.[7]

The world of medicine, in other words, tends not to believe

women when they say they are in pain, which in the realm of invisible illnesses like Marian's, is often the only symptom on offer. Fold in a host of known food-related disorders—anorexia, bulimia, etc.—and we can detect a general cultural tendency to label women's problems with food as little more than psychosomatic, mere psychological issues undeserving of deeper study, never thought to be exacerbated by external or environmental forces, or indeed to be outwardly provable in any way.

Marian never describes the full range of her bodily failures, either to another character or to her audience. It's a trick of Atwood's, to force the reader to believe a female character's version of events in order to follow a storyline. It also saves the character from the embarrassment that millions of other women have experienced, of being told—by acquaintances, loved ones, and doctors—that their illnesses are all in their heads.

◆ ◆ ◆

You've heard of celiac disease, a diagnosis given to two to three times as many women as men, in which the body's immune system attacks itself when triggered by the ingestion of gluten. Perhaps you've even reposted one of many articles claiming to debunk the wheat protein's link to physical discomfort on social media, a sharable, friendly way to discredit women's pain. (I know I have.)

However much the precise mechanics of the relationship between certain foods and autoimmune disease may not be understood, foodstuffs beyond gluten have been linked to certain autoimmune responses. Usually, autoimmunity is considered a medical mystery: for unknown reasons, doctors say, the body's immune system turns on itself in the same way it would attack a parasite, virus, or other foreign invader. The resulting inflammation causes pain as well as physical impairment. Yet some health practitioners—naturopaths, in particular—root autoimmune disease in food sensitivities.

There are several food-elimination protocols suggested for the autoimmune, therefore: some name-brand, like the Paleo Diet, and others more tailored to individual responses, like the low FODMAP diet (to cut down on short-chain carbohydrates), elimination programs (to identify problem foods), low histamine diets (to quell allergic responses), and rotation diets (for those who can't identify any specific food relationship to symptoms beyond ingestion). Such diets, however crazy they may sound to those who have not tried them, do tend to work for a large number of people.

Despite extensive anecdotal evidence, however, scientists have been slow to look into a relationship between consumption and autoimmunity. The reasons for this are likely myriad. While many in the post-Sanders campaign era would tend to blame Big Pharma's exclusive focus on profits for the holdup, it may equally be due to the gender of the majority of sufferers. Although medicating illness is profitable, there are surely enormous profits to be made in staving off illness, if the price point for continued health is set high enough. It seems more likely that the tendency of the sciences to overlook autoimmunity is rooted in the low numbers of women in STEM (Sciences, Technology, Engineering, and Medicine). Women chemists, for example, make up only 35.2 percent of the field, and women chemical engineers only 22.7, according to analysis by the National Girls Collaborative Project. Nor are there enough women funders to ensure such studies take place: only 4.6 percent of the 2016 Fortune 500 CEOs are women, according to Catalyst, an organization that tracks women in business leadership. Women, earning on average 77 percent of what male counterparts do in the same jobs (specifically making $15,900 per year less than men in STEM jobs, according to a 2013 report by the US Census Bureau) do not currently have the economic clout as a class to fund or demand such studies. Anyway, those who perceive a clear need may be too ill to mount a campaign, or already wrapped up in the sustaining care work of blogging.[8]

Only recently, therefore, has a connection been proven between food and these poorly studied ailments. A June 2015 report in the peer-reviewed journal Autoimmunity Reviews found that common food additives contribute to intestinal leakage, which creates the conditions for autoimmunity. These additives are named in the report: "Glucose, salt, emulsifiers, organic solvents, gluten, microbial transglutaminase, and nanoparticles are extensively and increasingly used by the food industry, claim the manufacturers, to improve the qualities of food," note authors Aaron Lerner, a professor at Technion Israeli Institute of Technology, and Torsten Matthias, of the Aesku-Kipp Institute in Germany. They also:

> *increase intestinal permeability by breaching the integrity of tight junction paracellular transfer. . . . It is hypothesized that commonly used industrial food additives abrogate human epithelial barrier function, thus increasing intestinal permeability through the opened tight junction, resulting in entry of foreign immunogenic antigens and activation of the autoimmune cascade.* [9]

In plain English, consuming these additives leads to intestinal breakdown—commonly called "leaky gut syndrome"—which allows for the autoimmune response to occur.

The report cites the rise in autoimmune disorders—many diseases have three times the diagnoses that they did three decades ago—that are primarily occurring in nations with high rates of processed food consumption. Also noted are the specific disease categories with rapidly rising numbers of diagnoses (neurological, gastrointestinal, endocrine, and rheumatic), as well as the geolocations of the diagnosed, which seem to indicate that environmental, and not genetic, factors are the primary reason for the uptick in these ailments. The report describes a corollary rise in the use of food additives, intended to increase "the world's capacity to provide food through increased productivity and diversity, decreased seasonal dependency and seasonal prices." (In Brazil, for example, the years 1987 to 2003 saw a 46 percent increase in the intake of processed food in the average household. Virtually unheard of three decades ago, today Brazilian rates of rheumatoid arthritis stand at around 1 percent of the population and incidents of psoriasis at 2.5 percent. Far more worrying is the Zika outbreak in the country, a virus that grew twentyfold between 2014 and 2015, and is linked to Guillain–Barré syndrome, an autoimmune disease that causes paralysis.)

To recap, the seven additives listed above are now being found in more foods. Those foods are eaten in more households around the world. And bodies in those households with previously healthy immune systems are becoming dysfunctional. Causality, the authors warn, "has not been proven"—the report only proves that these particular food additives contribute to leaky gut syndrome, from which the autoimmune response follows. "Precise mechanisms responsible for the development of nutrient-induced autoimmune disorders are unknown," the authors contend.

Still, recommendations based on these findings are in order. "[I]ndividuals with non-modifiable risk factors (i.e. familial autoimmunity or carrying shared autoimmune genes) should consider decreased exposure to some food additives in order to avoid increasing their risk," the report states. Additionally, strengthening FDA nutritional labeling standards—policies that have been designated "barriers to trade" by lobbyists and are being modified or dropped entirely[10]—and further studying the impact of food additives on immune systems are strongly recommended by the authors.

What this means is that individuals may be "going autoimmune" due to personal consumption habits. Yet autoimmune diseases in general—their worldwide spread, their increasing diagnoses, and their worsening symptoms—are likely triggered, at least in part, by the far-reaching machinery of globalized food production.

♦ ♦ ♦

A food industry reliant on additives to ease its own spread throughout the globe has become central to a socioeconomic system based on private ownership of the means of production. McDonald's stands as a shining example. In the decades since *The Edible Woman* first appeared, the chain has been documented using food preparation techniques from farm to table that are questionable at best and extremely dangerous at worst; exists now in outposts formerly hostile to Western presence; and—Marx would be impressed by the company's allegiance to his definition of capitalism—exploits the workforce to such a degree that the fight to raise the minimum wage to $15 per hour is commonly sited at the burger chain. (The company had just opened it's one thousandth restaurant and expanded to all fifty states when *The Edible Woman* came out; today there are over 36,000 restaurants in 119 countries around the world, according to the company's own website.)

Michael Pollan describes a visit to McDonald's in *The Omnivore's Dilemma*, where he muses on the poultry-like meal his son orders. "[T]he most alarming ingredient in a Chicken McNugget," he explains:

> *is tertiary butylhydroquinone, or TBHQ, an antioxidant derived from petroleum that is either sprayed directly on the nugget or the inside of the box it comes in to "help preserve freshness." According to A Consumer's Dictionary of Food Additives, TBHQ is a form of butane (i.e. lighter fluid) the FDA allows processors to use sparingly in our food: It can comprise no more than 0.02 percent of the oil in a nugget. Which is probably just as well, considering that ingesting a single gram of TBHQ can cause "nausea, vomiting, ringing in the ears, delirium, a sense of suffocation, and collapse." Ingesting five grams of TBHQ can kill.[11]*

The mainstream food movement in which Pollan plays a significant role has given us a contemporary understanding that the standard consumption habits of the Western world can be quite damaging to consumer health.

Of course, there is also a disease called consumption that in the nineteenth century killed as many as one in four Brits. Susan Sontag traced its earliest usage to 1398 in *Illness as Metaphor*. "Whan the bode is made thynne," writes John of Trevisa, "so folowyth consumpcyon and wasting."[12]

"Consumpcyon" was the common name given to tuberculosis, a disease that at one point was as mysterious and misunderstood as autoimmune diseases are today. Mysterious, but ever-present: the ill were described as langorous, hollow-chested, romantic, and pale. They appeared to be in the process of being consumed.

It's a markedly different metaphor than can be applied to the autoimmune, who have less a disease in the traditional sense than a dysfunction. However much autoimmunity may be triggered by food consumption—and despite the fact that many can control the negative effects of these disorders to at least some degree by restrictive diets—the autoimmune are not being devoured by any malevolent, outside force. The bodies of the autoimmune attack *themselves*. In some cases, yes, eating away at it, over time—but the immediate symptoms of inflammation occur at the site of self-generated attack. In fact, what is markedly different about autoimmune disorders as opposed to any other public health crisis in history is that the whole language of "fighting" disease does not apply: the body must instead be soothed into remission, must learn to lay down its weapons entirely.

This is the logic behind restrictive diets, that certain foods trigger attack more than others. This isn't an explanation that makes much sense to medical professionals, however. Doctors who don't outright laugh when asked about connections between autoimmunity and food are few; others are more tolerant, although one often gets the sense that one is being humored. ("There are people who feel better when they don't eat certain things," is a common medical response, if an unhelpful one). There are only a handful of doctors in the US, however, who believe food to be a primary trigger in autoimmune disorders that aren't situated in the intestines, like rheumatoid arthritis, lupus, and psoriasis. Even Lerner and Matthias' groundbreaking studies on leaky gut syndrome have been slow to filter through the medical world.

In some ways, the reluctance of the medical profession to acknowledge that disorders suffered by one fifth of the US population are partially triggered by modern food production is understandable. Recent changes to the global supply and processing chain were made, as Lerner and Matthias acknowledge, to increase nutritional access and limit hunger. Admirable goals, to be sure, and certainly one could argue that slight suffering among the few is a reasonable price to pay in pursuit of increased health for the many. Yet such a justification can only hold for so long before changes become necessary to restore public health. Incidents of type 1 diabetes rose 23 percent between 2001 and 2009, according to the American Diabetes Association, and to significant effect: autoimmune diseases as a class are thought to shorten a patient's lifespan by eight years.

Some have also found symptoms worsening and triggers increasing in number. Celiacs who have trouble managing their symptoms, for example, are now urged to avoid dairy as well as gluten, which some suggest is an indication that dairy proteins have begun to mimic the wheat protein. Others, already diagnosed, are simply accruing more diseases at a seemingly unstoppable clip, regardless of how well their original symptoms have been controlled through standard food restriction protocols, a possible indication that more foods trigger the autoimmune response than is currently suspected. On several concurrent fronts, the negative effects of globalized food production seem to be quickening at an alarming rate.

Marian solves her problem with a symbolic gesture: a small cake replica of herself that is offered for Peter's consumption. He doesn't want it, so she eats some—a miracle!—then offers the rest to another man. It's a joke about consumption. Who has the right, and obligation, to consume? The joke is on Marian, for she must be consumed, however symbolically. The unremitting inevitability of consumption is, of course, capitalism. Yet the joke is also on women like her, real-life women like Rachel. For Marian's symptoms went away following no medical intervention. Perhaps it was all in her head after all? The reader is left to wonder.

Not all readers, of course: millions of women around the world know that their bodies are failing not through any mental or emotional flaw, but because the system under which they live is causing damage. They feel it as clearly as Marian did. Today, bodies regularly grow intolerant of production lines, global distribution, and decisions made with only profits in mind. Like Marian, women throughout the industrialized world are no longer capable of consuming what is on offer. Their bodies, too, are rejecting capitalism.

An excerpt from this essay was published as "The Planned Cow" in Women's Review of Books.

CULTURAL IMPERATIVE
VALUABLE
YOU OWE
IMPORTANT BOOK
DEBT BONDAGE FOR DUMMIES
NOT ENUF
RE-PRODUCE!!
REQUIRED ~~READING~~ BREEDING
C
TM

I confess that I relied on the same party trick for nearly two decades: presenting as a well-educated, upper-middle-class white woman of able body, I'd engage in polite but witty banter with fellow revelers until the topic of The Future would arise, and what each of us desired from it. Then came my time to shine! It made no difference in what terms The Future was being discussed—political, economic, domestic—because in every scenario women are consigned to limited roles, and my trick hinged on this fact. When it was my turn to speak (I liked to build tension by pausing to apply a fresh coat of lipstick), I would reject the options presented me. "I want to continue doing exactly what I am doing," I would say. I was single, writing, and traveling extensively. "I am happy."

My declaration would first be met with silence (satisfied twenty- and thirtysomethings are apparently rare enough to stun). Then a well-intentioned and kindly voiced line of inquiry would emerge: "What about kids?"

"Kids?" I would say, gazing at a far corner of the room, as if pondering the existence of the younger generation for the first time. As if I hadn't been challenged on my disinterest in motherhood the night before, the week prior, the month previous, and for several consecutive years and now decades before that in a relentless social rejoinder to my autonomy. "No," I'd say thoughtfully, feigning consideration. "Not interested." And I wasn't.

Here, eyes would widen and throats would be cleared. Glasses might crash to the floor, a plane or two might fall from the sky. It seemed like it, anyway, for the gaiety would pause, and the mood in the room would shift. I'd failed to express a "healthy," "natural" desire to grow a baby in my tummy. Or however that works. What do I know? I've never done it. Perhaps worse: I had offered no apologies or explanations, and no defense of my position ever followed. For what else could I say?

At the party, a group of acquaintances, tongues loosened with liquor, would soon close in around me, a cacophony desperate to prove me wrong, inform me of my own naivety, or accuse me of lying. My desire to make use of my body for creation but not for procreation was denounced in every way imaginable. The barrage of proclamations—on why I should want to become pregnant or did secretly want to become pregnant or would eventually want to become pregnant but did not yet realize it—could last late into the night. Some of these conversations trailed me for months or years and were revived at later parties, depending on who I'd crossed paths with before and how they were feeling then about starting families.

Objections to my reproductive disinterest were telling in terms of volume and consistency, if not exactly logic. You see, the real trick wasn't the ease with which partygoers could be manipulated into haranguing me for an evening (this was too easy and, ultimately, boring). The trick was on me, on women: the illusion of control we have over our own bodies and lives is less effective and more emaciated than we've been given to believe. My very bodily agency, it turned out, was considered up for grabs, even among close friends and trusted associates, in the most relaxed circumstances, on any night of the week.

◆ ◆ ◆

Through years of cataloging arguments denouncing my desire to remain childless, I saw certain patterns emerge. The most glaring posited that I had accrued some form of social debt that required repayment. The foundation of this stance wasn't that I would "make a good mother" (no one ever suggested that I would) or that an additional child would somehow be of benefit to "the community" (for babies, in my circle, are not so rare). Rather, it was that I might "owe it"— to society, to my family, to my ancestors, to "my people"—to reproduce.

Those of us who navigate the world as women often encounter such hidden riders in the social contract, just as do nonbinary people, and even men, whether we acknowledge these expectations or not. For gender is a form of debt bondage: we agree to perform the labor of femininity or masculinity or both or neither. In exchange, we are offered certain compensation. What forms those rewards take, the conditions under which they are withheld, whether anyone truly owes anything to society in exchange for them, and toward what end the original agreement was negotiated and by whom are all worthy questions and deserving of an essay of their own. Here we will approach them only obliquely.

Let's focus now on how expectations of motherhood as the most appropriate form of productive contribution are often made explicit once someone read as female states a disinterest in bearing children. I'm certainly not the only ciswoman who has faced the bizarre charge that I am wrong to want what I want—or, more exactly, that I am wrong to not want to do with my body what I do not want to do with it. That bodily desire can be labeled as wrong is a foundation of homophobia, racism, transphobia, ageism, and ableism as well as misogyny, but here we set the limits of our inquisition by the role I assumed at parties—that of a well-educated, upper-middle-class white woman with no evident physical malfunction; I cannot speak of any other experience.

There are, of course, plenty of others like me. The point of this essay is that an overeducated mind in a healthy-appearing, young, white body replete with feminine markers (in my case, more glitter and skirts than ample breasts or hips) and upper-middle-class bearing (*classy* glitter and *knee-length* skirts[1]) is instilled with the message that she owes it to society to reproduce. Women like me, we're told—by grade-school teachers and college professors, church parishioners, friends in school, dinner party companions, or people we meet in the grocery store—are "well-bred" or "of good stock," and our obligation to procreate rests in part on the notion that we would raise the "right kind" of children. Judgments such as these stem from a particular mindset born of a particular context. In my case, perceived race, perceived education, and perceived class status mark me to some as the correct type of person to populate the planet. These exact phrases—"well-bred," "good stock," "right kind," "populate"—have frequently been used to outline my responsibilities as an American woman. It is only now, in writing them down, that I can fully acknowledge them as extremely problematic.

I should note that my disinterest in procreation to be a form of privilege. Children are not necessary to my survival, and I can, medically and legally, ensure that I will not have them. I live in a time and place where, although it is an economic challenge to remain unmarried, it is not impossible, and as an independent woman, I have no partner's desires to consider as I pursue my own definition of "family."

However, it must be stressed that pressures on me to bear children often appear to spring from a desire to shore up and extend the limits of this privilege to pass along to future generations imagined to emanate from my womb. This is a flattering but insidious form of elitism, class bias, and ableism, but most clearly I believe it to be rooted in—if not a fundamental mechanism of—white supremacy.

◆ ◆ ◆

It begins to seem possible to measure the value of my imaginary child, whose worth may rival or best my own, inclusive of my social and cultural contributions. For when presented with a future in which I must choose between bearing offspring and doing what I professed to enjoy at the time—writing, creating art, and traveling—I have invariably been urged to choose the former.

What makes this remarkable is that I am a reasonably well-respected (if modestly compensated) cultural producer, by which

I mean that my livelihood and vocation are to create things that reflect the world as I see it, and I am allowed to do so because the work seems to hold value for people, who support me in creating it. Yet when the notion of children arises—I cannot call it a question, because for me it's never been one—my life's labor is relegated to prelude, the sideshow act before the main attraction: an imaginary child. The message seems to be that I've exhausted my individual worth on the countless zines, articles, magazines, and authored and edited books I've produced (I don't even know how many total literary projects I've completed), so now it's time to settle down and get serious.

Except I have always been serious, have always known what I wanted, and was never swayed by anyone's suggestions regarding why I might be mistaken. Oh, I was still appalled by the arguments: the demand that I contribute to society invalidates what I may have already contributed to society, or whatever potential I felt at an earlier age I may have had to contribute to society eventually. That debt has been *paaaaiiiiiiddddd*, I thought, every time someone suggested to me anew that perhaps I might think about the next generation. (I've written several books for young people, and several more about my work with young people.) But the mechanisms of debt are insidious: a month after paying off a credit card in full, you will always get another bill reflecting the interest accrued between the time your payment was sent and the moment it was received, plus the interest accrued on that total during the time you were sitting around thinking your account was clear. By then, you may owe a couple hundred dollars, basically for your own hubris in believing yourself to be debt-free.

What I have come to understand is that instilled in the agreement to perform womanhood, or perhaps all of femininity, is an expected desire to be reproductive, even if one has already staked a claim for oneself as *productive*. Creating things outside of the body may be seen as preparatory to creating something *inside* the body: that no matter what one has experienced in the public realm, a woman should eventually retreat into the private domain, for it is her rightful place. You have done a good many things in the world and your work is strong, some partygoer or another always noted earnestly after I expressed my disinterest in having kids. But wasn't it time to do something meaningful?

◆ ◆ ◆

The line between society and culture is often indistinct, but I am under no delusions that culture is anything more than the messy material byproduct of people living in the world together and interacting socially—in fact, of society itself. So while culture may inspire many, often conflicting, definitions, the value granted cultural products in the United States is fairly straightforward. It is codified in a body of policy known as intellectual property, or IP, rights—laws that allow for economic, although not exclusively financial, gains and losses from the production of objects.

Consisting of trademark, patent, and copyright law, IP divides cultural production in the following manner: industrial language and methodologies are the domain of trademark law; scientific and design inventions are covered by patent law; and artistic creations are outlined in copyright law. Through a web of protections we consider rights, intellectual property is a primary conduit for the flow of capital around the world, the framework within which the trade in goods takes place. Yet what is protected under IP law is very specific: the tangible expression of an idea— the form—and not the idea itself. This is significant, and its ties to trade ultimately cannot be ignored: IP governs things and the ways they are made, because objects can bear price tags. Indeed, the clearly stated goal of IP law, as UC Davis legal scholar Madhavi Sunder writes, "is to promote the invention of more machines, from the Blackberry to the iPod, and more intellectual products, from Mickey Mouse to R2D2." The focus on the dissemination of tangible goods has a social and cultural effect, she argues in *From*

Goods to a Good Life, her look at the interpersonal reverberations of IP policy.[2]

Believe it or not, the human implications of object-based legislation are vast. Take for example the gulf between an idea and its expression—the period before which a concept is made tangible, before IP law can offer any protection. It's often called a pregnant space, or a space of gestation. (Creators awaiting copyright protection, inventors applying for patents, and businesspeople eligible for trademarks alike use terms like "birthing" and "baby" to describe pending projects.) This anthropomorphizing language matters. Particularly in IP law, where some potential forms of expression are wrangled into products and offered protection, while others are not. IP laws do not protect all potential expressions of ideas, in other words; they protect only the rights to certain ideas, when expressed in particular forms, and for the most part, when expressed by particular people. The equivalency between product-creation and childbirth adopted in artistic, business, and scientific realms is no coincidence: IP laws and the manner in which they are applied tend to be quite gendered.

Copyrights, for example, cover creative expression within certain artistic mediums, the list of which reflects the historic roles of men as breadwinners and women as homemakers, as well as the cultural value of work created in each of these realms and for each implied audience. So while traditionally masculine forms of cultural production such as sculpture, filmmaking, and architecture are all copyright eligible, traditionally feminine forms of cultural production including food preparation, garment creation, and quilting (considered domestic labor, because the products created are often intended for use in the home) are generally not. Patents, too, are offered more masculine players than feminine players: in 2012, the National Bureau of Economic Research found only 7.5 percent of all patent holders to be female, a figure that shrinks to 5.5 percent for holders of commercial patents. Not surprisingly, incidents of gender bias in patent application and approval processes are common and some quite blatant—as in the long history of patent lawyers who would take ownership of female applicants' patents in lieu of fees. (Trademarks, which protect brand names and business practices, are gendered, too—they cover products from which an overwhelmingly male group of CEOs profit—but because they are more specialized, do not figure strongly in this discussion.)

The gendered presumptions on which IP laws rest, I believe, play a significant role in the sense that women may owe some kind of debt to society. The truth is that my determination not to reproduce was met with a nearly despotic intolerance that did not waver with shifts in presiding politics or economics. I believe that the reason my prioritization of a productive role over a reproductive one was so roundly rejected is related to why and how IP laws were gendered in the first place, and how they have evolved since. My suspicion is that intellectual property rights work not only descriptively, defining traditional creator roles, but also prescriptively, consigning feminine players to one form of production and masculine players to another.

Echoing a concern of Sunder's, we might ask, how does a body of law that governs the production of things come to operate in relationships between humans? Of course capitalism, the economic system under which we operate, establishes a market to allow for survival through the trade of things. We—understandably—become emotionally invested in retaining the ability to have things available for trade or sale, since our survival seemingly depends on it. This ever-expanding market is where we buy in, literally, to the logic of legislation that governs the ownership of productive practices—federal policy as individually held values system.

There is no question that we may retain certain beliefs even in the face of evidence that they do not hold true. The productive drive is, at this moment, capitalism's most overbearing quality: the manufacture of clothing, food, and data in the United States has already far outpaced our desire for or ability to consume same.

Yet rarely do we question the need to produce more, or to be productive at all, and concerns that do arise about overproduction are quickly silenced by the accepted truth that economic security—for individuals and for the nation—relies on *producing things*. Stalled production under this values system is an indication of weakness, but failure to produce appears to be read as something far worse.

This is where the space we have described as pregnant between an idea and its tangible expression becomes most significant. In IP terms, women who express no desire to birth children are unprotectable because there is no potential expression of this idea: nothing is produced. (Men who express no desire to raise children have many other sanctioned means of production to fall back on.) While capitalism might simply mark the absence with a big, fat zero, the values system incorporated by humans living under an ever-expanding market logic seems to identify it as a threat: a black hole of potential, *horror vacui* to be warded off at every turn. Under capitalism, then, when one expresses a desire not to produce—whether on the production line or in the bedroom—one abdicates one's interest in protection. One proclaims oneself, it seems, valueless.

The implications of this extend well beyond my diminished capacity to escape a cocktail party without catching a drink in the face: they can be seen in the regular repeal of federal abortion and reproductive healthcare laws with glaring acuity. Politicians seem to unanimously agree that women's reproductive value must be secured for the good of the entire nation. Forget the myth of the biological imperative. The imperative to bear children seems to be cultural.

♦ ♦ ♦

The House Committee Reports on the Patent Act of 1952 declares "anything under the sun that is made by man" as its mandate of protection. Indeed, since the precursors of modern patents in sixth-century Europe (*litterae patents*, Latin for "open letters") up until quite recently, this description of the domain of patents—the driving force of the American economy—remained apt.

Originally official documents that granted privileges to their holders, early patents were especially useful to aid the exploration of foreign lands. As globalization scholar Vandana Shiva writes in her 2001 book *Protect or Plunder? Understanding Intellectual Property Rights*, patents were originally used "for colonization and for establishing import monopolies."[3] The more modern notion of patents, as pertaining to the realm of idea-fostered objects and systems, emerged nearly a thousand years later in Renaissance Italy. At that time, the "novelty" of a device was figured regionally—in this case, in the Venetian domain—as well as based on the stature, or visibility, of the patent seeker within it. Uniqueness of a creation was less prized than its availability, so one did not need to "invent" a device to obtain an early patent; one needed only to manufacture a device that no one else within eyesight was already making.

In our contemporary, globalized world, of course, patent law is often used, alongside other IP and trade agreements, to dissuade local creation of a preexisting invention in what is usually called patent or IP infringement. Arguably the same distinction is at work, a legal framework that simply shifted allegiance as economic power centralized over time. Shiva also suggests that the early encouragement of technology transfer throughout the world was eventually replaced by a regime that prevents the global transfer of technology, but she makes clear that fluid definitions of creativity and technology have always disadvantaged certain actors. When patents came to the United States, for example, they were written to benefit US players. Under Connecticut law, "invention" was defined as "bringing in the supply of goods from foreign parts, that is not as yet of use among us."[4] Only later were import patents distinguished from patents of invention. Until then, finders were not only keepers, legally speaking. They were also *creators*.

The ambivalence in early IP law between what is created and

what is found—the distinction between what is made versus what has merely been located and sited to a source discounted in some manner—highlights interesting economic incentives hidden in patent law to encourage ignorance, travel, and self-promotion. Multiple patents were awarded around the world in the late 1700s, for example, for steamship creation, use, and travelways, and a smart "inventor" could make a good go of business simply remaking the creations of others, domestically. (The sheer number of patents assigned to pre-existing inventions would testify to the likelihood that this happened quite frequently.) The ability to patent what has already been invented elsewhere offers financial benefits for the public life often granted masculine players but denied feminine ones. This is true in practice, certainly, if it is not inscribed directly into the law: women at the beginning of the 1800s stood a one in eight chance of dying in childbirth and bore an average of seven children in their lifetimes. Married women with the financial means to travel were surprisingly unlikely even to be able to get out of bed, much less locate a foreign invention to produce back home.

A quick accounting of the story of Samuel Slater can illuminate the ripple effect of gender biases in patenting. Born and apprenticed to a cotton miller in England, he departed for New York in 1789, after committing locally patented cotton-spinning secrets to memory with the intention of selling them in the States. For such plundering, he was called the "Father of the Industrial Revolution" by Andrew Jackson, although locals in his hometown referred to him as "Slater the Traitor." It's unclear what he was called by the laborers who worked in the factories he is said to have revolutionized, because as female members of the underclass and/or recent immigrants, their gender, race, and class deemed their specific contributions unworthy of publicly note. (This, of course, equally applied to their innovations to his designs, and explains their absence from his patent applications, although they are likely to have offered improvements fairly consistently.) Indeed, Slater may have been known as the Patriarch of the American Factory System, but what he really innovated—through theft—is textile manufac-turing. Today, around one in seven women who work outside the home labors in some aspect of the textile industry, a workforce that on average brings in far less than half the amount of money it takes to survive in the regions of the world in which they work. Slater can't be held exclusively responsible, of course, but his legacy includes a significant contribution to the global gender wage gap.

Due to the manner in which they foster and restrict global trade—indeed, how they limit those who might profit—patents, even more than other forms of IP (including copyrights, which have been around exactly as long), form the backbone of American-style capitalism. Thus our political economy rests on gendered constructs—and it always has. Yet since the first patent was awarded in 1790 for a potash-making process, a salt used in both soaps and artillery, patent protection has been described as an unbi-ased stimulator of creativity, a protective measure for the makers of products that offers exclusive rights to profit from patented goods.

Patents are uniquely aimed to incentivize cultural products, elements of processes, or technological solutions in "science and the useful arts," as the US Constitution explains. They are guar-anteed only on successful application and cover a significantly shorter period than copyrights (twenty years from date of appli-cation, in most cases). There are six main types of patents: utility patents, which apply to processes, machines, products, material, or a significant improvement to previous versions of any of these; design patents, which cover the ornamentation or decoration of a manufactured good; and three varieties of patents that, more or less, correct, update, or stand in for previously awarded or pending patents.

Theoretically, of course, exclusive rights to profit may spur makers toward innovations—or theft—but there's very little evidence to show that economic gain truly stimulates the creative process. And there's none to show that women and other marginalized folks have been offered similar incentives to create, however much they persist in doing so. In fact, the notion of patents as creativity stimulators is fairly quickly revealed to rely on an unproven logic that ignores inherent masculine privilege and confuses legal rights, financial profit, and free expression to create the myth of US ingenuity and entrepreneurship. More than anything else, patenting seems to uphold the myth that we Americans pull ourselves up by our bootstraps (#US 216544, patented by Henry M. Weaver of Mansfield, Ohio, in 1879).

Yet who made that boot? What patenting deliberately fails to acknowledge are the communities and contexts that often lead to what we call invention and discovery. "Histories of colonialism and cultural and racial stereotypes have often led us to overlook the knowledge contributions of the poor," Sunder summarizes. One of the noted areas in which the poor—farmers, in this case, often in developing nations—have seen contributions overlooked is in agriculture and medicine. Recently, herbs long known to promote certain healing effects in India, for example, have been patented to US companies. It's a situation that started in 1931, with the first plant patent, which covered distinct varieties of asexually produced vegetation. It was the first time that life forms became subject to intellectual property claims, but it was not the last.

In 1988, a sea change: the first patent was awarded for the ownership of and rights to profit from a living mammal. #US 4736866 was granted Philip Leder and Timothy A. Stewart of Harvard University for the creation of the OncoMouse™, a mouse they'd bred for cancer research. No longer were patents covering the vast domain of "everything under the sun that is made by man." For the rodent was at least partially "made" by an impregnated female mouse, unnamed in Leder and Stewart's application.

◆ ◆ ◆

Whether to mice or men, offspring-producing females ceded then their formerly exclusive domain, the creation of new mammalian life forms. The changes to patenting were significant, but also not, for the new patent revived earlier, ambivalent definitions of certain key terms: an "invention" could be found; a "novelty" could be elsewhere common. The new domain of patent ownership also revived an even older notion of patents, from the sixth century, when they were intended to aid exploration and colonization. Is it not colonizing to invent new forms of mice? So the patenting of mammalian life in 1988 hardly happened suddenly as much as it suddenly laid bare the gendered intentions of IP policy. But even that had a precursor, a quarter century earlier.

Up until the mid-1960s, most things under the sun that were "made by" women weren't truly owned by anyone at all. The forms of cultural production to which women were often consigned were not considered "authored" in the contemporary sense and were therefore not eligible for IP protection. Dinner just appeared on the table and clothes emerged from closets. Of course women were actively dissuaded from participating in patent-heavy STEM fields, partially because babies. And babies didn't require IP registration, they were simply birthed. Some of them grew into men, who could be said to be "made by" pregnancy, specifically, or maternity, more generally.

But in 1964, a patent (#US 1970000062143) was awarded William Wright and Ralph Meyerdirk for the first articulated arm scanner, also known as the sonogram machine. Heralded as a means by which pregnant women could bond with unborn fetuses, ultrasound technology had been commercially available since 1963 and had risen to popularity quite quickly. Sonograms made the previously hidden "mysteries" of "life" visible, although not exclusively to the women it was presumed weren't bonding with the fetuses growing inside them. Men—husbands, older brothers, male doctors, interns, medical technicians—were granted access to this previously unseen provenance, too. (I would be surprised if the female partners of pregnant women were regularly granted similar viewing rights.) This shift had a cultural parallel: in the 1950s, it was still common to announce, "We're having a baby!" while the sentiment two decades later would be expressed with the biologically less likely, "We're pregnant!" IP rights over an unborn creation may not have changed yet—they would, however, soon enough—but the cultural sense of ownership over pregnancy certainly did. Sex education adopted a spiritual tone, situating intercourse as the scientific foundation of life itself; the interiors of women's bodies were photographed, stripped of actual women, who became mere background to fetuses, the nonconsenting models on the covers of news magazines. The ownership of pregnancy, in other words, became cultural through the wonders of ultrasound technology.

If we accept that sonograms provide pregnant women the opportunity to increase their emotional attachment to growing fetuses—and I'm not convinced we should, although my bias against growing a fetus may be coming into play here—we can believe that it would elicit a similar response in male partners. Or, perhaps, in men in general. After all, recent studies indicate that social media—which facilitates interaction between physically disconnected social actors—does provide many of the same effects as in-person interaction.

The exact psychology at work, however, may matter less than the political impact of a technology that allowed men unhindered visual access to the interior of women's bodies. In 1988, twenty-five years after the patenting of the ultrasound machine allowed a broad swath of people greater insight into the mechanics of pregnancy, the first patent was granted guaranteeing ownership of mammalian life. Note that twenty-five is the exact minimum age required for election to Congress, which in 1988 was 98 percent male. So the men who voted on whether other men should have the legal right to own and profit from the creation of mammalian life forms were the first generation who from conception grew up—literally, and not metaphorically—under the watchful eyes of their fathers, all thanks to a device from which other men profited.

Masculine ownership of the means of reproduction, I suggest, was gradually normalized throughout the second half of the twentieth century. First in the early 1960s with the sonogram machine, and then as images of what the machine allows us to see were more and more circulated throughout popular culture. This was furthered in the late 1980s, with the patenting (indeed, even trademarking) of the OncoMouse™. And while before 1988 there may have existed such a thing as a biological imperative, a drive described as natural that some suggest lie at the base of their desire to have children, it's possible that maternity may have lost some of the purely biological veneer since. It could be (and has frequently been) argued that the planet no longer requires or even supports an expansion of humankind, and that the biological imperative, if it did ever exist, is no longer necessary, sustainable, or ethical. It may only be leftover, a relic of life before technology.

◆ ◆ ◆

These days at parties, I'm more likely to be asked how many kids I have than when I am going to have them, but my answer hasn't much changed. Sometimes I offer a spluttering recitation of my full life and active career, and sometimes I state dully, "I've written over ten books." I admit I have occasionally mentioned my cats. Whatever my response, I'm still expected to defend my selfishness, or confronted about my apparent disinterest in honoring my parents, or asked what is wrong with me. (While I do have several invisible chronic illnesses, not a single one of them played into my decision to remain childless, so they do not enter this conversation.)

Neither does the measure of my cultural production mitigate the implicit accusations, the sense (we all feel it) that I have erred. Still, weekly if not daily, I am called to explain my aberrational nature, of being a woman apparently capable of having children who won't. It's not only white cismen, of course, demanding justification. It's my South Asian immigrant neighbors, the attendees of lecture tours, my students. They may express considerable investment in my work, but remain reasonably convicted that it is not enough. In such conversations, I feel it most clearly: being a woman who is a cultural producer is clearly not sufficient to fulfill my obligation to society. I will not be valued, it seems, until I am a *reproducer*. I suspect this may be true as well for women incapable of having children, may contribute to the sense that women gain as they age that they are no longer of value to the world.

I submit this may be because, in a very basic way, IP has outlined a course of gender roles for masculine players and for feminine players and then policed them, at least partially, through the assignment of copyrights and patents. "We must understand intellectual property as social and cultural policy," Sunder rightly contends of the laws that govern who we value as productive and who as reproductive. "Increasingly in the Knowledge Age, intellectual property laws come to bear on giant-sized values, from democracy and development to freedom and equality," she argues. And indeed: these giant-sized values seem to show up in individual relationships—even between random partygoers, talking about the future.

My concern, and my frustration, is that this contributes to a sense that pregnancy for women is obligatory, but cast as biological. If the entirety of intellectual property rights were established as a counterweight to women's ability to birth babies, women must keep reproducing as long as men are producing. The logic of one proves the logic of the other. It's starting to seem to me to be a sad race to make more stuff and more people to make use of it, not out of desire or joy, but because we are told we must, in a logic so deeply instilled we write it all off as natural.

I came to Chicago at the tail end of 1993, a moment that has been described as one of the most exciting in American music history. I went, at the time, to two or three shows a night, right up until I moved west in 1999. I wanted to go off-grid then, to escape not the electrical grid, but the urban one: the physical division of space along right angles, featuring sequentially ordered lot numbers, a logic that allows you to look up from any outdoor location in the city and know exactly how many houses you are away from your own. You can easily calculate how long it will take you to get to your house, or anywhere else, and the best means of crossing that terrain. And suddenly your life is efficient, predictable, and you feel accomplished for having figured out something so complex, simply by looking at an address. Even if you have just stumbled out of a show at the Abbey Pub at 12:45 drunk as shit and are trying to get to the Empty Bottle to catch the headliners before they climb offstage. A later analysis will reveal that each of the performers you traipsed around town for that night had different careers by the following decade's end: one became an accountant, another joined the police force, two married and moved to a farm to raise twins.

You can calculate quite a bit about the future from any street corner in Chicago, but what you cannot predict is whether or not you will be happy there.

I found that first time away from the urban grid chaotic and distressing. Streets wandered aimlessly and adopted new names, there was no way of telling how long travel might take within the city, and people were often late for appointments. I returned to the grid four years later. I had to get on with my life. I wasn't getting any younger.

Chicago's grid system is more than a satisfying urban plan, however; it reflects the very origins of modern time, and the many efficiencies it birthed. Indeed, right at the intersection of Jackson and LaSalle downtown, there's a plaque celebrating the adoption of standard time in 1883. Here's a travel blog with details:

> *In the aftermath of the destruction of downtown Chicago by the Great Chicago Fire of October 1871, all of the central city was rebuilt, and pretty quickly, too. One of the architects in the city who got nearly more work than he could handle was W. W. Boyington, whose Chicago Water Tower and Pumping Station at Chicago Avenue and Michigan Avenue (then Pine Street) were among the very few structures that survived the fire. Among Boyington's commissions after the fire were two on Jackson Boulevard at LaSalle Street—a prestigious address as the financial district was being rebuilt in that area. . . . On the northeast corner of the intersection was the Grand Pacific Hotel, a very swanky hostelry that stood across the street from the newly rebuilt Chicago Board of Trade Building, also designed by Boyington. . . . Then as now, the CBOT building had a large town clock by which many in the financial district set their pocket watches. But how was the rest of the city—or, for that matter, the rest of the state or the region—to agree upon the time?*
>
> *Though it may seem strange now, there was no single national time system being used. Many towns and cities, especially along railroad lines, set their time according to the railroad's clock. The railroads themselves depended on local noon as the determining factor, but that resulted in more than a hundred different local time zones. You can see how this made setting accurate train schedules difficult. . . . So when the railroads decided they had to do something to standardize the time system, you can bet everyone was interested.*[1]

You've probably heard this story before: the railways developed, and then implemented, standard time in order to ease travel across great distances. And people, because they love being on time for things, responded enthusiastically. Any closer inspection reveals this is a bold-faced lie, which we'll get back to in a moment, but I can't let you overlook the significant presumption embedded in this tale: that agreeing on a single notion of time is, in any way, desirable.

There was a time when I would have concurred that it was. And admittedly, it is hard to imagine a world that functions without being able to say, "Let's all meet up here at 7:00 for this reading, and then I will read, and it will take between seven and ten minutes and then you can go home." But just because that is how the world functions now does not mean that other functioning worlds are not possible.

Back to our travel blog:

> [Boyington's] Grand Pacific Hotel II . . . was one of the first . . . big, important hotels built in Chicago immediately after the fire. It occupied a square half-block bounded by Jackson, LaSalle, Quincy, . . . and Clark Street[s]. . . . The Grand Pacific was designed . . . in the then popular grand palazzo style and served both travelers and wealthy permanent residents, some of whom did business across the street [at the Board of Trade]. It was here that in 1883, delegates from all the U.S. and Canadian railroads held the General Time Convention to find a better, uniform way of setting the time.

Note, please, who it was that we are told wanted time standardized: the robber barons that ran the railroads, the wealthy, and high-stakes financial investors. Let me take another moment to underscore *that*: the standardization of time did *not* emerge from a popular uprising.

A little over a century later, in 1989, an astronomer, employee of the US Army Laboratory Command, and time historian named Ian R. Bartky published an article called "The Adoption of Standard

Time." In it he revealed that standard time was not initiated by the railways at all, in fact it was initiated by *astronomers*, who preferred to let the private interests of the railroads both do the dirty work of and take the blame for the fundamental shift to the way US residents arranged their days and interacted with each other that standardized time would require. Of course this was calculated. People already hated the rich, who ran the railroads, but harbored few to no opinions about the scientists who looked at stars. Those scientists, however, needed a better way of communicating across great distances of land what was happening at the same exact time. Why not see if the railways would get on board this standard time thing, the astronomers figured, and do the dirty work? Pure science should not be sullied by such quibbles.

For it turns out that the standardization of time was enormously controversial. Bartky describes explosions and people shooting out the massive town clocks that the railways had installed—monuments to a hated temporal uniformity—in protest of the stripping away of individual determination over when things were going to happen.

What people were protesting the loss of, and how they got around *even on trains* before the introduction of standard time, was *talking to other people*. Business owners were angered by standard time because a centrally installed clock meant no one had to step into their stores to inquire what the local time was. Unmarried young people were sad because eligible hotties passing through had no excuses to start conversation. And train porters—perhaps the most frustrated of all—saw full minutes shaved off of needed rest stops at several different points in their already long, overworked days.

Before standard time, in other words, when you went somewhere new, you had to get to know people to figure out how things worked there. The locals liked it. It seemed to work for everyone, in fact—except the astronomers, the railways, and the rich, who collectively found it easier to track planetary changes and fire people for being a few minutes late to work or for taking lunch breaks for too long.

The plaque itself[2] commemorates Sunday, October 11, 1883, the "Day of Two Noons." On that date, the plaque explains, astronomers at the Allegheny Observatory at the University of Pittsburgh transmitted a signal at noon on the 90th meridian, and railroad clocks were reset to it. The plaque was presented to the Continental Bank from the Midwest Railway Historical Society on November 18, 1971. Note that the plaque simply restates what I have already told you: the astronomers gave the signal, the railways capitulated to it, and the banks celebrated it.

♦ ♦ ♦

A few years ago I accrued several debilitating diseases in a process some call "falling out of time." I now function on crip time, which, to crips, means that we operate on a different schedule. We require more time to perform certain tasks than is usually allotted under the regimented, efficient system of standard time. The phrase is also used disparagingly. If you are invited to an accessible event, perhaps with ASL translators or requiring complicated maneuvers to allow wheelchairs entry, the able-bodied man sitting next to you may joke about crip time, by which he will mean that the event is starting later than he would like it to.

I should mention that I was born on a reservation in South Dakota, where we had a similar concept named Indian time, but described it otherwise. Indian time is the awareness that time—standard time in particular—is a construct of capitalism, and the doings of animals like people are not beholden to patterns of efficiency or imperialism. Nothing need proceed until the various spirits beckon them to convene, which is why I once spent four days waiting for a guy to teach CPR to my camp counselors, so I'm not saying that it doesn't take some getting used to. Indian time is differentiated, in South Dakota at least, from slow time and fast time, because the latter refer to Standard Time Zones, that are sort of arbitrarily adhered to in certain regions of the state based mostly on whim. If one is late for a meeting, for example, one does not apologize by saying one is on Indian time; one says one has accidently set one's watch to slow time. For if one is genuinely on Indian time, there is no reason to refer to other formulations of time, because they do not matter.

This same concept is called something else in Latin America, and in the Styrian region of Austria, and outside of Tbilisi in the Republic of Georgia. From what I can gather they don't bother calling it much of anything in the provinces of Cambodia, because folks will just get to stuff when they're ready, if it really needs doing, and actually, why would you care what needs doing and what doesn't. Why don't you have a nap? It's hot out.

This is the basic principle at work in crip time. When you get sick, it becomes clear real fast when something doesn't really need doing after all. I'm finding, more and more, that what I don't need to do is calculate from any street corner how to get to my next destination. In fact, I no longer wish to be destination-driven at all. So, nearly twenty-three years after I arrived, I'm leaving the grid a second time. While it's still technically true that I'm not getting any younger, I no longer care that I am getting older. In fact, a certain number of disease diagnoses in, I've learned to relish it.

To my friends in Chicago, stuck on this grid for a while, or a lifetime, I leave you this thought: standard time, as natural as it now seems, has only defined certain humans for 135 years. It was implemented by scientists, bankers, and railway owners to ease their workloads and tax yours, in a decision that kept people from interacting with each other, from getting to know each others' needs and interests. Standard time need not last forever. Before its implementation, there were local times, and before that, crip time, or Indian time, maybe slightly different notions with separate sets of values distinguishing how we, as individuals, might prioritize our days. Nonstandard times still exist, everywhere, and serve to remind us that we matter as individuals, that our sense of well being and personal abilities may not be best served by zones, alarms, deadlines, or grids.

I'll leave you with this thought, sent by a friend in Uganda, where certain celebrations, like weddings, parties, and graduations, start late on purpose. The things that really matter deserve your patience, and starting on time might signal to the audience that they do not truly deserve the experience of the event.

"There is so much value," Asia writes from her home in Kampala, "in subverting standard time in big and small ways."

An excerpt from this essay was delivered at "First Time" at the Miss Spoken Reading Series at the Gallery Cabaret in Chicago.

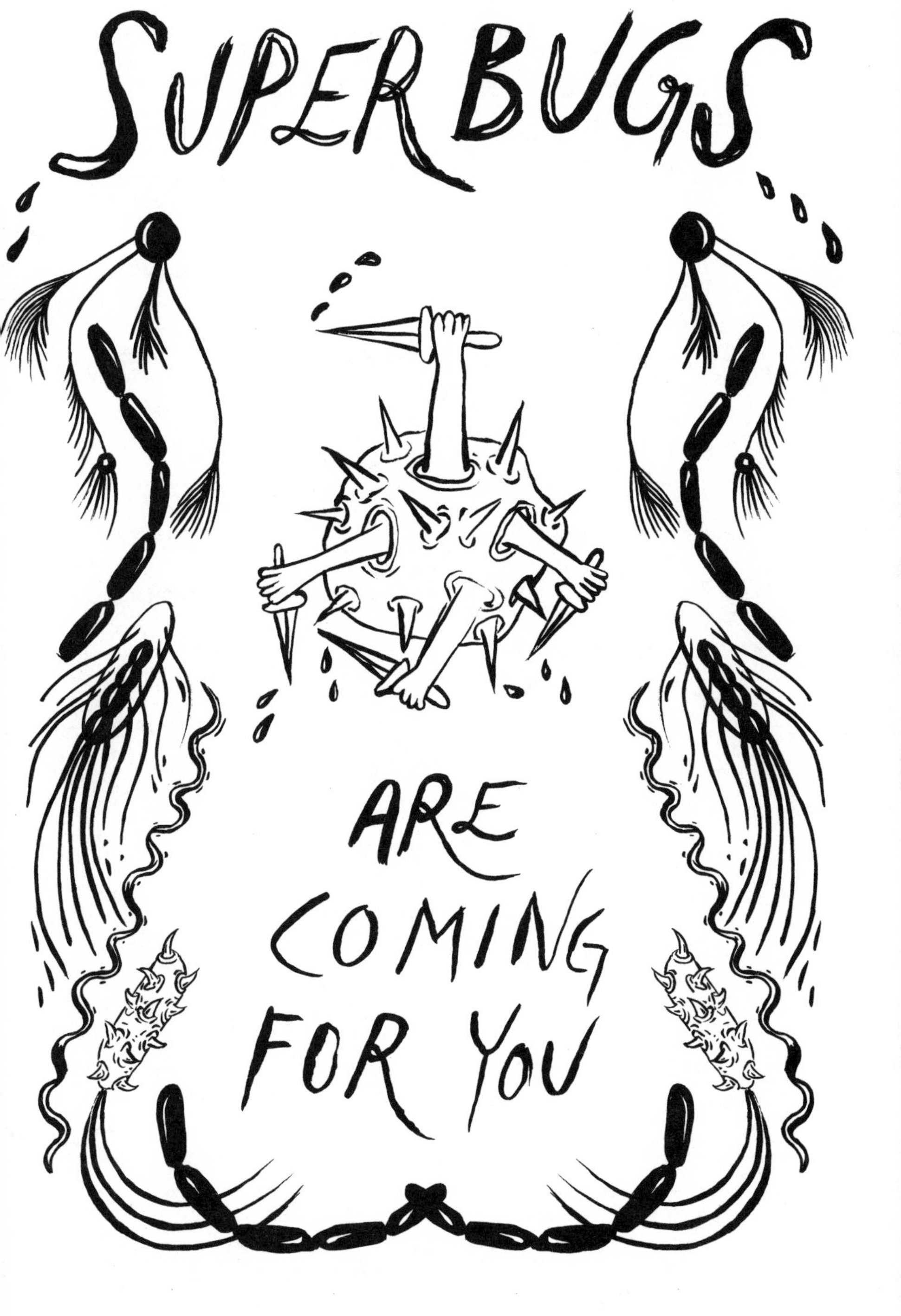
SUPERBUGS
ARE
COMING
FOR YOU

Already, bacteria are the stuff of nightmares: creatures invisible to the naked eye, able to hand off distinctive features without the generational lag of biological evolution—*oh, did you need a slightly more protuberous arm, or sharper teeth? Perhaps thin, pointed spikes that emerge from your core? Take mine, please*—and are estimated in sum to number somewhere between two and a half million trillion trillion (on the low side) and five million trillion trillion (although that, admittedly, seems like a lot). Some bacteria are shaped like hot dogs, desiccated after too many days in the sun, and others resemble extremely hairy tampons with reactive, probing tails. There are spherical versions, too, with barbed talons or smaller, welty growths, and crumply ovoids covered in abscesses, seemingly pre-wounded. Add that they've been living on earth for somewhere between 3.8 and 4.1 billion years, and *can be found inside your own body right now*, and your pulse may quicken. But superbugs—bacteria that use all forementioned abilities, experiences, and tendencies to ward off antibacterial drugs—inspire a particular terror. Every substance designed to eradicate them only makes them stronger.

So you're probably already quaking in fear over the pending superbug apocalypse, that not-so-far-off day when disease-causing bacteria develop genes to ward off all available and potential antibiotics, and humans become mere breeding ground for invisible foes. But if you aren't already a practicing or even latent germaphobe, a quick peek at the news might turn you, real fast.

Reports of the superbug apocalypse have been hard to avoid: "The emergence of 'superbugs,' and the devastating threat of antibiotic resistance, is no longer a prediction. Last month, for the first time in the United States, a strain of E. coli resistant to colistin, an antibiotic of last resort, was found infecting a Pennsylvania woman," read a late June 16, 2016, report from Boston.[1] "Superbug Is a Wake-up Call," echoed a headline in Pittsburgh early the next morning.[2] Around the same time, Mid-Missouri Public Radio posted this item: "'Superbug' Found in Illinois Meatpacking Facility."[3] The same day, the health-focused *Alternative Daily* ran "Move Over Zika: A Superbug Hits Brazilian Beaches"—in case you thought the enemy was confined to domestic shores.[4] In fact, the enemy is not confined at all. "One in three seniors is discharged from hospital with a superbug on their hands!" cries *Newsmax.*[5]

These are just a handful of the dozens of articles on drug-resistant bacteria published within a single ten-hour stretch, culled here to exemplify the overarching public narrative (in case you somehow missed it): SUPERBUGS ARE COMING FOR YOU!

It's far more than a media-constructed narrative, however, for the World Health Organization (WHO) issued a strongly worded warning about the perils of growing antibiotic resistance a few years back: "[T]his serious threat is no longer a prediction for the future," it begins. "It is happening right now in every region of the world and has the potential to affect anyone, of any age, in any country."[6] The concern at hand isn't merely that emerging and particularly dangerous bacterial infections can spread, either. It is that all previous infections, treatable and considered eradicated by modern medicine, will re-emerge. A WHO spokesperson elaborates: "The world is headed for a post-antibiotic era, in which common infections and minor injuries which have been treatable for decades can once again kill."

The threat is hard to square with our daily, lived experience of the workings of the human body, a gloriously designed and fiercely self-protective object, far more complex than any single-celled organism. When an invader—say, a knife or a virus—enters a healthy body, that body will launch a defense that continues long after the initial slice or sneeze. Our wondrous protector, the immune system, labors subconsciously and immediately. Once antigens (the knife, the virus) have invaded a body, the immune system springs into action—first identifying, then attacking, and ultimately eradicating the invader. The process hinges on a built-in intelligence network, an antibody that molds to each new incoming threat. If a once-bested antigen returns to launch another attack, the binary code set off by an antibody match triggers a swift response. That response can be final—this is why most people only ever get measles once, and why flu shots work. The second time an infection or virus appears, in the form of an antigen your antibodies recognize, you may not even feel it. It is an exceedingly clever system, so brilliant, in fact, that medical science cannot fully account for its workings. And so effective that many living under the careful watch of such a powerful and intelligent protector have never bothered to give the mechanism of their guardianship any thought.

For an increasing number of people, however, learning how these protective networks function has become a central concern of their lives, if only because their own immune systems have turned against them. Autoimmune disease diagnoses have risen so dramatically, the epidemic is best understood anecdotally: fifteen years ago, before the American Autoimmune Related Diseases Association (AARDA) was formed, approximately sixty-seven diseases were classified as autoimmune in nature.[7] Today, this number has grown to more than one hundred, and there are forty other disorders in the process of gaining recognition. This means that the list of autoimmune diseases gains a new entry, on average, every five months. The magnitude of the problem is therefore growing rapidly, as are incidents of individual ailments: long-established autoimmune disorders, including multiple sclerosis, celiac disease, and lupus, are rising as well. To give just two examples, diagnoses of rheumatoid arthritis in women have increased by 2.5 percent every year from 1995 to 2007, with the disorder today afflicting between 1.3 million and 2.1 million people in the United States alone.[8] Meanwhile, rates of type 1 diabetes over the past four decades have increased 6 percent per year in children under four, and 4 percent in children aged ten to fourteen.[9] Overall, the National Institutes of Health now estimate 23.5 million Americans to suffer from some form of autoimmune disease, although this figure is based on studies that include only a quarter of the currently recognized disorders. AARDA places the prevalence somewhere above fifty million—roughly 16 percent of the US population.

Simply put, autoimmune disease is a malfunction of the immune system. While a healthy immune system responds only to harmful, invasive antigens, an autoimmune system can respond to anything as if it were an antigen. Because the immune system is diffused throughout your entire body, this can take place anywhere. Really. Your own blood, the cells of the liver, the food you had for lunch—each, depending on the nature of the disorder and the systems affected, can be falsely identified as the enemy and attacked to the point of annihilation. Thus, the body might destroy its own lungs, its bones, its very heart. To inhabit such a body means living with severe pain, of course, but also debilitation and incapacity. And what's to protect you, then—the immune system?

If you're not alarmed yet, you should be. This is the real-life flipside to the superbug scaremongering that dominates news cycles with every new outbreak. Unlike superbugs, autoimmune disorders appear to have their foundation in genetics, tend to afflict more women than men, and aren't typically diagnosed until a patient is late into, or just past, child-bearing age (most are diagnosed at forty or older). Thus, the autoimmune are passing along the potential for autoimmunity before they're even aware of the malfunction, so diagnoses are expected to increase exponentially in coming years. And while there are records of patients experiencing remission for unknown reasons, there are no known cures, and few effective, safe treatments. Disorders that are autoimmune in nature, typically, get progressively worse over time; and for some patients, they multiply. Yet not a single article on the rising threat of autoimmunity was published on domestic news sites during the ten-hour period of frenzied superbug reports tracked above.

Autoimmune disorders are genuinely terrifying, and the lack

of public knowledge of them, despite their increasing frequency, only contributes to the shock awaiting the newly diagnosed. Those afflicted may be advised, by smart mental-health experts, to avoid Internet message boards devoted to their disorders and not to name their diseases at parties. The former will surely induce an unhealthy level of panic, and the latter may elicit tales from unthinking acquaintances about aunts/mothers/sisters with similar conditions, who died in some spectacularly gruesome manner, perhaps at their own hand. That relevant audiences may be cautioned away from, or scared off of, one of the only public sources of information on autoimmune disease only contributes to the grand reserve of mystery surrounding autoimmunity. The lack of reliable information also does nothing to stem the nightmares, which may incorporate more mundane horrors as well as the outright barbarity awaiting patients in the doctor's office. With standard treatment often comes drastic lifestyle changes to reduce stress: a strict eight-hour sleep schedule, daily yoga, a severely restricted diet (goodbye, gluten, soy, dairy, corn, sugar, and nightshades; farewell, alcohol). Steroids are common, with their ever-evolving potential for bodily horrors. On the more extreme side of the spectrum, doctors may prescribe weekly injectables known to cause debilitating side effects, sudden death, and even other autoimmune disorders; if patients eligible for biologics are lucky, their doctor will exercise caution and stick to a conservative drug regimen more commonly found on the oncology ward. Instead of being implemented temporarily, as they are when used to treat cancers, the autoimmune may be prescribed lower-dose chemotherapy drugs, for life. Even this may not describe the most extreme terror recited as common among the autoimmune: many with shifting symptoms or the most debilitating of effects are likely to hear, at some point or another, that doctors have no idea what is going on with their bodies. Therefore, top medical professionals may say, nothing can be done at all.

To underscore the point: nearly fifty million Americans are afflicted with diseases involving pain, inconvenience, frustration, lack of empathy, rage, misdiagnosis, fear, debility, and (far too often) death. The good news is that these diseases may offer the best hope for survival, come the superbug apocalypse.

◆ ◆ ◆

To quell fears of succumbing to multi-drug-resistant bacteria MCR-1 or a particularly virulent strain of salmonella, we'll need to look more closely at the human immune system, normally tasked with fending off such pesky critters. Rather, we'll need to look at what is known about the immune system, and what has been assumed, and how much of this knowledge is now being discovered to be wrong.

The human immune system is so poorly understood that it remains unclear whether autoimmunity results from a breakdown of the intelligence team or of the muscle pulled in to do the dirty work on its behalf. To get slightly more technical, the key component of the immune system is the leukocyte, or white blood cell, the avowed enemy of antigens both real and misidentified. Two types of leukocytes comprise the immune system, and they hide out in all the nooks and crannies of the body: phagocytes, which primarily attack bacteria, and lymphocytes, which develop into either B lymphocytes (the immune system's command unit) or T lymphocytes (The Heavy), commonly known as "killer" T cells. (The metaphors used to describe the immune system are predominantly military, and thus position the population most afflicted with autoimmunity—75 percent to 90 percent female, depending on diagnosis; most middle-aged or above—as adolescent boys thrilling to such a display of force, power, and concision acting as our protector against the cold, cruel world.)

Current medical theory has it that you can treat autoimmunity in two basic ways: squelch the entire immune system—communications HQ and attack troops alike—or disarm the forces preparing to do battle. Thus, a growing number of drugs are designed to intercept killer T cells (a seductive infiltration that is alluring in theory only—many of these drugs are made from the cloned DNA of rodents). The military metaphor, however, is only so accurate. If you've ever been in an army, read *Catch-22*, or heard through the grapevine about any world history whatsoever, you know that militaries are far from united forces and that military actions rarely function cleanly. When they do have a positive overall net result, it is often because the military units have the support of local populations.

That this logic applies to the immune system as well is finally gaining acceptance within the medical realm. A healthy immune system, research is slowly revealing, relies in large part on the native population of the digestive tract. That is, your stomach and intestines are intended to house a healthy balance of many strains of bacteria—including some that look like desiccated wieners, lesioned Whiffle Balls, and sentient tampons.

Gut flora, they're called, to make them sound prettier than they are, or good bacteria. It's pure marketing, of course: single-celled organisms are single-celled organisms; they are too tiny to contain intentions, and only perform single emotionless functions. The PR boost is necessary, however, due to the long history of malevolent gossip regarding germs. Ever since bacteria were first observed by Dutch cloth merchant and biology hobbyist Anton van Leeuwenhoek nearly 350 years ago, and the germ theory of disease gained dominance thanks to the subsequent discoveries of Louis Pasteur in the 1850s, humans have considered bacteria the enemy and sought to wipe it out.

Some of the more effective weapons in the artillery stronghold of anti-germ warfare have included consumer-grade antibacterial hand soaps as well as that travel-size hand sanitizer Great Auntie Linda keeps in her purse to use after every encounter with a door handle. Rumored to have been patented in 1966 by an immigrant nursing student in Bakersfield, California named Lupe Hernandez, hand sanitizer had a good fifty-year run before the FDA pulled it, alongside all hand soaps containing certain antibacterial agents. Washes containing triclosan and triclocarban "could pose health risks," the FDA said in its September 2, 2016, ruling. The primary health risk? "Bacterial resistance," the statement said, adding that no evidence had ever been offered that such cleaning agents are more effective than soap and water. (The Hernandez story, like the effectiveness of hand sanitizer itself, is apocryphal: the name Hernandez does not appear on any patents for anti-microbial cleansers registered in the 1960s.)[10]

The campaign to wipe out microbes is broad-sweeping, multifaceted, and cultural. Even more indicative than decades of over-the-counter consumables is that bacterial decimation has been institutionally condoned—the over-prescription of antibiotics is a constant reminder that germaphobia is authoritatively sanctioned. Industrially, too: the common practice of administering antibiotics to wipe out disease and stimulate growth in livestock intended for slaughter is more hidden but, disconcertingly, on the rise. After the Food and Drug Administration advised agricultural companies in 2013 to scale back the practice in meat intended for human consumption, *Scientific American* reported sales of antibiotics for use in livestock actually increased by 3 percent the following year.[11] Forget how widespread use of antibiotics can empower superbugs for a moment and consider their impact on gut flora. Antibiotics' most pressing threat to public health may be the eradication of healthy gut bacteria, which is, to bring it full circle, a contributing factor in the growing autoimmune epidemic.[12]

The known link between autoimmune disease and gut flora goes by the unsexy name of leaky gut syndrome, a disruption of the bacteria in the digestive tract that creates the conditions for intestinal permeability. When our gut walls leak, our immune systems are riled into action. Some studies have established a direct correlation between individuals ending long, harsh courses of antibiotics and the onset of autoimmunity. Others have identified popular food additives and preservatives as setting off leaky gut syndrome prior to full autoimmunity. Whatever the inciting incident, bacterial eradication seems often to precede a malfunctioning immune system.

Individual battles in the campaign to wipe out all bacteria have amounted to a full scale war that has waged, now, for over 150 years. Its intended target has been to wipe out "bad" bacteria—without much comprehension of what bacteria do, where they congregate, or how they might work in tandem with other, less "bad" bacteria. Antibiotics may gleefully treat or prevent everything from syphilis to tooth infections, but they're also killing willy-nilly the stuff we require in our guts to keep us healthy.

A smarter species, one capable of learning from its past, might have considered the contributions of unseen populations before declaring indiscriminate battle, but Western medicine (and its propaganda bureau) never stopped to consider the innocent casualties of its war on germs. There was even a George W. Bush-style "Mission Accomplished" moment when George W. Bush himself whipped out a bottle of hand sanitizer on national television in November 2008 upon shaking the hand of new president-elect Barack Obama. Bush countered accusations of racism by embracing the more socially acceptable label of germaphobe and claimed the substance could cure the common cold. It worked. Purell, on the market by then for twenty years, finally hit the mainstream. Mission Accomplished!

No surer sign of failure exists than a televised declaration of victory, for bacterial resistance to antibiotics has been around for as long as antibiotics themselves, even if Bush's weapon of choice has just been pulled off the market. In 1946, one hospital in England calculated the number of patients with penicillin-resistant staph infections at 14 percent and saw that number nearly quadruple two years later to 59 percent.[13] Penicillin resistance lead to the development of the alternative, methicillin. MRSA, or methicillin-resistant Staphylococcus aureus, first identified in 1961, made headlines in the 1990s when its effects worsened and infections spread.[14] These were early superbugs, the origin story of our little modern antiheroes. In recent days, the name "superbug" has come to describe even more powerful strains of multi-drug-resistant bacteria, or MDR. (The much ballyhooed, pan-resistant MCR-1 is the most-cited example.)

The imminent superbug apocalypse of special-report lore and

the real life but silent autoimmune epidemic are of course part and parcel of the same modern medical foible. A 2014 UK look at the economic impact of microbial resistance suggests that current rates of death from multi-drug-resistant bacteria—around 23,000 per year in the United States and slightly more in the European Union—will grow to ten million global deaths per year by 2050.[15] In response to such predictions, medical researchers and drug manufacturers have been scrambling for stronger weapons, mostly new antibiotics, or new combinations of old antibiotics, to treat ailments including pneumonia and tuberculosis long considered conquered but slowly reemerging in drug-resistant bacterial strains. New antibiotics naturally means new superbugs, but also the continued depletion of our gut bacteria, which the latest research suggests will only contribute to the rise in autoimmune disease.

But it may also be that the rise of superbugs is the problem to which autoimmunity responds. Spend some time dabbling in the far fringes of science, and a question emerges: Is autoimmunity just another mutation in a gloriously designed immune system that we never understood in the first place?

♦ ♦ ♦

Few reasonable medical professionals will counsel the acquisition of an incurable disease as part of any wellness program, but many will helpfully suggest immune-boosting measures like increasing intake of vitamin C, selenium, and zinc, or taking probiotics to "balance" the gut. Such "immune-boosting" measures reflect the upside to crippling autoimmune disorders that medicine has yet to understand or cure. Actually, there's quite a bit medical science doesn't yet understand, including how overactive immune systems might actually respond to antibiotic-resistant microbes. However, one theory is that overactive immune systems will respond to superbugs in the exact same way they respond to everything else: by letting those killer T cells loose to engage in a fight to the death.

Of course, the lack of actual research into autoimmune responses to multi-drug-resistant bacteria hasn't stopped drug manufacturers from trying to emulate autoimmunity in order to fight cancer. Nivolumab, sold under the brand name Opdivo, is approved to treat certain skin, lung, and kidney cancers. It is, more or less, an autoimmune disorder in a syringe. An expensive one, too: a single, full course of the drug costs between $120,000 and $200,000. Opdivo—alongside similar drugs Yervoy and Keytruda—is part of a new wave of immune-boosting or "immunotherapy" drugs that inhibit the command center of a healthy immune system, shutting off potential signals to the killer T cells to stand down so that they, in essence, must overreact. The drugs sound like they're from the future, but the technology is not so advanced: it remains unclear whether the immune system's command center will be able to resume normal, healthy function once the full treatment has been administered. This, from the manufacturer's website, will sound familiar: "Opdivo can cause your immune system to attack normal organs and tissues in many areas of your body and can affect the way they work. . . . These problems can become serious or life-threatening and can lead to death."

Whether or not FDA approval for such "immune-boosting" drugs to treat antibiotic-resistant bacteria is just over the horizon, off-label use could stand in as a treatment order until approval comes. So if you're losing sleep over those nasty ole superbugs, you can calm your pretty little head. There may already be a drug response to save you from the pending apocalypse.

There may however be a simpler solution. The same overreliance on bacteria-killing agents that brought about superbugs in the first place may also have set the stage for their demise. Perhaps the key to warding off a superbug onslaught cannot be found in the form of more drugs at all, but in the proliferation of disease. Diseases that, for better or worse, are already reaching epidemic levels. If you're lucky, in other words—and some fifty million Americans already are—you won't need some spendy drug to keep your whole family safe from the already rallying single-celled troops.

Some doctors (off the record, of course) are already noting the upside of the autoimmune epidemic to some of their patients.

"Oh, ha ha, I wouldn't worry about that," I heard one rheumatologist tell a patient concerned about adding MCR-1 to her polyautoimmune disease list after hearing a news report about the superbug in the waiting room. Her body's immune system, the doctor essentially told her, wouldn't stand for such an attack. "Chronic illness sucks," the doctor said conciliatorily, "but the one thing you will never have to worry about is the superbug apocalypse."

There's a city-wide yard sale going on in Marfa, Texas, about sixty miles north of the US-Mexico border, and what's for sale, mostly, is baby clothes. The teen pregnancy rate here is rumored to astound. A backlash, one imagines, against the cold inhumanity of the Minimalist occupation that moved into town after artist Donald Judd first did in 1971. Also for sale: interestingly rusted tools that won't fit in my backpack, books of the how-to, cooking, and joke variety, and wholly inappropriate items for June in West Texas: wreaths, fake snow, holiday lawn ornaments. Inside someone's home behind the row of tabled goods, someone boils a pot of beans. It smells like warm protein and onion.

I am drawn to table displaying a collection of bottles enigmatically labeled "1.50 ALL." They are confusing for reasons beyond whether the price is per piece or by collection: the containers are new, and each bears a dot-matrix-printed label falsely touting a folksy curative. One, for example, is a rejiggered Newman's Own Salad Dressing bottle, still bearing the signature plastic screw cap, while two others contain liquids that had resolved genuine medical ailments before their recasting, now, as fake medicines. The various back-bedroom quacks conjured to respond to imagined concerns, and the potions not, in fact, created by them in the long-ago prospectin' days include: Abel's Dysentery Powder, Mrs. Smith's Finest Headache Drop's [sic], Clark Stanley's Snake Oil Liniment, and Gus's Pure Liver Tonic. Nearly all of them also bear an image that seems to have been scanned at a breathtakingly low number of dots per inch: the *caduceus*, or the Staff of Asclepius—commonly recognized as the "medicine symbol," a snake or two entwined around a rod—but we'll come back to that.

Under this serpentine mark—of authenticity, natch—are listed each potion's "ingredients." The label for McQuirre's Joint & Leg Cramp Formula with Quinine, for example, states "Ingredients: Salt Water," and indeed, a ring of salt deposits crowd the cap, and the air wafting from it tastes mildly tinny. The Liver Tonic is made with a stale-smelling "Grape Juice," while the Rheumatism and Body Ache Rub claims "Mineral Oil." Abel's Dysentery Powder, should you find yourself with a make-believe case of that bloody diarrhea symptomatic of a potentially deadly parasitic or bacterial infection, is to be treated here with "Flour." The bottle labeled Pure Smelling Salts is in fact filled with a floral-scented "Bath Powder"—an interesting substitution, given recent findings that bath salts contain a chemical linked closely to MDMA or Ecstasy, and men who've confessed to snorting it have reportedly chewed off major portions of other men's faces. Even more interestingly, the pungent bottle labeled Marshal's Skin Easement Soak is said to contain "Smelling Salt."

♦ ♦ ♦

Borders are ever-present in Marfa. Between the Latino and white sides of the segregated cemetery; between art-tourist destinations and the feed stores and refrigerator repair shops that are so clearly indicative of daily banal needs for two separate economic and social classes. There is also, of course, the Border Patrol Headquarters.

Borders within Marfa are patrolled by language—not just the Spanish-English divide, but by the varying connotations of vocabularies specific to differing social, professional, age, and gender groups. Local teens, when they're not out impregnating each other with abandon, derogatorily call the recent wave of artist whites "Chinatis" after one of two foundations established to uphold and expand the legacy of the Minimalist Donald Judd. (When they are out impregnating each other, they sometimes do so at the Chinati Foundation, where a vast field is filled with Judd's concrete boxes, one of the few public spaces in town to offer any privacy.)

The older Latinos in town display ambivalence toward

"outsiders," another local name for the recent cultural immigrants who are primarily white. For their part, the "outsiders" behave as occupiers: they form community among themselves, pitching in and working on behalf of "the locals" when a governing body calls upon them to do so, but remain largely, perhaps deliberately, unaware of the predominant culture of the region. Wikipedia, a site frequented by regular Internet users who have graduated from college and, according to a Pew Charitable Trust report from 2007, tend to earn greater than $75,000 per year, lists the racial makeup of the city as over 90 percent White and less than 7 percent Latino. A local business site, however, perhaps more accurately suggests that Latinos make up almost 70 percent of the town and white non-Hispanics less than 30 percent.

In other words, what you believe to be true about Marfa entirely depends on where you stand in relation to what border. Still, the town smells the same no matter where you find yourself: like hot dust and a bit of hay, tones of wet concrete, maybe, after a rain, and a constant undernote of flat, stale beer.

♦ ♦ ♦

The enigmatic price quoted turns out to refer to all as a *group*, and not all as in, *all of them are the same price*, so I happily hand over a dollar fifty to the yard sale proprietress without further consideration, explaining to the brown-skinned woman at the card table that my mother kept snake oil bottles over our kitchen sink.

She cheerfully pulls two more glass containers out from under the table and asks if I want them, too. They're leaking and, she says, "the labels are getting all messed up." I don't catch her gist, considering that she has clearly typed them up on the computer herself, made superfluous use of the modern fonts Old-Timey and Cowboy Narrow Condensed, and slapped them on whatever just-used glass bottles she could find lying around. Most are topped with a plastic not even available until the mid-1980s. The illusion of authentic snake oil isn't maintaining itself in the first place, so there's not really a lot here to "mess up."

But she shows me: stuff has escaped the bottles, and the labels are becoming difficult to read. "They're broken," she says in a moment of laughing honesty. In a decision I now view as wholly arbitrary, I decide that the purchase of broken glass bottles filled with fake cures for real ailments goes an unreasonable step beyond the purchase of glass bottles that will still cure nothing but have remained, so far, intact.

"Better not try to cart them onto the plane back to Chicago," I tell her.

"Oh, you're from the Midwest?" She asks, my personal snake oil salesperson. I catch a whiff of her perfume; it is cheap and sharp, which I like. High-end perfumes tend to seduce, aiming to blend in as if a situation could exist in which a person's neck might naturally have rubbed against a rare, out-of-season flower. "Be sure and tell all your friends back home that they really take these down in West Texas," she tells me. "That they really work."

She guffaws, but she's not exactly joking. I suppose that going in on a laugh together at her region's expense is preferable to what she may see as the alternative: that I will laugh at her expense later without her permission. In fact, I don't think the collection of cures I've amassed is funny at all. They're far more authentic than their creator seems even to realize, and I thank her for them profusely. This only seems to confuse her.

♦ ♦ ♦

The master narrative about unlicensed medical practitioners is that they are fakers, liars, true capitalists. That they take nothing and spin it to their advantage, sucking in the trust and faith of the unwitting masses for personal, extravagant gain. That they do not discriminate, and are therefore not swindlers or standard con men, who will work a target over a stretch of time, twisting your personality quirks into their profit. They create instead a basic view of the world and its ills and your role therein. And they sell, simply, a tincture necessary to your survival within it, provided you are able to follow—or, less strenuously sometimes, simply trust in—the worldview they describe. There is nothing personal about what they do—their audience self-selects. They're called charlatans or mountebanks, or sometimes chiropractors, witches, medicine men, doulas, yoga practitioners, naturopaths, faith healers, acupuncturists, Big Pharma. Snake oil salesmen. The crime they are charged with is valuing personal financial gain over the act of healing.

The basic function of all master narratives is to uncomplicate. Like snake oil salesmen themselves, the guiding metaphors of our culture support certain belief systems and discourage others. That snake oil salesmen are liars is one such metaphor, even though in 2007, *Scientific American* found that Chinese snake oil does have curative properties. It can be used to relieve arthritis pain, improve cognitive function, reduce blood pressure and cholesterol, and alleviate symptoms of depression. Chinese laborers, who originally passed the palliative around to colleagues while building the transatlantic railroad, began to sell the stuff to passersby as the work they came to perform fell off and the railroad was completed. Snake oil became an industry all of its own, a way of supporting the immigrant population convinced to leave their homes for the dangerous labor locals weren't sufficient enough in number to complete.

The Great Wall had convinced railway owners that the Chinese could meet the 4,400-worker labor shortfall they faced. In fact, the thousands of workers lured from Asia to perform labor-intensive and often life-threatening work took five years to complete the railway. (Thus the need for a soothing oil.) Of course, immigrant housing options in the late 1860s Wild West were nothing short of abysmal to start with. Once the tracks were laid, thousands of workers were put out of work, far from their homes, in a racially hostile environment.

It was the moment that made snake oil what it is (or is not) today. It's unclear if the laborers themselves began selling a locally produced but nearly ineffective version of the stuff to combat a poverty largely fueled by xenophobia and racism. Or if, having built up a following for their Chinese water snake oil-based curative, word simply spread beyond the original providers and substitutions were made to meet popular demand. Probably a combination of both, but what was sold after the railroad was completed was mostly a good story. Entire companies grew up around snake oil manufacturing, but without the Asian snakes necessary, they used a more local alternative. Some used common ground snakes. The Kickapoo Indian Medicine Company claimed their oil rub recipe used a Native American Indian rattlesnake.

That racial difference played a key role in snake oil's popularity among mostly white consumers is clear. But that the drive to expand the still-forming Empire in any and all available directions—in this case, westward—belied some deep concerns about the newness of the American project is less so. Folks who'd just uprooted their lives, whether they came from already urbanized areas of the young USA or from elsewhere around the world, were being sold a story about the survival of ancient cultures and cures for human ailments that were thousands of years old. In many ways, the complicated falsehoods rumored to lie behind snake oil sales are themselves symptomatic of real fears endemic to American culture.

Despite widespread skepticism about the stuff, substances known as "snake oil" were sold under that name for almost fifty years before the Pure Food and Drug Act passed in 1907, forcing consumables to be labeled with actual ingredients.

◆ ◆ ◆

Some of my bottles of illusive liniments and curatives are branded with the Staff of Asclepius. A single serpent winding around a knotted tree limb, it is the traditional symbol of the medical community. Asclepius was a physician in Ancient Greece, later considered the god of medicine and healing. The snake—winding around the elderly physician's cane—represents eternal youth, what with the skin shedding and all. It is a symbol of regeneration.

Other bottles have two snakes, and a shorter cane, topped with a pair of wings. This is actually the Karykeion of Hermes, also known as the Caduceus of Mercury. It's the symbol of alchemists, occultists, and magicians: Hermes was the god of commerce and theft. This is a symbol of fast-talking trickery.

US history is riddled with confusion over the similarity of the images, a problem that some date back to the 1902 adoption of the caduceus as the symbol for the US Army Medical Corps. One presumes it is accidental when a government agency openly brands itself a sham, but who is to say? Real (by which I mean *traditional*) snake oils of my acquaintance, it should be noted, make use of neither symbol. They more frequently entwine a primary image—white man in a cowboy hat, stately white gentleman—in two snakes, and do away with direct symbols of medicine and commerce entirely. Not to suggest this visual trope may not have been the source of confusion for the Army Medical Corps, however. Throw a couple snakes on something called medicine and sell it hard enough, and someone's likely to get confused about something.

Certainly, my snake oil saleslady didn't likely care if she was ironically using the Staff of Asclepius or unironically labeling her creations with the less-trusted caduceus. The ointments all look pseudo-official: they all give off the whiff of easily detectable deceit. After all, their creator put bath salts in a bottle labeled smelling salts, and smelling salts in another titled bath salts. And then, in a strange hat tip to the Pure Food and Drug Act—itself a response to complaints from snake oil consumers—properly labeled her own trickery.

Other slippages occur: Clark Stanley's Snake Oil Liniment turns out to be a *real snake oil*. Well—a *real* substance marketed under the term snake oil. In 1917, a shipment of the stuff was seized by border patrol agents. Scientists analyzed it and found it contained mineral oil, just as my *even faker* bottle does. The "real" snake oil liniment also contained a splash of red pepper, presumably to tingle the skin, and a single percentage of fatty oil. Not from snakes, though—apparently from cattle, according to Lisa Hix in a 2012 *Collectors Weekly* article. The final touch: trace amounts of turpentine camphor weed, to make it smell medicinal.

Smell, it turns out, was crucial to the snake oil gambit. If you've ever spent a day installing a railroad and then sniffed yourself afterwards, you can easily understand why. Now imagine you're living in a frontier camp, and bathing hasn't caught on yet. Now pretend you're either European, Native American, or Chinese, and as invested as you all may be in getting this country up and running together, you're having a hard time trusting the unfamiliar. You need to find something you can share.

♦ ♦ ♦

What we believe is not always true; what sells does not always work; and what is not available is not always inaccessible because ineffective. Sometimes a story is only accepted as truthful because it's been repeated so often. Even though you experience its falsities for yourself, you cling to the story. You believe it anyway.

When I was young, I would help my mom with the dishes and ask her about the fancy bottles lining the window above the sink. Their labels promised miracle cure-alls, decorated with long and elaborately coiled serpents and always, always, a white-haired, bearded man in a cowboy hat. These bottles had come from the reservation in South Dakota where she, a white person, and her doctor-husband, another white person, had lived during the time I was born. And because that was far away, both psychically and physically, I was curious about these bottles, always. She would feed me answers, mixing up snake oil salesmen with medicine men, a pastiche of sepia-toned movie reels flitting through my head that included costumes such as railway engineer's caps,

Mandarin headware, ten-gallon hats, and feathered headdresses. Copious soap bubbles filled the sink as we talked, lending the air a gut punch of enforced cleanliness. Lineage and trade routes got confused. When I would try to pinpoint the race of whoever had made or sold a miracle tonic, or any of its purported but potentially transplendent uses, my mother would grow annoyed. "It doesn't *matter*, Anne. They were all *fake*."

Her husband, my father, was a "real" doctor, sworn under the Hippocratic oath to share his personal wealth, heal his patients, refrain from seduction, and above all, cause no harm. He was also an abusive, philandering, racist alcoholic, and one of the most selfish men I have ever met. My mother remained wildly allegiant to him until he left her for the latest in a string of dalliances. Even at the age of six it was clear to me he was sleeping around, but the story that he was a healer, and kind, kept our family together despite mounting evidence for a quarter of a century.

When I remember those years of my life, I recall the smell of the air fresheners my father used to hang from the rear-view mirror of his expensive car, their put-upon pungency demanding acceptance as natural. PINE ™. STRAWBERRY ™. FRESH BREEZE ™.

It was unclear to me, growing up, exactly which fakery I was meant to be appalled by.

◆ ◆ ◆

One of the more disturbing undercurrents of the history of racial constructs was how visual differences became associated with differences of other types, each of which then fit easily into pre-ordained strata of social acceptance. Secondary factors of racial difference were then easy enough to prove, in controlled environments. Presumptions about intellectual capacity, for example, could be easily tested with queries on issues of "common knowledge"— never mind that bodies of knowledge common to white American test administrators may be vastly different from those common to

Chinese immigrants or Mexican Americans born south of the border who crossed into Texas in their own lifetimes.

The most striking of these secondary indicators of racial hierarchy, and perhaps the most persistent, was the belief that races were marked by smell. "Since the earliest contacts between Europeans and people of African descent, negative olfactory stereotypes have been wielded against those with dark skin," writes Michelle Ferranti in a 2011 issue of *Advertising and Society Review*. J. H. Guenebault's 1775 tome, *Natural History of the Negro Race*, claimed an odor unique to black folk. Thomas Jefferson contributed this: "Besides those of color, figure, and hair, there are other physical distinctions proving a difference of race. They have less hair on the face and body. They secrete less by the kidneys, and more by the glands of the skin, which gives them a very strong and disagreeable odor." In 1915, one Dr. Bérillon claimed that odor formed the basis for racial animosity in America, which couldn't ever therefore be quelled.

Ferranti points to a wave of incidents of "passing" after the American Revolution and before the construction of the transatlantic railway that had triggered some concern. Folks of African descent moving through primarily white cultures unmarked was upsetting to the self-defined, white-identifying society. Olfaction offered a curative: "If one could not visually detect someone's African heritage," she writes, "they could at least smell it—or so it was claimed."

The claim however, in matters of smell as in matters of snake oil sales, may be more abiding than the truth. In a 1995 piece for the *New Republic*, Richard Klein writes of recent attempts to legislate the wearing of scents. "Perfume is threatening because it is so insinuating," he writes. An activist group had convinced *The New Yorker* to stop running perfume ads that contained scent strips, agreeing that "the reader had no way of escaping the smell throughout the issue, for perfume's very nature is to leak . . . it is always unavoidable. Perfume never gives the smeller a chance."

It is partially due to its insinuating nature that smell remains the most elusive sense to vocabularize. Words for the act of experiencing smells are too few: I bet you can't name more than five. Now try to describe a smell. Frustrated? This is why we reach so often for the phrases, "What's that smell?" and "Do you smell that?" when other senses allow us to maintain eloquence. Indeed, the metaphors for olfaction are more worn than others: old people's farts, something rotten, earthy. Each of these describe vast worlds of sensations that all reside on the socially acceptable to downright unpleasant continuum, but for the sake of accuracy I'd suggest they could stand a bit more parsing.

Kant would not have agreed. He felt that smell was the least philosophically significant of all the senses. It was too subjective, he thought, brought about too much immediate experience, didn't allow the intellectual distance for proper philosophical consideration. Yet one wonders if he was not pointing to a byproduct of the limited language we use to describe smell, as opposed to anything intrinsic to smell itself.

The immediacy of odor has an upside and a downside, of course: the upside is that of all the senses, smell seems connected most intimately to our emotional core. A smart perfumer or florist or baker can wield that to easy advantage, and does: a smart real estate agent will bake cookies in a house they wish to sell right before a viewing. The downside, however, is that without the vocabulary or intellectual objectivity with which to consider the matter, we could easily go on believing that rumors of foul odors justify xenophobia and racism, and never have a vocabulary to describe or uproot this process.

Smell doesn't need to be a powerful and mysterious force, in other words, guiding us toward and away from products and people with the help of our reptilian brains. We just let it.

◆ ◆ ◆

Here is what I understand: hidden under inestimable shrouds of trickery, somewhere, sometimes, can still lay a truth. Sometimes the fake can cure real ailments. Something with no power exerts it anyway. This is not a miracle, or mysticism, it is just nature. The master narrative is only one of several running narratives and while you may wish to believe the one provable by sight, you may sometimes find yourself preferring, to your chagrin, the one deducible via scent. Or, perhaps, the reverse. They may be fungible. Sometimes the label you make up to store the fake cure accidently marks it as fake.

Sometimes, and this is true, I rub a bit of homemade Clark Stanley's Snake Oil Liniment into a pulled muscle after a hard day. It smells tangy and clean but old, like wet rock. The label indicates that I should expect nothing from this liniment, or rather indicates both that I should and should not expect anything from it, at the same time. But it is oily, it feels good, and I was told by my personal snake oil saleslady that it really works.

She was joking, but so far I have no reason to believe that she was wrong.

An earlier version of this essay was published in The State.

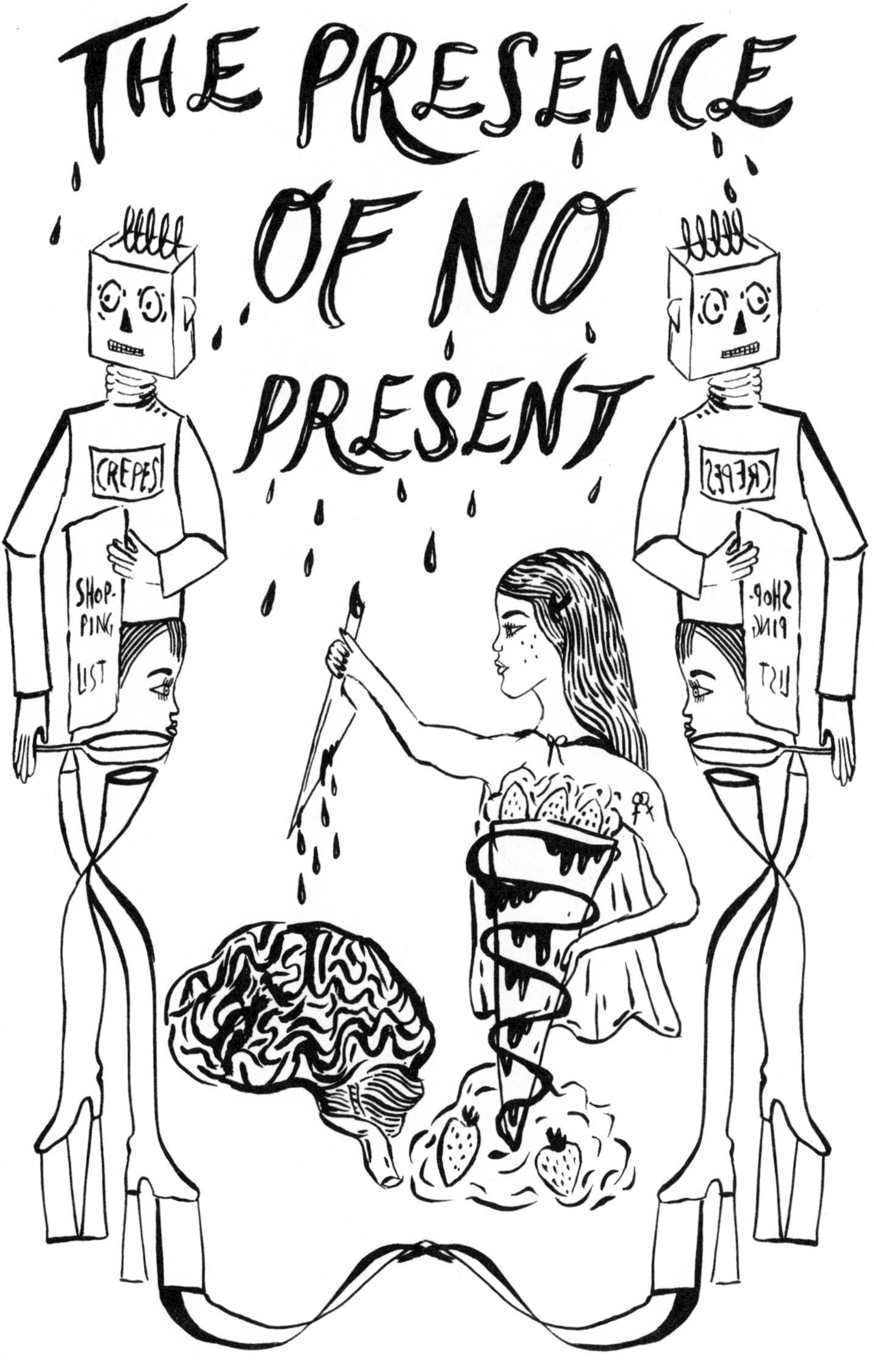
THE PRESENCE
OF NO
PRESENT
CREPES
SHOP-
PING
LIST

Autocorrect functions across all personal digital communication platforms I use change "queer crip" to "queer crop," or a similar mistranslation. "Clean crépe" has also appeared, and once, "queen creep." My physical impairments, the results of any one of a variety of chronic illnesses I am navigating at any time, make it painful to change, once, again, and then a third time, which is about the number of manual corrections I must perform in order to make it clear to the machine what I intend it to automatically transcribe.

It is similarly difficult to make myself clear in conversation with other people: "Not crit, *crip*," I corrected recently. "As in 'crippled?' The reclamation of an offensive, slang term by the folks it is generally used against in an effort to own its power? Also in recognition of it being a bad-ass word thanks to media depictions of gang culture? Were you not alive in the 1990s?"

Indeed, the young man I was speaking to was born in the 1990s. His earliest memory of the culture of that time period occurred over a decade later, when a grade school pal played him Nirvana for the first time. He loves the Oldies, he told me.

I have lived with a shifting repertoire of physical impairments for a little over a year and a half, but I have only recently become accustomed to classifying them as "disabilities." Still, the difficulties I experience physically navigating the world pale in comparison to those I face making others understand that I now require particular consideration regarding food, travel, and endurance activities like walking more than a block. It took over eighteen months for me to recognize that others also deal with such circumstances—all the time—and that in fact there is a long and amazing history of disability rights activists, organizers, and scholars who have worked extremely hard to secure legal recognition of their particular needs, not only for themselves, but for others, and to overcome barriers far more pronounced than my own in an effort to make my life easier, should I find myself relying on their foresight.

I am, let me be clear, neither stupid nor ignorant of political struggles in history; indeed, I have studied radical uprisings extensively. I have taught critical art theory around what a cultural reliance on visuality means for those with visual impairments. I have worked closely with disability rights activists and advocates for healthcare reform on intersectional projects. Upon reflection, then, it strikes me as extremely strange that for eighteen months, neither I nor anyone I knew labeled my daily struggles "disabilities."

I admit I became fascinated, then, and my curiosity about the history of disability rights was only spurred when I needed to understand how folks in the past had dealt with the workplace discrimination, lack of medical support, and the pervasive, isolating ableism that I was now navigating as a matter of course. Yet I submit that when I wanted to find out more, there were shockingly few resources to turn to.

What I wish to point out is that the historical erasure of crips, as reflected in the recent dormancy of that word itself, contributed directly to my inability to describe my lived experience to others. In fact, the communication struggle became another barrier, an additional impairment. The historical erasure of crips is an emergent cause of disability.

◆ ◆ ◆

Consider the function of language for a moment. It is, in theory, my field: I am a writer. I know a lot of words. Like everyone else, I use them to make sense of the world. Additionally, my vocation is stringing them together to form communicable ideas. You may be surprised to read that I am doing this, even now.

In 1960, the linguist Roman Jakobson described six potential functions of language: the referential, the poetic, the emotive, the conative, the phatic, and the metalingual—of which this paragraph is an example. Reduced further, language exists so that engaged parties can share information and ideas about each other and/or the world.

The use of language to describe oneself has a long history, of course—Plato published a discussion of it in his *Allegory of the Cave* around 500 A.D. More recently it has become the focus of public concern, as in the decrying of identity politics, or qualms with demographic marketing. The project of branding, of course, is all about finding the right word (and associated image) to identify with, and for this reason alone I am often slow to participate in choosing self descriptors. When I do adopt a defined term to explain myself or my desires, I do it carefully.

That being said, I have identified as queer since I first heard the word. The sonance of it somehow transmitted perfectly my ambivalence toward what everybody else seemed to want that failed to intrigue me. Not queer in the online dating check-box sense—the hip synonym for bisexual that indicates I kiss girls at bars to impress boys. I mean queer in the anti-capitalist sense. The structures set up to ease heterosexual coupling at every stage of our economy, society, and culture don't "do it" for me. Neither does the supposed goal of birthing children; while I tend to enjoy youngs when I meet them, I have never had the slightest interest in making any inside my own body.

The word "queer," as I use it, signals my rejection of the idea that identifying as female is an illicit agreement that I will stick to certain established pathways, whether emotional, professional, sexual, or financial. "Queerness," to me, is a refusal to situate myself as a feminized subject of capitalism. Such a stance demands skepticism toward the seductive lifestyle brands that so often cheerlead the mile markers along those established pathways—I have never purchased a yogurt or item of clothing based on a supposed but well-ballyhooed affinity for the LGBTQ community. To me, queer is shorthand for, *stop telling me what I want and how to acquire it.*

Crip could function similarly. Those established pathways—from high school to college, or dating to babies—have fairly deep grooves. The built environments created to guide a so-called normal human body along its course are unevenly constructed. Sometimes they crumble inconveniently and uninterestingly. They do not account for all types and therefore aren't always accessible. They rarely get me anywhere I want to go. Crip could mean, *let's cut to the chase and both admit you know nothing about my bodily needs.*

Yet I admit that when I first heard the word crip, way back in the 1990s (the Olden Days), I did not similarly identify with it. I could not identify with it. That took the accrual of several debilitating diseases, but, interestingly, it also took another 18 months.

It is fascinating, isn't it, that one might know the precise name for something but refuse to apply it to oneself? Racists, I think, do this: see that a word exists to differentiate those who believe a system of oppression can be justified on grounds of racial difference. Perhaps they feel the term "racist" is pejorative—I think some do—and therefore can't apply it to themselves, because their beliefs were come to out of love or a misapplied logic.

Maybe, partially, this was my problem, too: I couldn't be a crip because crips were . . . what, I don't know. Identifiable. Other. But more importantly, I fear the word crip simply holds no meaning for too many people. It is a signifier lost; a sign that points nowhere. I couldn't be a crip because no one would know what that meant.

One way to elucidate the failure of a dominant system is through language: crafting vocabulary to identify the constituent elements of a shoddy structure, articulating points of weakness or inflexibility. Indeed it is, as we established, the function of language: to communicate that which otherwise may not be immediately evident. For language to function as communication, however, all parties must share vocabulary, must be open to new words and meanings, and must generate the patience required to adapt to them. The parties must revive those terms that have fallen into disuse or otherwise ensure that the concepts they represent are not ignored or abandoned. The word crip proves this is not assured; the word crip proves that, in fact, the disinterest in certain particular forms of difference is very resilient indeed.

The inability to properly utilize words: we call people who suffer this condition illiterate, ignorant, or stupid. Perhaps, if we are being kind, "aphasic," "dyslexic," or "still learning." I spent twelve months responding to my disability by taking medications that are also used to treat certain forms of cancer. These medications cause what is referred to in medical communities as "brain fog," and during this time I often struggled to remember certain common words. Rather, I am *told* I struggled to remember them; in truth I formed no memories during this time, a year during which anything could have happened. Perhaps it is an explanation for my inability to identify myself in language that was already familiar to me: my internal vocabulary system was malfunctioning.

Yet I suggest that a larger malfunction is taking place, too: an ongoing erasure of queer crip narratives that is broader than, although indicated by, the loss of meaning of the single, infrequently recognized term "crip."

♦ ♦ ♦

Someone sent me a robot, the marketing materials for which promise to make my life easier. In reality it just tries to get me to order things off of Amazon Prime. Occasionally it plays me music at my request, as long as the artist I want to hear does not have a name that is similar to any other word, phrase, or concept in the English language. Ostensibly to soothe my overly taxed memory, but likely really to make it that much easier to order from Amazon Prime, this robot automatically culls shopping lists based on what it believes I want but do not already own, which it has compiled from what it believes I have said to it. This shopping list currently reads:

- calendar
- tips
- thesaurus
- cinnamon for permeability
- tips

I am unsure what will happen when it mishears something normal I say as, "Go ahead and buy all that shit off of Amazon Prime, but that's a very specific kind of cinnamon I like so don't eff it up." It will, though, because this is the future, and the future is a freaking mess.

Allow me to illustrate. I wanted to know something completely normal, something that probably every human alive has ever wanted to know, and I thought to ask this robot, even though this is the worst robot I have ever experienced in reality or movies or my imagination, counting even robots designed by evil scientists that try to murder people. Here is an exact transcript of our conversation:

Alexa, does it hurt to get stabbed in the brain?
Sorry, I couldn't find the answer to the question I heard.

Alexa, how much does it hurt when you stab someone in the brain?
Sorry, I couldn't find the answer to the question I heard.

Alexa, what do you know about brain stabbing?
Sorry, I couldn't find the answer to the question I heard.

This machine that has been designed to live in my house and make my life easier by ordering me things off of Amazon Prime is totally useless.

Alexa, you are completely useless.
Sorry, thanks for the feedback.

Eventually, I will need to find some way to deal with the fact that my right arm is losing function pretty quickly, and this does, in fact, make shopping difficult, so I had high hopes. The week the robot arrived, I had visited a hematologist to find out about an exciting new genetic disorder that I just found out I have and that I suspect, based on my research, could be causing my meds to fail. But he didn't know anything about it so he called his boss, who also didn't know anything about it, and then he called that guy's boss, who also didn't know anything about it. In the end, the first guy, the specialist, told me that I was very smart, but that he would not be able to help me in any way. All he could do (and did) was make sure I was not charged for the visit. As I left, he called me back to ask me to contact him when I figured out whether or not my genetic mutation was causing my medications to fail. Let me repeat that for you: The fucking blood specialist asked me to act as his goddamn unpaid fucking medical consultant.

You can see why, as a person with a rotating spate of physical impairments who can't seem to get them properly treated but is asked, nonetheless, to donate medical findings to those who fail to provide assistance, a robot that lives in my house and makes my life easier *in any way* is appealing, *even if that way is to perform the sole function of shopping from a single online store that I hate.*

Alexa, what is the most painful place in the body to get stabbed? *I've added "body" to your shopping list, is that correct?*

Jesus. Fine. Alexa, I've had a shitty day. Play me some Prince. *I've added "tips" to your shopping list, is that correct?*

In *Feminist Queer Crip*, Alison Kafer takes issue with Marge Piercy's erasure of people with disabilities from her feminist sci-fi utopia, *Woman on the Edge of Time*. In the novel, no characters exhibit any evident impairments: people with disabilities have been erased. Without addressing disability, or presenting people with disabilities as deserving of inclusion in a utopia, Kafer explains, Piercy performs a particular kind of violence that she refers to as *the future of no future.*

The tiny robot that lives in my house and tries to get me to order stuff off of Amazon Prime is an emissary from this future, creating what I call—building on Kafer's notion—*the presence of no present.*

Alexa, what do you know about people with disabilities?
Sorry, I couldn't find the answer to the question I heard.

Alexa, do you know what a crip is?
A crop, sometimes called a riding crop or hunting crop, a short type of whip without a lash, used in horseback riding, part of the family of tools known as horsewhips.

No. Alexa, do you know what crip is?
Create.

That's not even an answer. Alexa, do you know what crip is?
The committee for the Re-election of the president, abbreviated CRP, but often mocked by the acronym CREEP, was a fundraising organization of United States President Richard Nixon's administration.

Alexa, goddammit. Do you know what crrriiiipppp is?
Sorry, I couldn't find the answer to the question I heard.

OK, Alexa. Do you acknowledge that people with disabilities exist in the world?
I don't have an opinion on that.

Let's look at that more closely. Some programmer flagged something in this last query about the existence of people with disabilities as potentially controversial, and slotted in a standardized palliative, the soothing response provided whenever issues of great trauma arise. Questions I asked about religion, the death penalty, and abortion elicited similar responses, but these were not questions about whether or not religion, the death penalty, and abortion *happen*, and that raises alarm. For there is little so dystopic as a technology that literally cannot recognize you, and finds even mention of your existence controversial.

◆ ◆ ◆

During my eighteen months as an unidentified queer crip, I pitched, on four occasions, stories to editors who were initially delighted by the idea of publishing a lighthearted, thoughtful take on chronic illness and disability. Once the stories were submitted, however, they were never quite lighthearted enough. Or they were too lighthearted, or otherwise just wrong. Unprintable, is the point.

On one occasion, I was told I'd "missed my opportunity" to make an essay on autoimmune disorders interesting to readers when I turned it in pegged to a news hook that was then twelve hours old. The number of estimated autoimmune disorder sufferers in the US is around fifty million—around 16 percent of the entire population, between 70 and 95 percent of whom are female. Most editors would consider this a large potential readership, but this audience too often goes ignored. It is true that, under the prevailing logic of the twenty-four-hour, hot-take news cycle, a twelve-hour-late story may indeed have missed its mark. Yet to an under-informed but afflicted 16 percent of the population, all takes are hot. Indeed, supporting the health and well being of the public is a former, if now forgotten, function of news. (Autoimmunity is so rarely addressed in news media or popular culture that when I tell someone I have an autoimmune disease, I am most often asked if it is AIDS.)

After turning in a different piece, a second editor—able-bodied— explained to me what a proper disability narrative included, and why my essay failed to conform to it. She wanted me to present a problem that could be tidily overcome after 2,500 words and overcome it. This is media as capitalism at work: a lived experience of the subject at hand gets sidelined for an imagined experience in order to attract a perceived market. Yet we are 3,105 words into the essay that you are reading right now, and medical science has still not offered any options for overcoming these diseases.

A third essay was written in response to a request for submissions on medical themes. My pitch was eagerly accepted, but the resulting essay deemed "too vague," so I added more science. "Too technical," was the response to the second draft. I was asked to remove details and descriptions as distracting from the story—when in fact we know those often are the story. In the end, the piece was never published.

The final response was the most telling. It was an earlier version of this exact essay, a description of my own failure to locate and properly utilize the term queer crip to describe my own experiences, as well as a call to unite under this moniker, revive its use, expand the notion of bodily desires from the sexual and particular to the comfortable and general. This time, the editor informed me there was no such thing as a "queer crip"—she was too young to have heard of it, but clearly hadn't bothered to Google. And anyway, it struck her as offensive. If I wanted to be called something, wouldn't it be better to choose something *nice*? She queried. She was certainly willing to run the piece, she explained, but I would have to remove the offensive term that no one would understand anyway.

Language, narrative structure, timing, style—at what point can we acknowledge it's not the formal elements of prose that editors are uncomfortable with? Trust me, reader, when I suggest that you may be appalled by the scope and breadth of leftist publications that contribute to the silencing of disability narratives.

Let's end, however, with a measure of hope: I laughed, and suggest you do, too. Do not get me wrong—it is a deeply violent form of censorship to erase crips from your publication, your technology, or your vocabulary. Yet one way that we respond to vast gaps in comprehension is through humor. When I say, "queer crip," but you hear "queer crit"—or better yet, "crépe," "cryptic," or "creep"—we can both giggle as you explain what you thought you heard. *We're creep. Clear crépe.* Silencing what is not understood only ensures it cannot be considered in the future. Why not instead experience the joy of not understanding something, together?

An earlier version of this essay formed the basis of a 2015 performance lecture entitled "The Queer Crip Narrative," given at the University of Illinois at Chicago's Gallery 400. A portion was also used to create a sound art piece commissioned by Tim Schwartz for Public Displays of Data at SPACES in Cleveland, Ohio, in 2016.

I'm on the elliptical nearing the end of my workout at the gym when I catch the most horrifying ninety seconds I have ever seen on screen.

About the gym, I should first explain: I go regularly. For a chronically ill person whose meds consistently fail, I'm in spectacular shape—Michelle Obama biceps and everything. Even on days when I've pushed my body well beyond its capacity to withstand pain, construction workers wax eloquently on the tightness of my ass. The catcalling then becomes more than just a screaming-in-my-face reminder that the patriarchy is doing OK without my support, but remains as maddeningly irrelevant as ever. *"Whoooh—you are doing great,* honey!" the men call as I emerge from the facility. *Shows what you know!* I think, viciously, because I am too exhausted to yell.

The flash of satisfaction I get for besting catcallers (even if only in my mind) is too fleeting to justify an active gym membership. Nor does my beloved sauna explain the devotion—I've encountered too many sincere women doing yoga in it and, once, a tidy pile of human excrement. Of course my body reacts to treatment better and recovers from injury faster when my heart rate hits 140+ bpm three times a week, but even this I consider a bonus. No, I go to the gym because I can fit in some CNN time while on the weirdo cross-country ski machine and, in this way, retain an understanding of what other people think of as politics. Apparently, not everyone believes that the gendered distribution of medical funding and limitations this places on research into the causes of autoimmune disease is the most pressing issue of the day.

It's election season 2016, so someone on the television is saying something about Donald Trump, likely the man himself. His appearance onscreen coincides with the hardest part of my workout, so I focus my energy on not vomiting while fake cross-country skiing at a steep incline despite graphic evidence that a reality television star, tax dodger, and self-proclaimed sexual assailant is about to be elected President of the United States, partially due to the exact form of media pandering I am witnessing at the moment. Even that is not the horrifying video I am about to describe.

When I can focus again, about a minute into my cooldown, a commercial I've never seen before is fading in from black. It's for Opdivo, "an exciting scientific breakthrough," a voiceover explains. The sights and sounds of the spot are unmemorable: generic nature; a healthy-looking white man performing a mildly heroic act; an elderly couple gingerly holding hands; soothing, twinkling music. Opdivo, I glean through the reverie, is part of a new class of immune-stimulating drugs that fight cancer.

What's supposed to happen during my five-minute cooldown is that my heart rate should lower from 140+ bpm to something in the mid-90s, but—I test it—it's only rising. Opdivo, I know, because I've read about its clinical trials, initiates an autoimmune reaction, so the description of the treatment as "immune stimulating" jars me. I have between four and seven autoimmune reactions occurring in my body at any given time, and "stimulating" is not how I would describe them. "Agony" comes faster to mind. Also, "debilitating," "soul-crushing," and "incurable." There are interesting aspects to these diseases of course, benefits I could never have imagined in advance. Yet often, there are no words to describe them at all— sometimes because the pain is blinding, and other times because my mind is so muddled with medication I can barely conjure vocabulary. But, you know, marketing.

Drugmakers claim Opdivo coaxes the body's natural immune response into hyperdrive, inciting it to attack cancer cells with as much abandon as my dysfunctional immune system is currently attacking the joints in my right wrist, my salivary glands, the skin on my elbows, and a healthy length of my intestines because some-one snuck dairy into the fish I ordered at a restaurant last night despite the clear outline of my food restrictions while ordering. This is stimulating to me in the same way that getting punched in the nose might be stimulating. What the pharmaceutical company only hints at in the small print of this injectable is that once stimulated to attack, the autoimmune response doesn't stop on command. It may remain stimulated even if all the cancer cells it was called on to eradicate have been destroyed. (That's why autoimmune disorders are treated like diseases and not like add-ons at the spa.) Even if immune-stimulating drugs work on the intended target, they may provoke a system of autoimmunity that will go on to attack whatever was lying beneath, near, or beside it: your stomach lining, your blood, or your liver. Autoimmunity doesn't care.

I am gutted. What I am watching on television is an advertisement for some of the exact fucking diseases I am trying, at that moment, to survive.

On an intellectual level, the logic holds well enough. Harnessing the autoimmune response to fight cancerous growth is theoretically sound—and just the tiniest bit clever. However, medical science has never found a reliable way to reign in the autoimmune response for those suffering its worst effects, nor for anyone else. Other concerns flare up: Opdivo is approved to treat an advanced-stage lung cancer, renal cell carcinoma (kidney cancer), and certain melanomas (skin cancers) for which chemotherapy has not proven effective, and thus presents such "immune-boosting" treatments as alternatives to chemotherapy without acknowledging chemotherapy as a first-line treatment for several manifestations of autoimmunity. Here, let me help you out of this frying pan: Opdivo may treat your cancer after chemotherapy has failed, but you may also be stuck with a new chronic illness and even more chemotherapy, in addition to the several serious side effects of taking the drug in the first place. To me, this all seems a bit counterproductive (but who am I to tell you how to get over your cancer?).

Perhaps most insulting is the expense. A full, twelve-week course of biweekly Opdivo infusion treatments can run as much as $200,000. This is about twenty-five times what I pulled in last year, a pricey consequence for my particular combination of faulty genes, years of eating preservative-laden food, the occasional course of antibiotics, a high-stress lifestyle, constant international travel, and just regular old Life in the Age of Toxins. If you *really, really* want an autoimmune disorder—and all the cool kids have 'em—why not try a crap diet, skipping every third night of sleep, and doing a few shots of Purell? Whole thing'll net you less than $2000, for sure. At least until you start needing lab tests.

So there I was, at the gym, watching CNN condone and install megalomania as New World Order, when a commercial comes on, selling a disease or two that I was fighting at that moment to keep from doing more damage to my already compromised body. These are ailments I will have for the rest of my life, lit on screen by a soft, white light and accompanied by a lilting tune, and they are going for top dollar. That's not money that will fund research into treating autoimmune disease of course, but will instead fuel the project of making autoimmunity useful in the treatment of other ailments—proliferating disorders like mine as a result. And all of this is happening before my eyes, at the gym, without a shred of acknowledgement of how difficult, hopeless, and expensive these diseases can be to live with.

When I can breathe again, my first inhale is a gasp. The next is a sob. I begin crying then in horrible jags, angry as shit, my heart rate steadily rising, standing there on that lumbering machine. I've seen thousands of horror films, but the commercial terrifies me more than all of them combined.

♦ ♦ ♦

The 2014 film *Creep* opens with a bright-eyed, if slightly skittish, videographer arriving at a mysterious freelance assignment he picked up online. Aaron (Patrick Brice) has been offered $1,000 in exchange for a day's footage and "discretion." Josef (Mark Duplass), who posted the ad, clears up the mystery straightaway: "I am a cancer survivor," he says, describing a prior successful treatment. "[U]nfortunately two months ago . . . brain tumor, size of a baseball." Josef claims that the reappearance of his cancer means he has only two to three months to live. The video, a day-long document of his life, is intended for his unborn son.

Aided by the found-footage conceit of the film (we are watching Aaron's video), the videographer's anxiety, and Duplass's over-earnestness, the viewer is led on an eye-widening excursion of tiny scares over the course of the two men's weeks-long relationship that never seems to build to larger horror. That is, until just over halfway into the film, when it becomes clear that Josef probably isn't sick in the way he claims to be.

Horror films reflect society's deepest fears in absentia; that is, the presumptions underlying the safe version of the world destroyed in most horror films are often more telling than the scare tactics of whatever monster inflicts the destruction. Good horror movies exploit presumed bastions of comfort, universally held beliefs that, throughout the course of a film, we may come to understand are built on faulty or wholly false presumptions. *Creep* is a horror film— and quite a good one—based on the premise that cancer survivors are all of a type: they love and value life, are always truthful, and intend no harm. The inverse is also held to be true: that one does not lie about having the disease, that doing so is a violation of the highest moral order. *Creep* shows us someone inherently good and kind—but gullible—who deserves and receives punishment precisely because he believes the best of someone who claims to be dying of cancer.

The plotline calls to mind Susan Sontag's 1978 thesis *Illness as Metaphor*, which catalogs an affliction she was suffering, albeit through a critical historical overview of disease narratives; it is not a memoir. The narratives she explores, she argues, create unhelpful metaphors, storylines patients must rail against in lieu of their actual illness-causing agents. Sontag casts disease metaphors as dangerous, energy-wasting distractions from medical treatment that do far more harm than good.

Although the essay caused medical practitioners, psychotherapists, and naturopaths the world over to throw hissy fits in the ensuing decades—the hopefulness at the center of many disease metaphors does seem to aid healing—she did have a point. Sontag's ailment/muse, companion/foe was a disease around which many narratives have been constructed. In fact, so many that there has come to be a standard cancer narrative (beloved figure grows mysteriously ill, fights vainly, yet perishes, and the rest of us gain lessons about the value of life from the experience), or even standard narratives for particular forms of cancer (an unjust and cruel man is afflicted with an aggressive and untreatable cancer; an innocent child remains hopeful in chemo despite overwhelming odds). Individuals are said to be either standard or not standard cancer sufferers, just as particular diseases are thought to behave in particular ways among particular populations. A healthy vibrant athlete facing radiation therapy must be discussed in almost mystical terms, as if cancer does not regularly afflict the previously healthy; the patient being treated for lung cancer who never smoked a day in her life is thought to have been done a grave disservice. The metaphors all craft a sense of knowledge without actual knowledge: Cancer, we feel, is known. Cancer survivors are known. The manner in which we respond to cancer survivors is known. The negative medical impact of this "knowing"—a vague sort of caring, absent of curiosity—was Sontag's subject.

Although the medical field has advanced significantly since the essay's publication, many of Sontag's assertions still hold true today. That we automatically react to the specter of cancer with patience, kindness, and respect is so deeply baked into our culture that responding with questions or criticism would be unthinkable. It is neither my intention, nor was it Sontag's, to challenge an inherently humane response. But we should note that cancer comes to operate, culturally, as a safe harbor: the metaphors we still use today to describe the course of the disease—in truth, many similar-acting diseases—are reliable, somber, and predictable, however much the diseases themselves continue to defy true knowledge. This becomes tautological: when we treat dangerous elements of any kind as if we already comprehend them, we actively deny ourselves the opportunity to acquire new information about them.

The metaphors of disease can establish a culturally reinforced ignorance of its true dangers and mechanisms, Sontag argued. And this point remains true today. If you don't believe me, try saying to the next guy who says he has a brain tumor the size of a baseball, "Prove it." *Creep*'s Aaron didn't, and I'm not even going to tell you how horribly that turned out for him.

◆ ◆ ◆

When intellectual women become ill, they turn, invariably, to Sontag. This does not mean, apparently, that they all *read* her. An overview of literature referencing her work on illness reveals the most quoted passage to be the sly joke from its opening lines: "Everyone who is born holds dual citizenship in the kingdom of the well and in the kingdom of the sick. Although we all prefer to use the good passport, sooner or later each of us is obliged, at least for a spell, to identify ourselves as citizens of that other place."[1]

It's the one solid, original metaphor we can pull from Sontag's groundbreaking work—by authorial design. She references the easy glitz of the image herself in the introductory paragraph of *AIDS and Its Metaphors*, the 1988 addition to the Picador reprint of the essay:

> *Saying a thing is or is like something-it-is-not is a mental operation as old as philosophy and poetry, and the spawning ground of most kinds of understanding, including scientific understanding, and expressiveness. (To acknowledge which I prefaced the polemic against metaphors of illness I wrote ten years ago with a brief, hectic flourish of metaphor, in mock exorcism*

of the seductiveness of metaphorical thinking.) Of course, one cannot think without metaphors. But that does not mean there aren't some metaphors we might as well abstain from or try to retire.

Not all metaphors, she acknowledges, presaging social media-level criticism by a good twenty-five years and responding directly to her detractors in the wellness field. She also lays bare larger intentions of the piece never elucidated in the original. The essay aims, she writes, to consider the "mystifications surrounding cancer" through a review of the literature that set them in print, stopping first to outline the mythology of tuberculosis in light of the medical evidence that has since emerged to disprove most of its purported truths. She wanted, she explains, to avoid another first-person autobiographical tale of yet another triumphant cancer survivor. "A narrative, it seemed to me, would be less useful than an idea," she writes. In support, she quotes Nietzsche: "To calm the imagination of the invalid, so that at least he should not, as hitherto, have to suffer more from thinking about his illness than from the illness itself—that, I think, would be something! It would be a great deal!"[2]

The desire to remove the psychosocial burden of illness from the physically ill person, Sontag explains, is "practical":

It was my doleful observation, repeated again and again, that the metaphoric trappings that deform the experience of having cancer have very real consequences: they inhibit people from seeking treatment early enough, or from making a greater effort to get competent treatment. The metaphors and myths, I was convinced, kill.

Time has since proven a good number of her assertions correct, and many cancer treatments popular in the late 1970s were ultimately withheld, abandoned, or improved in response to the concerns raised in her book. Breast cancer treatments, for example, became more localized and less invasive, as researchers and patients alike began demanding more accurate, individualized responses to the disease. As medicine progressed, it became clear that there was not, in fact, a "cancerous personality," a theory popular when Sontag was diagnosed; the evil were not stricken with the disease because they had erred (and would therefore succumb to it) and the good were not immune (and would therefore be cured if they mistakenly fell ill). The metaphors and myths surrounding cancer, without a doubt, caused a great many deaths that could easily have been prevented, as scientific breakthroughs fostered a more accurate understanding of the causes and treatments of various forms of cancer. This remains consistent with Sontag's authorial intention. The focus of the patient, the healthcare team, and those who seek to describe the diseases in question, she argues in *Illness as Metaphor*, should stay on scientific fact and medical research. Period.

Without going full-bore, counter-intuitive Camille Paglia on you, I'd like to suggest that, today, those with a more proliferative disease than even cancer may be suffering from the exact opposite dilemma. With autoimmunity, it is a total *lack* of metaphors and mythology surrounding these diseases that kills. Many may even be dying in service to the cancer research that Sontag so rightly championed.

◆ ◆ ◆

A description of the popular milieu surrounding autoimmunity is easy enough—a brief overview of contemporary literature is extremely brief, indeed. Minus self-help books and blogs—of which, in truth, there are a great many—we're left with surprisingly few references, whether literary, journalistic, or popular, for a set of disorders also considered epidemic.

Even Laurie Edwards's *In the Kingdom of the Sick* (Bloomsbury), a 2013 cultural history of chronic ailments named for Sontag's joke about the seduction of illness metaphors, strangely offers little to no deep thinking on the subject; neither do characters with unnamed diseases littered across sci-fi narratives that seem, often, to reflect autoimmunity. Donna Jackson Nakazawa's 2008 nonfiction book, *The Autoimmune Epidemic* (Touchstone), pays more engaged attention to the topic (occasionally too much for me—I cried heartily out of naked fear that each horrendous disease described would be the next to appear on my hospital chart) and is an excellent read of case studies and medical theory surrounding autoimmune conditions. For a time, it fostered in the press a mild interest in the rise of autoimmunity. This died out quickly—faster even than folks perish of "Bellini's lymphocemia" in season one of Fox's sci-fi series *Fringe* (2008–2013). The fictional autoimmune disease is inflamed by anger, and causes peoples' heads to explode.

If you want metaphors for autoimmunity, in truth, you will find them most frequently on television, particularly on the Fox series *House* (2004–2012), where autoimmune disorders are often first assumed and then rejected as diagnoses by the eponymous Dr. House. Lupus, which is notoriously difficult to diagnose, even became something of a running gag on the program. "It's never lupus," the pill-popping sociopath mutters more than once to his medical team. The phrase became the program's unofficial tagline, then a meme, then a joke that spread throughout pop culture. As Sontag predicted, such jokes have real-world effects. This one became an ever-ready cultural dismissive for a disease that predominantly affects low-income women and people of color—groups that often have trouble accessing healthcare services and even more trouble being taken seriously within the medical system.

"What's Graves' disease?" Kate Micucci asks a weed dealer in the first (and only) season of IFC's 2014 women-led comedy, *Garfunkel and Oates*.

"Oh, that's what you get if you're a grave robber and you go in and you take the body for some sort of nefarious, scientific purpose, and then you find out that you have some sort of fungal infection on your finger," he replies. The joke, of course, hinges on the fact that Graves' is a lesser-known autoimmune disease that causes anxiety-producing hyperthyroidism, the effects of which are suppressible by marijuana-smoking.

Autoimmune diseases are played for only slightly fewer laughs in *The X-Files*, another Fox program that ran from 1993 to 2002. In an episode toward the end of the second season, a string of characters are diagnosed with Creutzfeldt-Jakob disease, a degenerative neurological disorder thought to be related to autoimmunity. In this case, the disease resulted from the consumption of chickens from a commercial processing plant where feed consisted of human sufferers of the disease who were murdered to cover up the ... well, it gets a little confusing. The episode ends with a bizarre, colonialist depiction of tribal cannibalism in New Guinea, scary masks and all, lending autoimmunity an exoticized provenance that has no basis in reality.

In the sixth season of Showtime's *Nurse Jackie* (2009–2015), Edie Falco's titular character treats an ER patient with only a tote bag full of medications for ID. The woman turns out to have a host of autoimmune diseases, and Jackie—habitually drug-addled herself—turns solemn. The patient's sole problem turns out to be medical incompetence: she's been prescribed multiple prescriptions for multiple diagnoses with no centralized oversight. "Not one of her doctors came down," a nurse explains to Jackie. "I'm on hold with the rheumatologist right now."

The nursing staff tricks the physicians into a group consultation by telling each respectively that their mothers have just been admitted to the ER—unethical, perhaps, but based on my experience, a believable depiction of what it might take to get various specialists together to address a single patient's panoply of autoimmune conditions. The episode ends before any incisive medical advice is handed out, but the characterization of autoimmunity as deadly serious but complex beyond the abilities of modern medicine is clear.

BBC's *Orphan Black* provides the most recent, and currently most watched, depiction of autoimmune disease in popular culture. An untold number of clones—some kind of corpo-government invention—are programmed with an endometriosis-like disorder to prevent pregnancy that, unfortunately, appears to spread and turn malevolent in the body of each clone. The search for the cure is a journey of self-discovery for each of the identical victims, of course, as well as a cloak-and-dagger intrigue replete with military, scientific, and private business interests all competing to conceal, nab, or supply knowledge about the clones' diseases, genesis, and creators. That disease was programmed into the clones' design seems a fitting acknowledgement of real-world conspiracy theories about autoimmunity; few medical, scientific, or holistic explanations make as much sense. (Some suggest, in fact, that autoimmune-adjacent Lyme disease is a government invention that leaked from a military water source, while the infamously contentious Agent Orange is, in fact, autoimmune in nature.) But that the diseases on *Orphan Black* are mysterious, suddenly triggered, serve the functional purpose of controlling a secret government invention, and appear (at least so far in the series) to be chronic does little to dispel the wider myth of autoimmunity as unfathomable, incurable, and even impossible.

In sum, popular representations of autoimmunity are almost wholly consigned to sci-fi and comedy television—even though they've been acknowledged by the medical establishment now for decades. These are diseases of the future, the metaphors run. They are *incomprehensible* and *ridiculous*. And that's where the metaphors stop.

◆ ◆ ◆

The impossibility of knowing autoimmunity to the same degree that we know cancer, it turns out, is a metaphor with a history. German physician and scientist Paul Ehrlich set the theory in motion in the early 1900s with his research into the immune system.

Ehrlich's scientific distinctions are many: he developed tissue-staining methods that allowed labs to distinguish between types of blood cells; he developed the first effective medicine to treat syphilis; he even initiated and named the concept of chemo-therapy. In 1908, his work on immunology earned him a Nobel Prize. His immunological studies, however, led him to some fascinating conclusions. One, still surprisingly pernicious today, was that auto-immune disease could not possibly exist.

Ehrlich's 1898 attempts to immunize animals with the blood of other animals from their own species, and then with their own blood, failed to produce autoantibodies; that is, the blood did not appear to be rejected even when removed from and reintroduced into the body. "This led Ehrlich to postulate the existence of what he termed *horror autotoxicus*," Arthur Silverstein notes in the journal *Nature Immunology*, "the unwillingness of the organism to endan-ger itself by the formation of toxic autoantibodies."[3]

Ehrlich's precise judgment of the concept of autoimmunity, noted by Silverstein, was that it was "dysteleologic in the highest degree"[4]—fully purposeless, without function. (I recognize the validity of this argument, although the makers of Opdivo would cer-tainly disagree.) When called on in later years to respond to emerg-ing evidence that, however purposeless, autoimmunity did in fact exist, Ehrlich dug in his heels. Horror autotoxicus (literally, the hor-ror of self-toxicity), he explained, did not prevent antibodies from forming against the self—the evidence he was given to examine—it merely kept them "from exerting any destructive action," accord-ing to Silverstein, underscoring Ehrlich's own vague explanation, "by certain contrivances." Thus, Erlich dispelled the possibility of autoimmunity, at least in his mind, for good. Others paid note, too.

"Ehrlich's absolute dictum that autoimmune disease cannot occur would resound throughout the decades and prevent full acceptance of a growing reality," Silverstein contends. As recently as 1954, despite scientific reports pointing to the emergence of at least six autoimmune disorders, horror autotoxicus was still consid-ered a law, with holdings as absolute as the law of thermodynamics or those set out by Newton to describe motion. "The ruling immu-nochemical paradigm," is how Silverstein more democratically refers to Ehrlich's now disproven theory, noting that the possibility of autoimmune disease was still an open question in the 1960s and just starting to be addressed as a medical reality in the 1970s.

How could an inaccurate (and frankly, wholly unprovable) theory hold such sway for so long? In short, the immune system was thought to contain within it a range of emotional responses—aggression, clearly, as well as acceptance—and one of them was "horror." The sheer terror the body would naturally feel at the possibility of self-attack was presented as the medical reason autoimmunity was impossible. The logic of this must have seemed, at the time, unassailable. There is no biological reason for a human body to self-destruct—it is, truly, dysteleologic in the highest degree. I can barely imagine it, and my inability to imagine it *should* by all *rights* be mirrored in my body's inability to perform it. Except that my right wrist and left foot are swollen and achy today—bodily evidence that Ehrlich was wrong.

The idea of the immune system turning on its host is terrifying. It is one thing if the guards fall asleep on the job, but once your knights start invading your castle, what's a king to do? Call a meeting to remind them of their duties? Throw the knights an appreciation party? The king would be lanced immediately. It is the combination of the terror of the idea, I think, and the easy accessibility of the medical theory to justify it, that mounting evidence of the existence of the autoimmune response throughout the twentieth century was ignored or considered aberrant to the "truth" of horror autotoxicus.

Autoimmunity went unacknowledged for generations not because it was too horrible to consider, but because it was assumed to be so thoroughly horrible that *the body couldn't possibly allow it*. We believed our biggest fears were impossible, and there's something quite charming in that. As much as I'm aware that this is why no drugs have been developed that can keep my hand from hurting as I type, something deeply trusting lies at the base of this falsehood. It's only too bad how much damage the falsehood continues to cause.

◆ ◆ ◆

The inexplicable and rampant growth of cells might be considered fascinating, if you have never seen the effects of it in yourself or others. Certainly, the cultural response is fascinating. We talk about beating cancer, run a Race for the Cure, buy pink to fund cancer research. "Fuck cancer!," we say, and we mean it. These are narratives that we are familiar with and that we invest in, financially and emotionally. Color-coded ribbons and sympathetic head-shaving rituals are among the ways we indicate to one another: here is a thing that must be endured, and here is the manner in which I am connected to it. The metaphors may not always be apt, or terribly effective, but they act as scaffolding for further exchange. Even Sontag eventually conceded that such metaphors acted as "the spawning ground of most kinds of understanding."

Unlike the community that rallies for the eradication of cancer, prescription pills for the treatment of cancer are quite toxic; if you touch them, you must wash your hands immediately afterwards. Because ingesting a drug without touching it can look ridiculous, I sometimes explain to people when I toss back a few pills directly from the bottle, "These are chemo meds." I say this to avoid looking like a crotchety pill-popping sitcom character knock-off, but my statement has no calming effect. Immediately, whomever I am with will look concerned, or sad, or alarmed. Until I add, "Oh, I don't have cancer," and then they look relieved and everything proceeds as if nothing unusual occurred. As if there was nothing wrong, as if there was nothing else to know.

Autoimmune disorders are also fascinating diseases; they are less about the quantity of cells than their behavior. They do not create inexplicable growths—they incite cells to attack and to attack any available cells they can find. This is what makes autoimmunity the perfect response to cancer: an autoimmune system will attack until there is nothing left, and potentially well beyond that. Autoimmunity offers unrelenting but often invisible violence:

the sick don't usually appear ill, diseases may lie dormant for years before emerging through symptoms, and tests are only administered once patients complain—or rather, once their complaints are taken seriously by presiding medical staff, which can sometimes take years.

Little is known, thanks in large part to Paul Ehrlich, about why these diseases start, how they function, or what triggers them. What is known is that they cause disability, dysfunction, and death, by which I do not mean that they are all fatal—in fact, the number one cause of death of those who've received a diagnosis of autoimmune disease is suicide.

The most significant source of frustration for the afflicted is how few effective treatments have been developed to respond to autoimmune conditions, which is why most of the drugs prescribed have other primary uses. One I took for awhile prevents malaria; another, that I do not take, is just gold, injected into the muscles. (I don't know how this came to be a treatment for autoimmunity, but because I like ridiculous things and was willing to try anything, I requested it. My doctor unfortunately refused to administer it to me, saying it sounded, "Stupid, like it came out of a comic book.") No one knows why most of the frontline autoimmune drugs work, in fact, because no one fully understands why the immune system goes haywire in the first place. The chemo meds, for example, are simply thought to throw the body into such extreme distress that it stops attacking itself. If you need these drugs, you quickly get the sense that you should feel lucky anyone bothered to find any treatments that help at all.

The National Institutes of Health (NIH) funded autoimmune disease research at a measly $850 million in 2016, a drop from 2012's $867 million, since which time diagnoses of individual autoimmune diseases rose between 2.5 percent and 6 percent per year, depending on the condition. Today, around fifty million Americans suffer autoimmunity, according to the American Autoimmune-Related Diseases Association, so an increase of 2.5 percent would mean 1.25

million new cases; an increase of 6 percent would indicate three million more cases.

Far more funding, of course, goes to the study of effective cancer treatments. In 2016, the NIH dedicated $6.3 billion to cancer research, representing a healthy increase over 2012's $5.6 billion. However, new cancer diagnoses didn't increase much during that time—there were 1.6 million new cases in 2012, compared to 1.7 million new cases in 2016, according to the American Cancer Society. An increase of less than 1 percent.

Note, please, that there's not even enough funding to effectively track the number of new diagnoses of autoimmune disease on an annual basis. Yet even the most conservative estimates suggest that one in twelve people—one in nine women—will develop autoimmunity over the course of their lives. Only one in fourteen, according to the National Center for Health Statistics, will develop cancer, research for which was funded last year at nearly 7.5 times the funding for autoimmune diseases.

In this way, understudied diseases that afflict some fifty million Americans *are* researched, although primarily for their potential to be used by the makers of such drugs as Opdivo to treat the cancers of some twenty million Americans.[5] Sontag's initial concerns clearly still hold true. The metaphors we use to describe illness limit our imaginations—not to mention the political force and funding pools required to develop effective response to rapidly spreading illnesses. But the mythology of cancer she explored was rich and elaborate— even if ultimately limiting—compared to an autoimmune disease, about which little to nothing is known.

Cancer is known, while autoimmunity remains unknowable. Yet the unknowable has use, it seems, when put to service of the known.

Part of this essay was included in a 2015 performance at the University of Illinois at Chicago's Gallery 400 called "The Queer Crip Narrative."

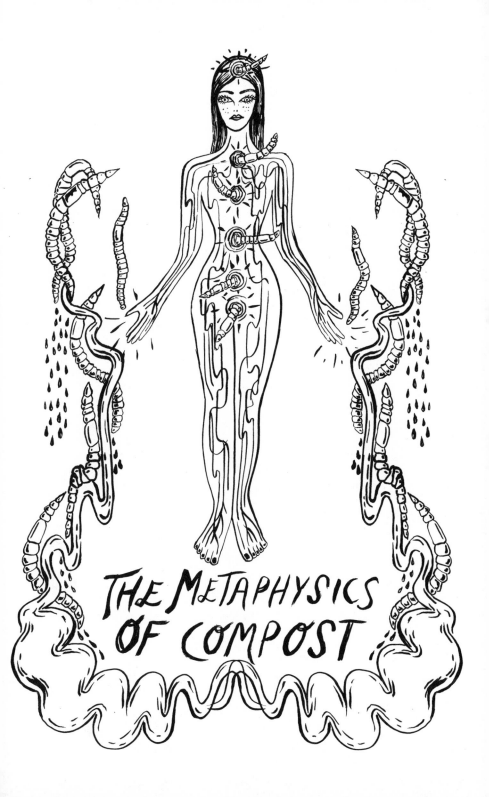

THE METAPHYSICS OF COMPOST

I don't want to go into it all over again right now, so let me just start by explaining that I almost died, like, eighteen times last year, so I pretty quickly got used to thinking about death in a functional way. Not as something through which I will personally be able to function—that would be ridiculous. Rather, death as an aspect of existence, as a likelihood, even as a future, um, event. One we may never "like" on Facebook, but that we will all attend anyway. More interestingly, I grappled last year with death so frequently, and in such a short period of time, that I started mulling over ways that it might hold value for me, now, while I am alive. Death as imminent, and not wholly unfriendly. Not to say that I am eager to personally embrace it as a state of being, mind you.

What I am saying is that death—being inevitable, apparently—became at some point for me an intellectual banality, a scheduling concern, a daily consideration. Then, shortly after I became slightly bored by the concept, I got . . . intrigued. High school biology classes teach that the cessation of life is the first stage of a whole other process, one that starts with decay, and then becomes nourishment, which is life-giving. See where I'm going with this? None of this *Live every day as if it were your last* business. More like: *Live every day as if, at the end of it, something new and exciting was going to happen.* I started preparing for death, then, materially as well as emotionally. Not mine precisely, but in general.

In other words, I started a worm bin.

♦ ♦ ♦

My move to a Bengali neighborhood in Detroit in May 2016 after more than two decades split between Chicago and various hotel rooms, couches, and flats around the world presented an opportunity to re-establish the foundation of my life without inconveniencing anyone else through divorce, marriage, or birth. I saw the house I was given as a reward for having won The Big Coin Toss, as an acknowledgment that my survival had neither been guaranteed nor would it prove to be permanent. So with little fanfare, I packed up my worms, drove five hours east, and dug my new foundation in the unsolid principles of useful decay. It seemed an appropriate metaphor for that particular moment in my life, after several serious health crises, as well as for the city that has come to symbolize urban ruination around the world. Decay not exclusively as *death*, then, but as both the end of life and the future life that ruination fosters. That's the part politicians ignore while warning constituents away from becoming the next Detroit.

I put seeds in the ground before I'd unpacked a single box and found that I had become a gardener. Not merely one who drops a couple beans in some front plots of dirt to see what will happen, although I have the utmost respect for folks who can keep their hobbies in check. I planted seedlings, invested in literature, and joined associations. I bought books—first one, soon a small library. I eschewed my work—writing, I remind myself sometimes—for projects like stump eradication and research into companion planting. Of course from these efforts naturally emerged the time-consuming lunch experiments, the driving inquiries behind which quickly evolved from "how can I best prepare this vegetable that I recognize and could purchase in the store?" to "this sort of looks like food and did come out of my garden, so I'll just pop it in my mouth and see what happens." *What's the worst-case scenario here, it could kill me?* Runs a query through the back of my mind. *Get in line.*

Most significantly, I crafted a compost bin from a couple concrete slabs in my back yard, and then another slightly larger one next to it. I daily fill one or the other with food scraps and cover those with a thin layer of soil. My chronic illnesses come with an array of food restrictions, so I've banned what I can't eat from both my kitchen and my compost bin. Conversely, I've forged a pact with my co-conspirators in this life-cycle project—all microbes, insects, and worms—and have eliminated most of what cannot be composted from my diet as well. One should never feed anything to friends, single-celled or otherwise, that one wouldn't consume oneself.

I recently added a third bin, about two feet wide by ten feet long, for turning yard waste into usable soil. In sum, then, I manage three distinct plots of land, each devoted to meeting requirements for draining all vestiges of life from particular forms of organic matter for, ah, microbial re-use. There is more physical space in my immediate environment right now devoted to enabling processes of decay than to any of my other obsessions except "books."

My composting habits are not even limited to the yard. Indoors, I keep the worm bin, a two-tiered contraption that, in theory, allows the European Red Wigglers I ordered from the internet to feed on fruit scraps in the top bin, safely nestled in some wet-newspaper bedding, until their home fills with waste and I avail them to move house. Then I place bedding and food scraps in the bottom bin and the worms—again, in theory—make their way through the holes that I have drilled in the bottom of each container to their new abode. The notion is that the two-tiered bin allows me to make easy use of their leavings.

In reality, however—and this is important to the process, I think—the "leavings" we are talking about are worm poop, and the worms like living in it. So when I require some "vermicompost," I scoop it out and place it directly under a seedling. After snuggling that worm waste in next to some food I'm hoping will eventually happen, I pluck the worms from it, one by one, with my bare hands, and return them to their proper locale.

The neighbor girls have screeched at this, their parents exclaiming out loud in Bengali at the sight of me digging worms out of some poop that I have just placed next to some vegetables, possibly because they know I will eventually try to get them to eat those vegetables with their mouths. I do not blame them. It is disgusting. There are ways to make the process less disgusting, of course, but I forgo them. They are distractions, I feel, from the process of ensuring that the beings I have enlisted in my agenda of useful decay are well cared for and enjoying their work. I can't say for sure that I know when my worm friends are happy, of course, but they seem to like banana peels and being left alone in their bin. They are particularly important to the composting process: their waste is especially nurturing for young plants. I treat the worms with care, therefore, and give them only the foods they seem to like, which I gauge by noting how many of them crowd around certain scraps in a wriggling mass, the sight of which cannot be described as anything less than "stomach-churning." Like the snake-pit scene in *Indiana Jones and the Temple of Doom*. It's playing out in my kitchen right now.

It became clear over the last year that the world as it exists does not facilitate my survival. What I am doing in Detroit is nudging an entire tiny ecosystem toward a state that will allow my participation, crafting a mini biome with millions of other beings. My worms are my closest collaborators in this project; an added benefit is that they keep the process visceral. It is one thing to bury food scraps in the back yard, it turns out, and another to keep pooping worms in your pantry. The latter can churn the stomach, which is only appropriate. A whole, new ecosystem *should* be felt in the gut.

Both backyard and vermiculture composting have captured the imaginations of a growing number of folks in recent days, alongside a rise in urban farming and the popularity of the sustainable food movement. It is not uncommon to heap a healthy dose of hyperbole in with the food scraps for the backyard bin, either: composters tend to infuse their talk of rot and decay with grandiose notions of life-force sustenance and metaphors for Important World Events.

The *LA Times* predicted the trend with a short piece of compost boosterism published in 1989, just as the Berlin Wall began to fall:

[R]ecent events in Eastern Europe notwithstanding—among the several things about which Karl Marx was right is the

uncontestable fact that consciousness is determined by one's
relationship to the means of production. And what finer
method to approach the consciousness of one's garden than
to partake in its death and regeneration.[1]

Hyperbolic, maybe, but provable. Among the many rewards of composting listed are the horticultural (of course), the political (which we'll address in a moment), and the metaphysical. I'll personally attest to this last: I know I've never felt more connected to the spiritual cycle of life—the one that exists beyond sight, taste, smell, sound, and touch—than when I am digging around in one of my several delightful piles of rotting gook and poop and death and pondering my own demise with a certain measure of serenity and hopefulness.

♦ ♦ ♦

The metaphysics of compost, according to writer and researcher Kim Hall, is more than just a woo-woo guide to backyard gardening: it may help inscribe justice into a mainstream food movement currently distracted by inherently capitalist notions like sustainability and consumption. Food often acts as invitation, a means of sharing both physical space and a nourishing—potentially educational—experience. Considering food within this larger sociocultural context allows us to envision it not as mere site to improve the minutest impact of globalization, but as an easy access point to politics that are rooted in resisting oppression.

Consider that recent darling of the mainstream food movement, the farm-to-table restaurant. These serve what's often called "pure" food, sourced from local growers in a manner termed "sustainable." Such establishments are often chided as elitist, and they are, but farm-to-table eateries pride themselves on crafting healthful meals that provide pleasure.

Yet charges of elitism aren't just tossed out over the high cost of locavore dishes: such facilities are often unlikely to respond to individualized food needs, a stance that quickly privileges the able bodied over those who may have more pressing reasons to seek healthful food options. I've heard more than one server suggest that if I don't "like" ingredient X—one that may trigger pain or dysfunction, but which the chef has determined is a part of how a meal tastes best—I should probably just eat at home. This same suggestion was once offered a friend who has no food restrictions, but is larger-framed than I and requested an untiny table that she could more easily access, so even the built environment seems to cater to a particular variety of eater. Many restaurants, too, fail to install ramps for wheelchair access or other devices for mobility assistance; few offer large-print menus for the visually impaired; and I've yet to enter a restaurant that offers American Sign Language as a matter of course. Far from mere oversights (and occasional violations of the Americans with Disabilities Act), such tendencies build to a pattern that infuses the mainstream food movement with ableism, centering it on a desire to ward off—instead of treat existing—disease and disability. (Hall reminds us that nutritionless but cheap fast food is served in ADA-approved facilities and often available for extended hours, which gives us a solid glimpse why the drive-thru may arguably be more "sustainable" for people with disabilities than the average farm-to-table eatery.)

There are grander implications to positioning food as "pure," too, even besides the mythos of white supremacy the term calls up. I'll attempt to outline an economic argument based in my own experience. Let's grant a normal, healthy body—one capable of gaining all the nutrients it needs from meals—a weekly food budget of $100, and assume that, for the sake of argument, to be standard. Folks with any sort of health concerns, however, are likely to have a diminished ability to process certain nutrients, whether from illness itself or as a side effect of a treatment program. Supplements can be expensive: mine cost approximately $120 per month, or $40 per week. Which leaves me with a starting (imaginary) weekly food budget of only

$60. So when food is presented as healthful, but not priced with budgetary diversity in mind, it appears to be targeted mainly toward those who are already free of serious health concerns. The "purity," of the sustainable food movement then, is not an attainable state for all clientele: it is granted only some, perhaps before even entering the establishment, and they must guard it carefully.

Yet everything, we know, must end in decay, and Hall writes of eating, disability, and the myth of sustainability in this context. We are, she reminds us, messy: how we eat, and, even more, how we navigate relationships around eating. "Food practices are sites where the meanings of community, identity, relationship, and food itself are materialized and negotiated," she writes in her essay, "Toward a Queer Crip Feminist Politics of Food."[2] The notion of purity, she argues, or even untrammelled longevity, has no place in how we really eat. Even tastes change over time, after all.

Food politics that center on justice, Hall contends, would hold the relationships forged by what we eat and how we acquire it as equally important to the nutritional properties of what is ingested. In real terms, the labor practices at that farm-to-table restaurant would come under consideration as another aspect of our health. Does a restaurant that touts sustainability see providing for its employees as important as nourishing its customers? Is an eatery that fails to respond to the needs of customers with disabilities or food restrictions truly concerned with ecologically necessary biodiversity?

The metaphysics of compost, according to Hall, "understands bodies and food as . . . contested sites where boundaries are questioned, negotiated, and open to transformation, not fixed." She urges us to consider food as a complex of relationships. Between my worms, for example, and my neighbors; between me and the microbes that live in my backyard; between local restaurants capable of responding to individualized diets and farmers reliant on sound environmental practices; between the potential interactions that could be formed if high prices and swanky design did not prohibit a diversity of bodies from gathering in any particular locale. (I have taken, of late, to hosting parties in my new home to which no one is allowed to bring other food. Because I wish to ensure others can eat, too, I communicate with each individual in advance of the gathering, requesting dietary concerns and other requests necessary to ensure physical comfort. These are extremely time-consuming activities, this is true, but they allow for an unusual intimacy to emerge quickly in a roomful of strangers.)

Hall calls for a movement centered, therefore, not on a metaphysics of food, but on a metaphysics of compost. "There are no pure bodies," she writes, summing up her argument for why even food itself should be situated within the ecosystem that supports both its growth and its decay. "No bodies with impermeable borders."

Hall may have been a bit ahead of the game, but the data is now catching up to the theory. Critic Jonathan Weiner writes in the *New York Times* last year:

> [A]s you read these words, trillions of microbes and quadrillions of viruses are multiplying on your face, your hands and down there in the darkness of your gut. With every breath you take, with every move you make, you are sending bacteria into the air at the rate of about 37 million per hour—your invisible aura, your personal microbial cloud. With every gram of food you eat, you swallow about a million microbes more.[3]

Science has finally moved beyond "germ theory"—the presumption that all microbes cause disease—and is beginning to understand that important bodily systems depend heavily on the microbes that inhabit them. The immune system, for example, a malfunction of which is the cause of my own ongoing ailments, turns out to rely almost fully on what Weiner refers to as "immigrant microbes."

"According to the latest estimates," he writes, echoing Hall, "about half of your cells are not human—enough to make you wonder what you mean by 'you.'"

The metaphysics of compost offers a food politics centered on the health and needs of the diversity of beings that contribute to—and turn out to largely constitute—"you."

♦ ♦ ♦

Material evidence can be found in Detroit that the metaphysics of compost is not unimplemented theory, but already daily practice. It is a city filled with friendly people but associated internationally with images of ruin and decay; crumbling building are quickly overtaken by vegetation both planned and accidental. On my block, largely inhabited by immigrants from Bangladesh, most backyards are filled with herbs and vegetables from home countries that most certainly foster microbial life forms foreign to my system. (I will note here that these immigrant microbes are not only delicious, but kindly intentioned.)

This city is often called to represent failure; in fact, it turns out that narratives about the need to rebuild Detroit have been circulated several times in the city's history, casting it in an impossibly permanent state of decay, fully oppositional to any notion of sustainability. In that, Detroit also points to the flaws of a politics rooted in sustainability, serving as a geographic reminder that all processes do end.

What we know in Detroit, and what I am experimenting with daily—alongside my neighbors, some worms, and a million friendly microbes—is that decay truly is useful, and must take place for life to flourish.

An earlier version of this essay was published on the Write A House *blog.*

Three months after emerging from your deathbed, you may find that you wonder why you bothered. You will have just survived a remarkable medical feat, perhaps with no explanation, and you are expected to be filled with gratitude. You try. Many days, you shed tears of relief, or unprocessed fear. On other days, you cry because for however long—three months, maybe—you had wished yourself off your deathbed under the unshakeable belief that something bigger and better was awaiting you. Now you see that it was not. What terrifies you most after emerging from your deathbed is realizing how little difference your death would have made; how little difference it didn't end up making, after all.

You may become angry with yourself; in fact, you will. You are an ungrateful shit to have survived such trauma and emerge from it with only malaise. How dare you take this hard-earned gift of life and treat it so unkindly? When you watched movies on your deathbed, which you did quite often, and characters said unthoughtful things about the meaninglessness of life or ending it all, you would cringe, or yell, or cry. Remembering a friend's casual joke about wishing she were dead on the day your doctor gave you bad news about your heart function still makes you wince. Now you say such things yourself. Your anger compounds: for you are not only an ingrate, you are also a hypocrite. Perhaps you should have died, perhaps you should die now, because you are so horrible.

At the three-month mark, perhaps you will remember how you used to cope with your always precarious future, before it came under direct threat. You may recall, too, how you used to make plans with friends to ward off rare stretches of unstructured days, how you enjoyed the company, the conversations that moved freely from topic to topic. Even remembering that you used to do this is a sign that your enthusiasms are returning. You also used to apply for things: opportunities, awards, jobs. You did this to exercise intellectual promiscuity. It felt expansive. You used to plan trips, some you would not even take. And work! You used to love it, although you cannot now remember why. You used to read things that had nothing to do with your immediate physical survival, or eat foods because they seemed interesting and not because they contained healthy elements your kidneys or muscle tissue could not do without. You will remember this, and begin to wonder if you will ever have the excess of energy required to do it again. To make plans as if you had all the time in the world, as if you could follow through with them. You had forgotten what it was like to operate without a deadline, or that it was possible to do so.

Your friends, especially if they are middle-aged, will say: *Oh, I know. What is the point. I feel exactly the same way. It is the politics/ the season/climate change/the economy.* You will say, *Yes, but also I almost died.* And they will say, *Oh yeah. I'm glad you're feeling better now.* You will feel disappointed by this, although it is unclear why. You completely understand why your friends would be bored by your recent medical drama. You, too, are bored of it. You also understand that they are middle-aged, and you are middle-aged, and maybe really it is a phase of the life you just saved that you cannot escape: malaise. Maybe the thing about emerging from your deathbed is that it ended up mattering so little, your survival, that you are still beholden to the same whims and extravagances that fill regular people's lives. Maybe your life, in fact, is just like everyone else's, deathbed or no.

You might visit a therapist. If you had been seeing a therapist while on your deathbed, the therapist will remind you that you have made remarkable progress, will exclaim that just so many weeks ago you did not know if you could make plans to see friends or if you should bother buying groceries. The therapist will remind you that the increase in energy required to meet all the minimum daily upkeep tasks you now perform to stay alive displays an enthusiasm unprecedented in recent days; that you can even consider taking a long view at this time and pondering the worth of it all shows great progress over a few short months earlier. The therapist will ask you to refrain from taking a critical view of your life right now. Unfortunately, the therapist will have no idea who you are, really, no idea what your life was like before the deathbed, no idea that a little over so many months ago, you could never have invited such feel-good meaninglessness into your life. It is not an excess of bitterness you sling in the therapist's direction, but a real and relevant question: If I survived all this, why?

In other words, you do all the things at the three-month mark that indicate emotional healing. You take steps to consider and improve your worldview. (That the worldview itself does not improve seems only to bother you.) You maintain a daily regimen of physical health, however minimal. (Although privately you calculate its cost and purpose.) That you get out of bed at all seems enough for everyone around you. Was it ever enough before? The people congratulating you now have attended your book release parties, your art openings, your award ceremonies, your graduation events. Were they faking it then, by saying that they always knew you were capable of greatness? Or are they faking it now, by telling you that they are just happy you are alive?

One day, three months after you emerge from your deathbed, a friend will invite you to sushi. He once abandoned you at a moment of great need. He had failed to recognize the danger you were in while you were on your deathbed, and remained wrapped up in his own drama when you needed him to concentrate fully on yours. But it is much easier to forgive him for these transgressions than to forgive yourself for having become sick. So you agree to go to meet him and to eat sushi with him.

As you sit down to order, you will remember about sushi. It will be the first time in many months that you have considered the wonder of eating raw and perfectly prepared seafood: the coldness of it. The extraterrestrial aroma and sharp, clear colors. The perfect alarm of wasabi and the clean, earthy warmth of long-grained rice. The delightful nuance of flavors in fresh-caught fish from different parts of the world, subtly complemented with saltiness, tanginess, sweetness. You have not even ordered yet but looking at the menu will stir something in you. The restaurant will be busy and the couple sitting next to you appear to be on an awkward first date. They have come to the best sushi restaurant in one of the best sushi cities in the world, and you will be reminded about all the minor life choices that it took for you to even know about this place: how you found yourself living with your friend in an art residency on the east coast, how you became close under unlikely circumstances and then, under even more unlikely circumstances, ended up visiting him on the opposite end of the country on a fairly consistent basis. You weren't sure whether or not you would ever actually be friends, or who this person even was, until one day he put a banana in his pocket as you were piling into a car to attend a group function and he sat next to you. You made a joke: *Is that a banana in your pocket or are you just happy to see me?* The joke then became something else, not about erections or men being inappropriate or fruits that look like penises or even an unspoken attraction between you two, but a joke about carrying bananas around town, because in the end that was the funniest part: that someone might ever, for any reason, be carrying a banana around in their pocket.

You will be reminded of the hilarity of the banana joke while reading the menu, which will contain everything you have ever wanted to eat in that moment, and there it is, open in front of you. In a list. You can tally how many of each piece of sushi you want and they will bring it to you, and the wonder of this catches you at the base of your throat, somewhere above your left lung. You are overwhelmed with gratitude, shaking with it. You will order everything, you actually will, but there is a particular thing that you like there that combines deep-fried rice and spicy tuna and when it arrives and you take a bite of it you can feel the soft fish and the sharpness of the chili peppers and the hard, sweet crunch of the rice. You will be eating across the table from your friend, next to a couple on a first date that doesn't seem to be going very well, in a crowded restaurant, but you will also be crying. Giant tears will be dropping from your eyes at the sheer overwhelming wonder of this exact moment, and how lucky you are to experience it.

Then—as does everything, eventually—that moment will pass. When you glance down at the table, your tears are there, still pooled. Partially to distract your friend from your tears, but also because it is true, you will ask your friend, "You know what fucking sucks?"

He will look at you blankly. He has just been expressing concern about his own life and you are being a dick by interrupting him and averting the attention to yourself. But you could not fucking care less because you are alive and you have thought of something true to say.

"One thing that fucking sucks is thinking you're going to die every day for three months." You will say this venomously, like how people exaggerate meaningless things for the sake of comedy. Except here there is no exaggeration, no joke.

Your friend will burst out laughing anyway. He has a loud laugh, the laugh of a man who is secure in the world, a comforting laugh. The entire restaurant will respond to his laughter; some people will smile along with him. Then you laugh, too. You had forgotten about laughing the way you had forgotten about sushi. You laugh hard and long. Your laugh is frenetic, contagious. It always has been; it has just been dormant. Hearing it now makes others laugh, too. Soon everyone in the whole restaurant is happy, including the couple sitting next to you, and no one realizes that this is because you did not die. You had forgotten how easy it is to make people happy, how easy it is to be happy, yourself.

"That shit is the worst," you will say to your friend, before picking up your chopsticks to begin eating again. You will roll your eyes for emphasis. You will both laugh again, because it is true.

Then it will be over. You will no longer be someone who has just emerged from a deathbed. You will just be an alive person, whole again, living your life.

ACKNOWLEDGMENTS

I have always written about difficult subjects, even before my own medical issues became one of them. I am often asked how I can stomach the issues I write about, the stories I hear, and the events I experience. Below are listed the precise individuals who make my work possible, as well as the institutions who supported this particular effort.

I wish to thank my editor Naomi Huffman and my agent Dawn Frederick, as well as the editors and friends who helped shape the pieces herein—particularly A. S. Hamrah, Lauren Kirchner, Daniel Kraus, Chris Lehmann, Irma Nuñez Sless-Kitain, and the truly lovely readers of my weirdo newsletter that shares a name with this project. I must also thank the brilliant illustrator Xander Marro, a sharp thinker that I am honored to work with and be inspired by in this and other endeavors.

I remain grateful for the teams who have published the work included in this volume, particularly *The Los Angeles Review of Books*, *Women's Review of Books*, *The State*, *Talking Points Memo*, *Salon*, *The Baffler*, and elsewhere, as well as the curators at the University of Illinois at Chicago's Gallery 400, the Miss Spoken Reading Series in Chicago, and SPACES gallery in Cleveland, Ohio, who allowed me to further explore the ideas herein. As always, Nick Butcher, Nadine Nakanishi, Reinhard Puntigam, Tim Schwartz, and my cats Thurber and All Girl Metal Band put in no small amount of emotional labor to ensure that you would eventually have access to my printed thoughts on such significant matters as talking vaginas, sanitary napkin disposal bags, and straight-up lady cannibals, and for this I offer them my deepest apologies. Finally, I must thank the Salims: thank you, kindly, for all you do to ensure my health and happiness.

Part of this book was made possible by a Kone Foundation grant, which plopped me at the Saari Residency in Finland and gave me a few hours to write between other projects. Another part of this book, a big part—the part where you take the idea for a book and turn it into some paper that is covered in words and available for purchase at bookstores—was made possible by Write A House. This unique, permanent residency program, founded by Sarah Cox and Toby Barlow in Detroit, Michigan, did not merely offer me the gift of permanent publication storage for the first time in my life, but stuck me with the kindest and most healing neighbors a girl could ever dream of. The staff, board, volunteers, and donors will forever have my gratitude.

Body Horror, an introduction

1. The cartoonist Gabrielle Gamboa and I made a comic to illustrate some data we'd pulled during the #31HorrorFilms31Days Twitter challenge annually posed by Daniel Kraus at *Booklist*. Hashtag contributors are urged to watch a film every day in October and then tweet a review/summary. In 2012, a few of us (Rob Kirby's contributions stand out, alongside the above participants) further took note of basic demographic data on cast and crew, as well as key plot points. Further content analysis I performed on my own, because I secretly love doing math. "The truly scary politics of horror movies," Gabrielle Gamboa and Anne Elizabeth Moore, October 29, 2013, Salon.com. Retrieved October 21, 2016: http://www.salon.com/2013/10/29/the_truly_scary_politics_of_horror_movies/

2. In her long-running comic strip *Dykes to Watch Out For*, Alison Bechdel has two characters in a strip from 1985 discussing the minimal criteria for attending a film: that it include at least two female characters talking to each other about something besides a man. Even Bechdel was surprised, years later, to discover it still had currency. "I feel a little bit sheepish about the whole thing, because it's not like I invented this test or said this is the Bechdel test. It somehow has gotten attributed to me over the years. It's this weird thing. Like, people actually use it to analyze films to see whether or not they pass that test," Bechdel told NPR's Terry Gross on *Fresh Air*. (For the record, Alison Bechdel credits her friend Liz Wallace with these rules, and would prefer it be called the Bechdel-Wallace Test.)

3. "Tom Six: In 100 years people will still be talking about my human centipede films," Hannah Ellis-Petersen, July 2, 2015, *The Guardian*. Retrieved October 24, 2016: https://www.theguardian.com/film/2015/jul/02/human-centipede-director-tom-six-i-have-this-very-sick-imagination

4. "'I don't like human beings': A chat with *Human Centipede*'s Tom Six," Rich Juzwiak, March 21, 2015, *Defamer*. Retrieved October 24, 2016: http://defamer.gawker.com/i-dont-like-human-beings-a-chat-with-the-human-centi-1706049658

5. "Deadgirl—Interview with Gadi Harel," Michael Guillén, March 8, 2009, *ScreenAnarchy*. Retrieved October 24, 2016: http://screenanarchy.com/2009/03/deadgirlinterview-with-gadi-harel.html

6. *Deadgirl*, in truth, does offer an interesting and knowing view on misogyny, for a film about a group of young men finding a young woman and mutilating her is, fundamentally, about what culture suggests is acceptable for men to do to women's bodies. It is, however, a far cry from being a feminist film, in content or in production.

7. I suspect this has so far kept most filmmakers from making body horror films about nonbinary individuals, relying overmuch on the questionable notion that stripping away gender equates to a loss of personhood.

8. "Film review: *Contracted*," Dennis Harvey, November 8, 2013, *Variety*. Retrieved October 25, 2016: http://variety.com/2013/film/reviews/contracted-review-1200810688/

The shameful legacy (and secret promise) of the sanitary napkin disposal bag

1. For more on this, see Vern Bullough's, "Merchandising the Sanitary Napkin," in the University of Chicago Press 1985 release *Signs*.

2. "Why don't women patent?" Jennifer Hunt, Jean-Philippe Garant, Hannah Herman, David J. Munroe, March 2012, National Bureau of Economic Research. Retrieved October 28, 2016: http://www.nber.org/papers/w17888?ntw

3. "The wage gap is stagnant in last decade," September 2012, A factsheet from the National Women's Law Center. Retrieved October 28, 2016: http://www.nwlc.org/sites/default/files/pdfs/poverty_day_wage_gap_sheet.pdf

4. "Women aren't held back by an ambition gap. They're just held back," Bryce Covert, November 14, 2012, *Forbes*. Retrieved October 28, 2016: http://www.forbes.com/sites/brycecovert/2012/11/14/women-arent-held-back-by-an-ambition-gap-theyre-just-held-back/

5. "The most hazardous spot in women's restrooms," Ann Germanow, 2009, *Building Services Management*. Interestingly, the original letter has disappeared (http://www.bsmmag.com/Main/Articles/2009/09/FeminineCareProductDisposal.htm) since I published this piece with *The Baffler* in June 2014, although it was archived in February 2012, by the Internet Archive, retrieved October 28, 2016: https://web.archive.org/web/20120228181704/http://www.bsmmag.com/Main/Articles/2009/09/Feminine%20Care%20Product%20Disposal.htm

6. These are tallied by way of Google Patents; gender was determined by name and further online investigation. Both processes are somewhat flawed.

Women

1. For the remainder of this essay, I will use the term "misogyny" to refer to all gender-based violence afflicting folks outside the strictly masculine end of the gender spectrum. I have no wish to erase trans and nonbinary folks, not even in language, but it is the term under consideration in the works of the artists I address here. I also desire the language that I use reflect the world as I genuinely experience it, and my experience suggests that femininity in any degree, regardless of the gender identity of the performer, is the real target of misogyny. (I may, however, be in error.)

2. All Despentes quotations come from the 2010 English-language edition of *King Kong Theory*, published by the Feminist Press in New York, and translated by Stéphanie Benson.

3. "*I Spit on Your Grave* movie review," Roger Ebert, July 16, 1980. Originally published in the *Chicago Sun-Times*. Retrieved November 2, 2016: http://www.rogerebert.com/reviews/i-spit-on-your-grave-1980

Model employee

1. "Does fashion week exploit teen models?" Jennifer Sky, September 9, 2014, *The Daily Beast*. Retrieved October 28, 2016: http://www.thedailybeast.com/articles/2014/09/14/does-fashion-week-exploit-teen-models.html

2. "Jennifer Sky, Fashion week and exploitation," Jennifer Sky, September 10, 2012, *Guernica*. Retrieved October 28, 2016: https://www.guernicamag.com/daily/jennifer-sky-fashion-week-and-exploitation/

3. Pop-up ad on the Model Alliance website circa 2015. Retrieved October 28, 2016: http://modelalliance.org.

4. "Models: Occupational Outlook Handbook," December 17, 2015, Bureau of Labor Statistics (United States Department of Labor). Retrieved October 31, 2016: http://www.bls.gov/ooh/sales/models.htm

5. See my in-depth analysis at *Truthout*: "The fashion industry's perfect storm," April 4, 2012. Retrieved October 31, 2016: http://truth-out.org/news/item/8307-the-fashion-industrys-perfect-storm-collapsing-workers-and-hyperactive-buyers

6. "Yes, you should feel bad for models: we're being told to diet—or go broke," Sara Ziff, September 9, 2014, *The Guardian*. Retrieved October 31, 2016: http://www.theguardian.com/commentisfree/2014/sep/09/models-diet-go-broke-modeling-industry?CMP=twt_gu

7. "Protect children in the fashion industry from exploitation," Jennifer Sky, February 3, 2014, YouTube. Retrieved October 31, 2016: https://www.youtube.com/watch?v=kKJ99GhOUN0

8. For more on these fascinating, denationalized zones, see my comic with Melissa Mendes at *Truthout*: "Zoned," November 12, 2013. Retrieved October 31, 2016: http://truth-out.org/opinion/item/19977-ladydrawers-zoned
(Also included in my 2016 book *Threadbare: Clothes, Sex & Trafficking*.)

9. This rose dramatically by the 2015 report, when $13.23 was listed as the median hourly pay for models. Unfortunately, the living wage in New York rose just as dramatically, to $14.52, which narrows the gap between earnings and living wage only slightly.

10. Check MIT's Living Wage Calculator, retrieved October 31, 2016: http://livingwage.mit.edu/states/36

11. "Stealing from the poor: wage theft in the Haitian garment industry," Worker Rights Consortium, October 15, 2013. Retrieved October 31, 2016: http://www.workersrights.org/freports/WRC Haiti Minimum Wage Report 10 15 13.pdf

12. "About," May 2012, *Vetan Chori Band Koro* (Campaign to Stop Wage Theft). Retrieved October 31, 2016: http://vetanchoribandkaro.wordpress.com/about-2/

13. "Walmart warehouse contractor to pay $21 million to settle wage theft allegations," Dave Jamieson, May 14, 2014. Retrieved October 31, 2016: http://www.huffingtonpost.com/2014/05/14/walmart-warehouse-wage-theft_n_5324021.html

14. Admittedly, this is only one in a sea of hundreds or thousands of class-action lawsuits filed against Forever 21, distinguishable only by its association with a particular warehouse. "Forever 21 employees file class action lawsuit," January 19, 2012, *Los Angeles Times*. Retrieved October 31, 2016: http://articles.latimes.com/2012/jan/19/business/la-fi-mo-forever-21-lawsuit-20120119

15. "Yes, you should feel bad for models: we're being told to diet—or go broke," in *The Guardian*. (Ibid.)

16. "Fashion week's models are getting whiter," Jenna Sauers, February 18, 2013, *Jezebel*. Retrieved October 31, 2016: http://jezebel.com/5985110/new-york-fashion-weeks-models-are-getting-whiter

17. "Despite gains, the Fall 2016 runways were still less than 25 percent diverse," Jessica Andres, March 16, 2016, *The Fashion Spot*. Retrieved October 31, 2016: http://www.thefashionspot.com/runway-news/685109-runway-diversity-report-fall-2016/

Vagina dentata

1. "Pride and Prejudice," Zöe Heller, September 27, 2012, *New York Review of Books*. Retrieved October 27, 2016: http://www.nybooks.com/articles/2012/09/27/pride-and-prejudice/

2. "Interview: Wolfgang Büld," MJ Simpson, February 9, 2013, *MJ Simpson: Film Reviews and Interviews*. Retrieved October 27, 2016: http://mjsimpson-films.blogspot.com/2013/02/interview-wolfgang-buld.html

Consumpcyon

1. This and all other Atwood quotations come from the 1999 edition of *The Edible Woman*, published by McClelland and Stewart in Toronto.

2. "The epidemiology of irritable bowel syndrome," Caroline Canavan, Joe West, and Timothy Card, February 4, 2014, Clinical Epidemiology. Retrieved October 31, 2016: https://www.ncbi.nlm.nih.gov/pmc/articles/PMC3921083/

3. "The girl on the wedding cake," Millicent Bell, October 18, 1970, *New York Times*. Retrieved October 31, 2016: https://www.nytimes.com/books/00/09/03/specials/atwood-edible.html

4. Page 16, *The Omnivore's Dilemma*, Michael Pollan (London: Penguin), 2007.

5. "Laying off the pizza for awhile," *My Life with IBS*, Rachel, December 2, 2009. Retrieved November 1, 2016: http://ibsrachel.blogspot.com/2009/12/laying-off-pizza-for-while.html

6. "The girl who cried pain: A bias against women in the treatment of pain," by Diane E. Hoffmann and Anita J. Tarzia, in Volume 29 of the *Journal of Law, Medicine and Ethics.* Retrieved November 1, 2016: https://papers.ssrn.com/sol3/papers.cfm?abstract_id=383803

7. "Why do doctors take women's pain less seriously?" Mary Jo Dilonardo, October 23, 2015, *Mother Nature Network.* Retrieved November 1, 2016: http://www.mnn.com/health/fitness-well-being/stories/why-do-doctors-take-womens-pain-less-seriously

8. Those invested in mainstream feminism could and should ask why autoimmune disease is not an issue of concern on the level of reproductive health, but I won't spoil the fun for you by explaining it here.

9. "Changes in intestinal tight junction permeability associated with industrial food additives explain the rising incidence of autoimmune disease," Aaron Lerner and Torsten Matthias, *Autoimmunity Reviews*, Volume 14, Issue 6 (June 2015).

10. "Food labels and the trouble with trade deals," May 20, 2015, *Los Angeles Times.* Retrieved November 1, 2016: http://www.latimes.com/opinion/editorials/la-ed-food-labels-20150520-story.html

11. Page 113, *The Omnivore's Dilemma.*

12. As quoted on page 9, *Illness as Metaphor and AIDS and Its Metaphors*, Susan Sontag (New York: Picador), 1978.

Cultural imperative

1. It may be interesting that my actual class status changed at this time: family relationships disintegrated, so I had no economic foundation to rely on, concurrent with the disintegration of my health, although that wouldn't become evident for a few more years. I looked the part, in other words, but it was already evident to me that the way I was read had little to do with the resources I had access to.

2. Page 23, *From Goods to a Good Life*, Madhavi Sunder (New Haven: Yale University Press), 2012.

3. All Vandana Shiva quotations come from the 2001 edition of *Protect or Plunder?*, published by Zed Books in London, originally published as *Patents: Myths & Reality* by Penguin Books in New Delhi that same year. Page 12.

4. Page 17, *Protect or Plunder?*

On leaving the birthplace of standard time

1. "Route 66 history: welcoming Standard Time and time zones," Marie Traska, *The Curious Traveler's Guide to Route 66 in Metro Chicago*, November 4, 2014. Retrieved November 1, 206: https://curioustraveler66.com/2014/11/04/route-66-history-welcoming-standard-time-and-time-zones/

2. Which sits approximately twenty-three blocks south and twelve blocks east of where I first delivered this piece on the near north side in Chicago; a distance it takes me an hour and a half to cross.

Superbugs are coming for you!

1. "The superbug incentive," Ankit Mahadevia, June 16, 2016, *Boston Globe*. Retrieved November 2, 2016: https://www.bostonglobe.com/opinion/2016/06/16/the-superbug-incentive/GVLeEwKjliHoeN3zFAeU4O/story.html

2. "Superbug is a wake-up call," Matthew Wellington, June 17, 2016, *Pittsburgh Post-Gazette*. Retrieved November 2, 2016: http://www.post-gazette.com/opinion/2016/06/17/Superbug-is-a-wake-up-call/stories/201606130014

3. "'Superbug' found in Illinois meatpacking facility," Kristofor Husted & Harvest Public Media, June 17, 2016, KBIA. Retrieved November 2, 2016: http://kbia.org/post/superbug-found-illinois-meatpacking-facility

4. "Move over Zika: a superbug hits Brazilian beaches," Katherine Marko, June 17, 2016, *The Alternative Daily*. Retrieved November 2, 2016: http://www.thealternativedaily.com/move-zika-superbug-hits-brazilian-beaches/

5. "One in three seniors leave hospital with superbug on hands," June 16, 2016, *Newsmax*. Retrieved November 2, 2016: http://www.newsmax.com/Health/Anti-Aging/hospital-infection-senior-superbug/2016/06/16/id/734257/

6. "WHO's first global report on antibiotic resistance reveals serious, worldwide threat to public health," April 30, 2014, Geneva, World Health Organization. Retrieved November 2, 2016: http://www.who.int/mediacentre/news/releases/2014/amr-report/en/

7. "Comprehensive Report on the Global State of Autoimmune Diseases Released for National Autoimmune Disease Awareness Month," March 30, 2010, American Autoimmune Related Diseases Association. Retrieved November 2, 2016: http://www.prnewswire.com/news-releases/comprehensive-report-on-the-global-state-of-autoimmune-diseases-released-for-national-autoimmune-disease-awareness-month-86187622.html

8. Numbers are based on a 2010 study published in *Arthritis Care Res*, which estimated diagnoses based on relevant walk-in clinic visits. There is, unfortunately, little funding available to track autoimmune diagnoses any more closely.

9. "The Autoimmune Epidemic: Bodies Gone Haywire in a World Out of Balance," Donna Jackson Nackazawa, March 18, 2008, *Alternet*, (an excerpt from Nackazawa's book of the same name). Retrieved November 2, 2016: http://www.alternet.org/story/80129/the_autoimmune_epidemic%3A_bodies_gone_haywire_in_a_world_out_of_balance

10. In fact, the research trail for Hernandez only goes as far back as 2012, and appears to originate in a student paper posted online that names as source material a now-removed ehow.com article on hand sanitizers.

11. "Antibiotic use in food animals continues to rise," Tom Polansek, undated, *Scientific American*. Retrieved November 2, 2016: http://www.scientificamerican.com/article/antibiotic-use-in-food-animals-continues-to-rise/

12. See the scientific paper, "Gut microbiota, immunity, and disease: a complex relationship," by Michele M. Kosiewicz, Arin L. Zirnheld, and Pascale Alard in *Frontiers in Microbiology*. Retrieved November 2, 2016: http://www.ncbi.nlm.nih.gov/pmc/articles/PMC3166766/
For more on this, read the essay "Consumpcyon," in this volume.

13. "Superbug: An Epidemic Begins," Katharine Xue, May-June 2014, *Harvard Magazine*. Retrieved November 2, 2016: http://harvardmagazine.com/2014/05/superbug

14. "Antimicrobial (drug) resistance," National Institute of Allergy and Infectious Diseases. Retrieved November 2, 2016: https://www.niaid.nih.gov/topics/antimicrobialresistance/examples/mrsa/Pages/history.aspx

15. "Antibiotic/antimicrobial resistance," Centers for Disease Control and Prevention. Retrieved November 2, 2016: https://www.cdc.gov/drugresistance/

Fucking cancer

1. Page 3, *Illness as Metaphor and AIDS and Its Metaphors*, Susan Sontag (New York City: Picador), 1989. This and all other Sontag quotations are taken from this edition.

2. From Neitzsche's *Daybreak*, as quoted in Sontag (page 101).

3. This and the following Silverstein quotations appear in "Autoimmunity vs. horror autotoxicus: The struggle for recognition," Arthur M. Silverstein, 2001, *Nature Immunology*, Volume 2. Retrieved November 16, 2016: http://www.nature.com/ni/journal/v2/n4/full/ni0401_279.html

4. As quoted in Silverstein.

5. Cancer statistics come from the CDC's 2014 Summary Health Statistics.

The metaphysics of compost

1. "An organic theory of composting," December 31, 1989, *Los Angeles Times*. Retrieved November 2, 2016: http://articles.latimes.com/1989-12-31/opinion/op-464_1_compost-pile

2. "Toward a Queer Crip Feminist Politics of Food," Kim Q. Hall, Summer 2014, *PhiloSOPHIA* (State University of New York Press: New York). Retrieved November 3, 2016: http://www.academia.edu/7703970/Toward_a_Queer_Crip_Feminist_Politics_of_Food

3. "Human cells make up only half our bodies. A new book explains why," Jonathan Weiner, August 15, 2016, the *New York Times*. Retrieved November 3, 2016: http://www.nytimes.com/2016/08/21/books/review/i-contain-multitudes-ed-yong.html?_r=3